To Myra,

in affection.

from

Torsten

(who started to write up his
contribution to this book
during an extended visit to
Stanford)

Dalarö, Sweden, August 1980

Educational Research and Policy

How do they Relate?

Other Titles of Interest

L. K. COMFORT
Education Policy and Evaluation

A. KORNHAUSER *et al*
Chemical Education in the Seventies

T. HUSÉN
An Incurable Academic

R. M. THOMAS
Politics and Education

M. NIESSEN & J. PESCHAR
Comparative Research on Education

V. MALLINSON
The Western European Idea in Education

Journal of related interest

EVALUATION IN EDUCATION

An International Review Series
Edited by T. Neville Postlethwaite and Herbert J. Walberg

The journal publishes important studies in methodology and technique and presents an up-to-date assessment of education. It is designed to facilitate the exchange of information on evaluation methods and techniques which are frequently used in a wide range of different national systems and sub-systems of education.

Educational Research and Policy
How do they Relate?

TORSTEN HUSÉN
University of Stockholm, Sweden

and

MAURICE KOGAN
Brunel University, UK

OXFORD · NEW YORK ·TORONTO · SYDNEY · PARIS · FRANKFURT

U.K.	Pergamon Press Ltd., Headington Hill Hall, Oxford OX3 0BW, England
U.S.A.	Pergamon Press Inc., Maxwell House, Fairview Park, Elmsford, New York 10523, U.S.A.
CANADA	Pergamon Press Canada Ltd., Suite 104, 150 Consumers Rd., Willowdale, Ontario M2J 1P9, Canada
AUSTRALIA	Pergamon Press (Aust.) Pty. Ltd., P.O. Box 544, Potts Point, NSW 2011, Australia
FRANCE	Pergamon Press SARL, 24 rue des Ecoles, 75240 Paris, Cedex 05, France
FEDERAL REPUBLIC OF GERMANY	Pergamon Press GmbH, Hammerweg 6, 6242 Kronberg-Taunus, Federal Republic of Germany

Copyright © 1984 Pergamon Press Ltd., Institute of International Education, University of Stockholm

First edition 1984

Library of Congress Cataloging in Publication Data
Main entry under title:
Educational research and policy, how do they relate?
Reports and proceedings of a four-day symposium held at Wijk, Lidingö-Stockholm, June, 1982, and sponsored by the Bank of Sweden Tercentenary Foundation, the National Board of Education, and the National Board of Colleges and Universities.
1. Educational research – Management – Congresses.
2. School management and organization – Decision making – Congresses.   3. Universities and colleges – Administration – Congresses.   4. Education and state – Congresses.
I. Husén, Torsten, 1916 – II. Kogan, Maurice.
III. Stiftelsen Riksbankens jubileumsfond.   IV. Sweden.
Skolöverstyrelsen.   V. Sweden. Universitets- och högskole-ämbetet.
LB1028.2.E38 1983   379.1'54   83-13370

British Library Cataloguing in Publication Data
Educational research and policy, how do they relate?
1. Educational research – Congresses
2. Education and state – Congresses
I. Husén, Torsten   II. Kogan, Maurice
379.1'5   LB1028
ISBN 0-08-030820-1

Printed and bound in Great Britain by
William Clowes Limited, Beccles and London

Contents

Editorial Note

The two main parts of this Report were initially planned to be published separately. The first part consists of an account of the proceedings at the four-day Symposium that took place at Wijk, Lidingö-Stockholm in June, 1982. Professor Maurice Kogan kindly agreed to serve as the Rapporteur. In preparing his account he worked under the assumption that the invited papers, which provided the inputs to our discussions, would be published separately under my editorship. However, the Symposium was part of an ongoing study which I conducted on how researchers and policy-makers in four countries related, and in taking stock of this study it was felt that it would be advantageous if the entire project was reported in one volume. Therefore, I considerably expanded a paper on issues emerging from the comparative study which I gave at the opening of the Symposium. This has been placed as an introduction, before the Rapporteur's account, where references are also made to the invited papers which in revised form make up the second major part of the Report.

I want to express my gratitude to the Bank of Sweden Tercentenary Foundation which provided the financial means along with the National Board of Education and the National Board of Colleges and Universities, which made it possible to publish this comprehensive Report.

Torsten Husén

Foreword

A couple of years ago when a *Festschrift* for Torsten Husén was suggested by some of his colleagues at the Institute of International Education, University of Stockholm, a group of Swedish scholars proposed something more constructive. When the idea of a Symposium in his honour was suggested, no topic could be considered more suitable than "Researchers and Policy-makers in Education: How do they Relate?".

Since 1953, when Torsten Husén was first appointed to the chair of education at the University of Stockholm, his research has to a large extent been policy-oriented. As the first holder of the Chair of Educational Research at the Stockholm School of Education from 1956 to 1971, he was deeply involved in policy research tied to Swedish school reforms. The Institute of Educational and Psychological Research grew very rapidly to become one of the leading institutions of educational research in Scandinavia. From the early 1960s, Torsten Husén's research dealt more and more with international problems in education. In 1961 the International Association for the Evaluation of Educational Achievement (IEA) was founded and since then he has been very active in this Organisation in different capacities. He served as its Chairman from 1962 to 1978.

In 1970, Torsten Husén was elected Chairman of the Governing Board of the International Institute for Education Planning in Paris where he became increasingly concerned with educational problems in the developing countries. In 1971, a new Chair in International Education was established at the University of Stockholm and through the years the Institute of International Education has been a centre for international and comparative educational research.

On behalf of present and former colleagues, we wish to thank Torsten Husén for his willingness to engage in both great and small problems of research. We have always regarded him as a generous human being; and we hope that this publication will help scholars all over the world to better understand the relationship between research and policy-making.

The Symposium reported in this book was made possible with grants from the Bank of Sweden Tercentenary Fund, the Swedish National Board of Education and the National Board of Universities and Colleges, for which we are very grateful.

We also want to thank Professor Maurice Kogan who, expeditiously and to a tight schedule, undertook to write a report of the proceedings.

INGEMAR FÄGERLIND   INGRID MUNCK

Stockholm, January, 1983

Issues and Their Background

TORSTEN HUSÉN

Background

A considerable part of my research career has been spent on research related to the Swedish school reforms. I have reported on this in detail in Husén and Boalt (1968) and Husén (1978).

My involvement in policy-oriented research began in the mid-1940s with a series of studies of the so-called "reserve of talent" (Husén, 1946, 1947, 1948). These studies were self-initiated by-products of my work as a military psychologist which gave me access to test scores and information on formal education for nationwide age groups of twenty-year-old men who were tested and interviewed in connection with their conscription for military service. By relating test scores to the level of formal education and by studying the overlap between the distributions of scores on the various levels of education I was able to make rough estimations of how many with the requisite ability did not proceed to upper secondary and higher education. These studies were referred to by two Government Commissions and were quoted in the 1950 Education Bill, which presented a blueprint for a pilot program of comprehensive education.

These investigations, conducted on a rather unsophisticated theoretical base, gave rise to a fruitful methodological debate (Ekman, 1949, 1951) that resulted in both increased theoretical sophistication and methodological refinements, for instance by Kjell Härnqvist (1958). It was therefore appropriate that the OECD conference on "Ability and Educational Opportunity" was held in Sweden (Halsey, 1961). Provisions of equal educational opportunity by then began to be one of the major goals of educational policy in OECD countries.

A second type of experience I acquired from the work in Government Commissions in Sweden from the early 1950s to the mid-1960s. These commissions sponsored research relevant to the issues they were supposed to come to grips with. My experiences relate particularly to the 1957 School Commission which, during 4 years of intensive work, tried to take stock of the outcomes of the pilot program and the continuous evaluation of the comprehensive education. The over-riding issue was that of differentiation of educational provisions at the lower secondary level (Husén, 1962). In its recommendations the Commission proposed the establishment of a Bureau of Research and Development in the National Board of Education, the central administrative agency supervising

1

school education in Sweden. During these years I also had an opportunity to follow the research commissioned by Royal Commissions in England, such as the Plowden Commission which conducted a big survey of eleven-year-olds, their school achievements and what accounted for them (HMSO, 1967). I also studied the Robbins' Commission and was invited to meet the Public Schools Commission. This involvement in policy-oriented survey research was transferred to the international scene by the IEA studies, first the mathematics project (Husén, ed., 1967) and then the Six-Subject Survey (Walker, 1976).

A third set of experiences relates to the OECD reviews of national policies in education. I have been involved in three such reviews, the ones of France, the Federal Republic of Germany and the United States, respectively (OECD, 1971, 1972, 1980). The one of the United States was confined to the policies for compensatory education, where, in my role as the rapporteur of the review team, I had to go through the massive literature on evaluation studies that had been conducted from the mid-1960s with Head Start, Title One and other programs. Social science expertise in the United States had been mobilised in an unparalleled way (Aaron, 1978). Just one example: tens of millions of dollars were spent in evaluating the Follow Through program. The Harvard Educational Review (House *et al.,* 1978) devoted an entire issue to the theoretical and methodological problems encountered in evaluating this program.

I am referring to these personal experiences, because they form the background for my comparative study of the relationships between researchers and policy-makers in education, which was sponsored by the Bank of Sweden Tercentenary Foundation. The issues will be dealt with in what follows.

Countries Included in the Study

In 1980 I received a research grant from the Bank of Sweden Tercentenary Foundation to conduct a comparative study of the relationship between researchers and policy-makers in education. The study was planned to be comparative with four countries, Sweden, the Federal Republic of Germany, Britain and the United States, as cases.

Why select these countries for a comparative study? The highly personal reason was simply that I have since the 1950s been trying to follow the role of educational research in policy-making in all four of them.

1. *Sweden* was an obvious choice, since I had myself been one of the actors on the research scene and had also over many years interacted with Swedish policy-makers (Husén, 1983).

2. In 1952, I was invited by the American High Commissioner to participate in a six-week workshop at the *Hochschule für Internationale Pädagogische Forschung* in Frankfurt, *Germany.* This Institute had newly been established jointly by German and American authorities, with the purpose of serving

German schools by means of cross-disciplinary research in education and by long inservice courses for teachers who wanted to learn research methods appropriate for tackling important problems in German school education. The majority of the participants in the workshop were German colleagues, but some came from countries outside Germany.

The problems that the German school system was faced with and the need to reform it were discussed within the framework of what educational research could do in order to extend the knowledge base. Several of the chair holders in education at German universities had their disciplinary origin in philosophy and history and had very little, if any, background in empirical studies. The workshop focused mainly on what learning, differential and developmental psychology could contribute.

In 1964, I became a member of the Scientific Council (*Wissenschaftlicher Beirat*) of the Max Planck Institute for Educational Research in Berlin. The Institute was founded to conduct more fundamental research in education on an interdisciplinary basis that could be part of the background for educational reform in Germany. Leading scholars at the Institute, such as Hellmut Becker and Friedrich Edding, were later instrumental in the *Bildungsrat* (the Federal Education Council), the organ in charge of planning the educational system of the country. Germany did not have any ministry of education until 1970. Before that, there was the voluntary cooperative organ between the *Länder* called the Permanent Conference of the Ministers of Education (*Ständige Konferenz der Kultusminister*) which finally acquired a comprehensive secretariat with a large staff. It had, however, no formal authority and was there only in order to coordinate between the *Länder* on the basis of voluntary agreements. No official planning at the national level took place before 1970. A study in the early 1960s revealed that there would be such a shortage of teachers in the Federal Republic that even if all upper secondary school graduates enrolled in teacher training programs they would not suffice to cover the demand for new teachers. This created a panic, and talk about "educational catastrophe" (*Bildungskatastrophe*). In the wake of this a Federal Ministry of Education with the prerogative to plan was set up.

3. In *Britain* I followed the role of the Department of Education and Science in promoting educational research in connection with attempts, particularly during the term of office of Anthony Crosland in the 1960s, to introduce comprehensive education at the secondary level.

Britain is for two reasons a particularly interesting case. In the first place, a deliberate policy was introduced in the 1960s, particularly by Anthony Crosland, to multiply the resources available to the social sciences with an eye on what they could do to strengthen the knowledge base for policies and their implementation in welfare and education. Secondly, thanks to the long interviews conducted by Maurice Kogan for his book "The Politics of Education" (1973) with Edward Boyle and Anthony Crosland, we have on record how two leading ministers of education perceived the role of educational research as an input for a reform of secondary education.

Maurice Kogan conducted long conversations with Edward Boyle, a "reluctant conservative", and Anthony Crosland, a "cautious revolutionary". The conversations plus his analysis are published in "The Politics of Education". As formally a conservative, Boyle was somewhat lukewarm *vis-à-vis* comprehensivisation, whereas "going comprehensive", as pointed out by Susan Crosland in her biography of her husband, was on the top of Crosland's political agenda when he took office as Minister of Education.

Both ministers in retrospect make reference to the research that I and my co-workers had been conducting. Boyle deplored the short time span available for a minister in Britain with his usually short period of office. He refers to Swedish social democratic planning covering "a cycle of twenty years over which a major piece of social engineering was achieved": first 5 years of planning, then "five years of research by Husén", etc (Kogan, *op. cit.,* p. 77). Boyle evidently thought that research played a pivotal role in the Swedish school reform and regretted that, given the lack of long-range political stability, this was not possible in Britain. Crosland, as is clearly evidenced by Kogan's interview, also held educational research in high esteem, to the extent of inviting me to come to London in August, 1965 and meet for a full day with him and his advisers at Curzon Street when he was contemplating his famous Circular 10/65 to the Local Educational Authorities on plans for the re-organisation of secondary education. But he held a more realistic and in a way more cynical conception of the role of research. In response to Kogan's question on why the Circular was not preceded by research he said (Kogan, *op. cit.,* p. 190):

> It implied that research can tell you what your objectives ought to be. But it can't. Our belief in comprehensive re-organisation was a product of fundamental value judgements about equity and equal opportunity and social division as well as about education. Research can help you to achieve your objectives, and I did in fact set going a large research project, against strong opposition from all kinds of people, to assess and monitor the process of going comprehensive. But research cannot tell you whether you should go comprehensive or not – that's a basic value judgement.

4. In the *United States* I have taken particular interest in the role played by the Federal government in promoting educational research. These attempts have to be viewed within the context of the strong belief in the early 1960s not only in educational research but particularly in what education in general could do for social betterment (Aaron, 1978).

At the Federal level in the United States it all started with the Cooperative Research program administered by the U.S. Office of Education. This program operated with a modest annual budget of some 6 million dollars but managed to support several significant studies, such as the Project Talent. Suddenly under the provisions of Title 4 in the Elementary and Secondary Education Act the Federal funds for educational research, conducted in R & D centres or as proposed projects, grew to far more than 100 million. A massive attempt to improve education by means of research was envisaged by the architects of this program (Keppel, 1966).

* * *

Two of the countries selected for the comparative study, Sweden and England, have more centralised systems, England however far less than Sweden. Two countries, Germany and the United States, have a federal system where the educational prerogatives in principle are with the states (*Länder*). It appeared to me that it would be of interest to compare the relationships between social scientists and educational policy-makers within different settings of governance and administration. Both Sweden and England had ministries of education which possessed certain prerogatives simply because according to certain regulations, they provided funds for the local school systems. In the United States the Office of Education already in the 1950s had certain functions with a national impact. This can be measured by the percentage of school funds coming from that agency. From some 4 per cent of the operating funds in 1960, the relative contribution doubled within a decade due to the Great Society legislation on education.

The "golden years" for educational research in the four countries under study occurred in the 1960s and the early 1970s. It was assumed that systematic and massively financed research in education would be able to do what it had achieved in industry: increased efficiency and productivity. The expectations about what could be achieved were high both on the part of researchers and policy-makers. In 1971 the Select Subcommittee on Education in the U.S. House of Representatives toured Europe in order to find out what role research played in some European countries. In the Introduction to the report from this trip the chairman of the committee, John Brademas, is quoting Charles Silberman's "Crisis in the Classroom":

> The degree of ignorance about the process of education is far greater than I had thought. Research results are far more meagre and contradictory, and progress toward the development of viable theories of learning and instruction is far slower.

Brademas points out that, in defence, about 10 per cent of the budget is spent on research and development, and in health 4.6 per cent.

> Yet when we come to education, as important to the life of the mind as is defense to the Nation or health to the body, we find at all levels of education in America spending an aggregate of less than one third of one per cent of their budgets on the processes of research, innovation and planned renewal. (Educational Research in Europe, p. 3).

The Subcommittee conducted its fact-finding tour in connection with the legislation about the National Institute of Education (NIE) that was later set up. NIE was thought of as a better instrument for improving American education than the system of research grants and R & D centres run by the U.S. Office of Education.

The situation by the end of the 1970s was characterised by criticism and disenchantment about education in general and about educational research in particular (Husén, 1978). This was reflected in the levelling off, or even reduction, of funds going into educational research.

Conduct of the Study

When I submitted a proposal on a comparative study of how researchers relate to educational policy-makers, I had given little thought to the conceptualisation of such a study. By making it comparative and by conducting it in countries with different settings for both policy-making and research I hoped to be able to identify crucial factors affecting the communication between researchers and policy-makers.

Lack of initial theoretical sophistication could, of course, only partially be compensated by a long experience of involvement in educational research, a considerable part of which had been policy-oriented. Quite a few studies initiated by myself turned out to have unanticipated implications for educational policy. This applied, for instance, to the surveys on the "reserve of ability" in the 1940s referred to above.

When the study was begun I was indeed groping. Interviews with key actors in the field of policy-making and research, as well as unstructured questionnaires sent to a larger group, constituted the main approaches in collecting information about how researchers and policy-makers perceived their relationship. The first two interviews were conducted with Francis Keppel, now at Harvard University and U.S. Commissioner of Education when the educational programs in the Great Society package were in the design stage, and Benjamin Bloom, then President of the American Educational Research Association and consulted in 1965 about the research program which was launched under Title 4 of the Elementary and Secondary Education Act.

Later I had opportunity to interview Maurice Kogan, author of "The Politics of Education" and then in the process of finalising a study on interaction of researchers and policy-makers in the Department of Health and Social Services in London; Harold Howe, U.S. Commissioner of Education when major legislation on Federal involvement in school education had to be implemented; Michael Atkin, Dean of the Graduate School of Education at Stanford; Michael Kirst, former Chairman of the California State Board of Education and Professor at Stanford; David Krathwohl, former President of the American Educational Research Association, and William Turnbull, for many years President of the Educational Testing Service, Princeton.

In late 1980, I approached some 20 colleagues in Germany, England and the United States by mail and asked them to respond to a series of questions which I had deliberately put under the heading Questionnaire (at end of chapter). I wanted their perceptions of how they related to policy-makers who, one way or another, had been "consumers" of their research products. The 10 questions I had listed should serve as guidelines for their answers. I despatched the same questionnaire to all my colleagues at the professorial level at the Swedish universities and/or colleges.

In early 1981 I went to Stanford University as a Visiting Professor with the purpose of working further on my study on how policy-makers and researchers communicated. Furthermore, I knew that the Center for Policy Studies as well as the Center for Studies in Higher Education at Berkeley with Professor Martin Trow were involved in policy studies. When I came to the Bay Area, I discovered that the research topic which was to be my major concern for the next couple of years was a timely one. I met a number of people both at Stanford and Berkeley who were conducting related studies.

In the first place, Professor Maurice Kogan of Brunel University had sent me his preliminary report on "Government's Commissioning of Research" (Kogan *et al.*, 1980) which was a case study of the research conducted under the auspices of the Department of Health and Social Services in England. Kogan happened to be at Berkeley, which provided me with an opportunity not only to interview him about his experiences with British governments but also to discuss with him some of the issues I wanted to tackle.

In the Institute for Research on Educational Finance and Governance at Stanford, where I was accommodated, Professor Klaus Hüfner of the Free University in Berlin was a visiting scholar. With a background of German experiences he was conducting a study of the role of educational research in educational policy formulation and planning.

One of my interviewees with considerable experience of policy process and the forces affecting it at the State level as former Chairman of the California State Board of Education was Professor Michael Kirst at Stanford, who was then spending a year at the Center for Advanced Study in the Behavioural Sciences working on a study of "policy issue networks". There were several important changes in state legislation that had spread rather rapidly over the states in the U.S.A. in the 1970s: such as equalisation of school finance and minimum competency testing. How did it happen that, for instance, minimum competency testing within the short time span of 3 years was legislated in 32 states? The hypothesis was that certain cross-state networks were operating and had succeeded in achieving effective dissemination. A study of how policies spread might have something of importance to tell those who study the role of educational research in policy formulation. Together with a group at the Graduate School of Public Policy at the University of California at Berkeley, Kirst was also working on a study of educational policy-making with research information being one of the input components.

In May, 1981 the Dutch Foundation for Educational Research sponsored an international conference on "Educational Research and Public Policy

Making" (see Kosse, ed., 1982) with contributions, among others, by Carol
Weiss of Harvard University, who in recent years has conducted studies of
research utilisation by government agencies and has contributed seminal
papers on how research gets into the decision-making process. Her two basic
ideas are the following. In the first place, research is not directly in a
"linear" way "utilised" in policy formulation and administrative decision
making. It affects policies much more diffusely and indirectly than assumed,
usually by heightening the awareness of certain problems and reshaping
others or by contributing certain facts that give new aspects to existing
problems. Research is a "creeping" endeavour which serves an "enlightenment" function *vis-à-vis* decision-makers. Secondly, decision-making is more
like an accommodation or "accretion" process than a clearly identifiable
"decision" here and now (Weiss, 1980).

"The Two Cultures"—Researchers and Policy-makers

The Different Actors

Maurice Kogan and his associates (Kogan *et al.,* 1980) have, as mentioned
above, been conducting a case study of how researchers and policy-makers
relate to each other in the research program sponsored by the Department of
Health and Social Security (DHSS) in England. He distinguishes between
three kinds of actors in the DHSS research: 1. The researchers, 2. The policy-
makers/planners, and 3. The middle-men, professionals who are part of the
Ministry and who serve in a liaison function. The last group rather quickly
tends to become socialized into the orientations and opinions prevailing
among administrators and/or policy-makers in the Ministry. Therefore it
would be justified to distinguish between two main categories only:
researchers and policy-makers. However, professionals with research
background in ministries or central agencies represent a new and proliferating
species. They not only play the role of liaison officers with the divided loyalty
implied in that role but also, and more predominantly, the one of research
managers. They are closely related to the research analysts, who can serve on
the staffs of legislators and in government agencies. As a distinct category
with a particular type of training they are as yet mainly to be found in
America. Martin Trow discusses their role in his paper (p. 261 ff.).

The Field of Interaction

When it comes to sponsored and/or commissioned research, it is
convenient to conceive policy-makers and researchers in the roles of
customers and sellers, respectively. This was the perception of the Rothschild
Commission in Britain (HMSO, 1971), who assumed that research could be

"purchased" according to the rules of a free market economy. But, as Kogan points out, there is, when it comes to research, neither a "free market", nor is there a parity of power between government and researchers. Government in the DHSS case possesses a virtual monopoly in buying certain types of research. It has its hands on the pursestrings, and decides whether a research grant should be forthcoming or not. Thus, there are no free negotiations. The researcher-seller is not free to sell his commodities elsewhere if he is not satisfied with his customer's bid. The customer role further implies that government has a clear conception of what it wants. But it is in the nature of research that its products are largely unknown until the study is finished. It is part of the task of the researchers to help the customer-government to find out what he wants. The researcher, even in taking on strictly policy-oriented research, has to help the customer to redefine the issues in order to make them researchable.

Different Conditions for Policy-makers and Researchers

As pointed out by Levin (1978), the tension between researchers and policy-makers derives from constraints under which policy is shaped and implemented, constraints under which university researchers usually do not have to operate.

1. *Policy-makers* demand that research should address problems which are on their agenda, i.e. problems whose solution is relatively urgent. Issues such as private schools, busing, and voucher system, have taken on a quite different importance in U.S. policies under the Reagan than under the Carter administration. Politicians have party allegiances which dictate not only what they regard as relevant, innocuous or dangerous research but also to what extent they are willing to take research findings into account. Research addressing itself to major issues is easily regarded as "useless" by one side in the political power game if it does not support its views. Politicians, like advocates in a court, tend to select the evidence they interpret as supporting their views.

2. Policy-makers are concerned with advancing policies in a particular area of their own experience as politicians, and tend to disregard its connections with other areas. Thus, educational policies have been launched in order to solve what basically are problems in the larger social context, for example, compensatory education programs in the United States where enormous funds are made available to states and local schools as "categorical aid" (Husén, 1981a).

3. Policy-makers are as a matter of course not familiar with educational research or social science research in general, nor with the language that researchers use to present their methods and findings, a language that at best is precise in communicating to the scholarly world what the researchers want

to say and at worst is empty jargon. This imposes on the researcher the task of trying to cast his findings in a language understood by "ordinary people" but at the risk of being unprecise.

4. Policy-makers very often want to have access to findings immediately. Research findings have to be made available in time for policity decisions. Research that takes years to conduct cannot be considered if the timetable of policy-making requires the knowledge base to be presented "here and now". This dilemma is a reflection of the duality of tasks that faces planners and policy-makers in a government agency. On the one hand, strategic planning is going on. On the other hand, operational decision-making is a continuous process. In performing the latter decisions have to be taken without waiting for "relevant research", even the one that has been specifically commissioned in order to produce "relevant facts" of a rather simple and straightforward nature.

There is a tendency to favour the second, operational task which leads to an emphasis on the "needs of the field". Many administrators involved in policy-making perceive research as something that should be strictly field-oriented and pursued with narrowly-defined instrumental purposes. The researcher is required to provide clearcut information that could help the practitioner in his daily task of making decisions. Those at the top of the decision- or policy-making hierarchy might have less narrow expectations and more often expect researchers to help them in understanding the context in which policies are shaped. The professional middle-men, particularly those responsible for long-term planning, expect research to help in identifying new problems.

*   *   *

1. *Researchers* are usually performing their tasks at universities, but in recent years to a growing extent also at institutions which are part of public agencies. They tend to conduct their research according to the paradigms to which they have become socialised by their graduate studies. Their achievements are subjected to peer reviews which they regard as more important than assessments made by their customers in public agencies. Status among researchers is determined not primarily by seniority or by position in an organisational hierarchy, but by the assessment of the quality of their research by the scholarly community in their field of specialisation.

2. Researchers operate at a high level of specialisation, which means that they tend to isolate a "slice" of a problem that can be more readily handled than more complicated global problems.

3. Researchers are much less constrained than policy-makers in terms of what problems they can tackle, what kind of critical language they can employ and how much time they have (or think they have) at their disposal to complete a study. An investigation by the Dutch Social Science Research

Foundation (Kosse, ed., 1982) showed that the great majority of the projects the Foundation had financed were lagging behind the timetable agreed upon in the contracts. In order to conduct empirical field studies properly much time is required. Most projects typically take several years. One cannot without detriment to the quality of the project skip any stage in its conduct. The relevant research literature has to be reviewed, the problem and the research design have to be conceptualised, data have to be collected, processed and analysed, and sufficient time has to be allowed for writing up and waiting for criticism in the scholarly journals.

Tensions Between the Two Cultures

Above the field of interaction, with its tensions between researchers and policy-makers, different values loom large. There is some reason to talk about an academic versus a bureaucratic ethos.

The university-based academic is brought up in the tradition of the "imperial, authoritative and independent" Research, with a capital R. There is an anecdote about a meeting in the Royal Society of the mathematicians representing pure mathematics. The session was followed by a formal dinner during which the chairman raised his glass and proposed a toast to pure mathematics, adding: "And may it be of no use to anybody!". Fundamental research without particular concern about applicability traditionally carries high prestige. No problem area should be closed for the researcher even if the potential applicability (e.g. "genetic fix") would appear to be dangerous. The researcher feels that he does not carry any responsibility for the use that others might want to make of the insights, methods and facts generated by him. The autonomy of the researcher is cherished above all else and is often regarded as a compensation for low salary and insecure employment.

The practitioner in political office or as a planner/administrator in a public agency tends to regard research almost entirely as an instrument in achieving certain policy, planning or administrative goals. The quest for academic freedom is hardly understood, and often perceived as self-serving pretentiousness. Research should be focused on the priority areas of current politics (see, e.g. Shellard, 1979).

No wonder, given the constraints and the differences in value orientation, that there are tensions between researchers and their sponsors, something which in itself is not necessarily a bad thing. In order to discharge their task properly, academics, particularly if they are social scientists, have to adopt an independent, critical attitude. Therefore, the way researchers are institutionally anchored is a matter of great importance. Many of them are promoted to protected and tenured positions, mostly at universities, by means of peer reviews. In a way, they are paid to perform a critical function that is part of the intellectual lifeblood of a democratic society.

As we have seen above, researchers' needs are by nature different from those of the policy-makers. They view problems differently; they have other time frames and they interpret findings differently. Thus, it is not surprising that policy-makers often feel that the research products badly fit the policy agenda. Even specified, commissioned research is frequently accused of this deficiency.

Differences in value-orientation and outlook tend to colour the interaction between the researchers and policy-makers all the way from the initiation of a project to the interpretation and dissemination of its findings.

It should, however, be pointed out that by no means all research is initiated in interaction with policy-makers and planners. Universities usually have certain funds at their own discretion or grants from research councils, where the "research-worthiness" of a proposal in principle is assessed on the basis of "immanent" research criteria. Studies are initiated without any particular glance at the applicability of findings. They are conducted for the sake of extending the frontier of fundamental knowledge.

Disjunctions Between Research and Policy-Making

Tensions and conflicts that can lead to disjunctions between research and policy-making are implicit in what has been said above.

One could at some length quote evidence about frustrations stirred up in policy-makers by discrepancies between expectations and actual performance of research. The Committee chaired by Roald Campbell, which evaluated the work of the National Institute of Education, Washington, D.C., stated that "improvements in the learning and the behavior of the students are difficult to demonstrate" as a result of research endeavours. (Quoted after Shellard *et al.*, 1979, p. 18.) The committee pointed at three reasons for this: 1. The low level of sophistication of the social sciences (one would suppose in comparison with the physical sciences) that deprives them of "the luxury of predictable results"; 2. Problems of bringing about and measuring changes in human learning and behaviour are "vastly more complex" than those of technological change, and 3. The need for improvement in education is so great that expectations of educational R & D have been put much higher than the "limited results" of research can live up to.

There might be some truth in all this, but the crucial thing is that research and development *cannot provide answers to the value questions* with which social issues, including educational ones, are imbued. That explains why research at best can provide a system of enlightened communication. Information of relevance to policy via other channels has to be merged with findings. (Carrick, Australian Minister of Education, in Shellard *et al.*, 1979, p. 32.) Carrick also quotes Gene Glass as saying that there is far more knowledge stored in the nervous system of ten excellent teachers of how to manage and promote classroom learning than an "average teacher can distill from all the educational research journals in existence" (*ibid.*).

*   *   *

Given the background above, one could tentatively identify the following four reasons why "disjunctions" occur.

1. Research does not "fit" the particular circumstances. The problem dealt with in a given project or study is not part of or directly related to any political issue. Women's equal rights was for a long time a dead issue. But once it became an issue it almost instantly began to spur an enormous amount of research. On the other hand, research might address itself to urgent issues but come up with findings that are out of phase with policy-making process.

2. Findings are inconclusive from the policy-makers' or researchers' point of view, or both. This is more the rule than the exception. It is in the nature of the process of making an issue "researchable" that the overall problem has to be broken down into part-problems that more readily lend themselves to systematic investigations.

3. Dissemination is ineffective, so that findings do not "percolate" to decision-makers and practitioners. Researchers seeking recognition among their academic peers place high premium on reports that can enhance their academic reputation, and look with scepticism upon "popularisation". This makes the role of "middle-men" so important. They can be of various types. Carrick (see Shellard, 1979) talks about the role of the "research broker" who conveys to the policy-maker research that relates to issues he has to face. Trow (p. 261 ff.) describes the training and professional role of the policy analyst. A particular type of broker is the researcher who conducts what Glass refers to as "meta-analysis" of research, tries to review critically existing research pertaining to a particular problem and comes up with a digest of what can be regarded as relatively valid conclusions from the entire research body in a particular field.

A special case of bad dissemination is the way many reports have been written up with undue emphasis on the technical jargon. Without compromising professional values it is possible for researchers, sometimes with the help of journalists who have specialised in writing on research in a particular field, to present their findings in reports with readable language. The technical aspects can then be relegated to appendices or separate publications. A typical example of such a presentation is Jencks *et al.* (1972) on inequality. Irrespective of the opinion one holds on the scientific merits of this book, its policy impact and its influence on public debate was due to the way the investigations were presented and interpreted, with the technical problems dealt with in appendices.

4. Research findings that contradict or do not support the policy that a

decision-making body or an agency wants to pursue is, indeed, a frequent reason for disjunction. Policy-makers want to use research in order to legitimise a "pre-fabricated" position, only to find that the findings are not supportive or are even used as ammunition by adversaries. This is something that social research, given its fields of inquiry, has to live with and can take with a certain magnanimity, as long as its results are available to all interested parties.

The role of social science research is in the last run to help not only the experts but the general public as well to shape their model of social reality. This model derives its realisation from *many different sources, of which research is but one.* This should lead the researchers to a certain humility and prevent them from overselling their contributions and hopefully in the long run also contribute to much more realistic expectations on the part of the policy-makers about what research can do for them.

Research Utilisation and Research Communication

Before discussing various models of research utilisation it would be in order to define what is meant here by policy-makers and researchers, respectively.

1. *Policy-makers* comprise mainly three categories of people: (a) Politicians, elected representatives of larger constituencies, parliamentarians; (b) Top administrators in government agencies; (c) Top people in national associations representing various interest groups, such as trade unions; (d) Experts, mostly academics, serving as consultants or staff members for categories a–c.

2. *Researchers* are academics at (a) Universities, public or private; (b) Research institutions which are part of government agencies; (c) Private research institutions, and (d) "Middle-men" in administrative agencies.

In a study of how educational researchers relate to policy-makers we are confronted with two problems, of which the latter is largely part of the former: 1. How and to what extent research conducted by social scientists is *"utilised"* in the policy-making process or in day-to-day actions of administrators who have to implement policy decisions, and 2. How research is *communicated* to policy-makers. In order to make the study of interrelationships and interactions between policy-makers and researchers more fruitful in terms of understanding the processes one has to widen the perspective and try to clarify what could be meant by "utilisation" of research conducted by social scientists.

Carol Weiss (1979), who has thoroughly studied the problem of the use of social science research in policy-making, has advanced 7 different "models" of research utilisation in the social sciences. I shall briefly comment on these models.

The *first* model is the classical, *"linear"*, one that has dominated the picture of how research is utilised in the physical sciences: basic research →applied research → development → application. I would prefer to call this the "pure-to-applied-research" model. Some "fundamental" knowledge seems to have bearings on a particular "practical" problem. Applied research is conducted to test the feasibility of using the finding. In case the test yields favourable results, some development work is launched with the aim of devising a new technology, whereupon more wide-scale application can take place.

Weiss points out that this model has hardly any wide application in the social sciences where "knowledge does not readily lend itself to conversion into replicable technologies, either material or social" (p. 427).

The *second* model is the *problem-solving* one. The most common conception, or rather expectation, of how social science research is used is the "direct application of the results of a specific social science study to a pending decision" (p. 427). The social scientist is expected to provide the empirical evidence or research conclusions needed in order to solve a given policy problem.

The problem-solving model can schematically be described as follows:

> identification of missing knowledge → acquisition of social science research findings either by drawing on existing body of knowledge or by commissioned research → interpretation of research findings in the context of decision options → choice of policy.

This is – I would suggest – the classical platonic "philosopher-king" conception. Researchers are supposed to possess or otherwise acquire the knowledge (and wisdom) from which direct guidelines for policy-making can be derived. The researchers sometimes like to think that they communicate to the policy-makers what "research has to tell", which implies that the latter should act according to the advice given by the researchers (Husén, 1968).

This model, again, reflects what sometimes goes on, say, in electronics technology or in immunology on the basis of research in physics and biochemistry, respectively. But in both examples very little policy-making in the traditional sense is involved. In these cases those who are going to apply fundamental research findings are more seldom confronted with policy than by professional options. Sometimes policy-makers are called upon to contribute subsequently only when ethical conflicts arise.

The problem-solving model in the social sciences is based on the implicit assumption that there is a consensus on goals. It assumes that social scientists and researchers agree not only between themselves but also within the respective groups, something which, of course, is not the case when it comes to social issues.

The problem faced by social scientists, when there is no consensus of goals, can be illustrated with the following, typical example. While spending a few months as a visiting professor at Stanford University I received a letter from the head of one of the divisions in the National Board of Education in Sweden. He wanted my expert help in "solving" the problem of bilingual education in Sweden, where there has been a heavy immigration since 1960 from Finland and the Mediterranean area. More than 10 per cent of the children of school age now come from homes where Swedish is not the mother tongue. There are two, highly divergent, opinions aired both among researchers and parents of the immigrant children about to what extent instruction in the mother tongue should be provided. I encountered similar controversies when conducting the OECD policy review on compensatory education in New Mexico, where there was intense disagreement about to what extent Spanish should be used as a medium of instruction (Husén, 1981a).

Carol Weiss rightly points out that the expectations about what research expertise can do in solving such problems merely by providing "facts" are "wildly optimistic".

The *third* model is the *interactive* one. It assumes no "linearity" from research to utilisation but rather "a disorderly set of inter-connections and back-and-forthness". This model assumes the existence of a dialogue between policy-makers and researchers, not necessarily only in face-to-face situations but through intermediaries as well.

The *fourth* model is the *political* one. What often happens is that a social issue after having been debated for quite some time has led to firm and entrenched positions that will not be shaken by new evidence. Research findings then become ammunition for the side that finds certain research conclusions congenial with its standpoint. A rather frequent case is that policy-makers have already taken their decision and commission research that hopefully will back up their standpoint.

Social scientists often note with dismay how their research is utilized in the political battles without their being able to "explain" what their findings "really" mean. However, they can take comfort from the fact that their findings usually are available to *all* parties involved in the policy debate. Thereby, they can contribute to sharpening the issues and/or reformulating the problems.

The most typical example from my own experience of the political model refers to the debate and research conducted in Sweden on the issue of "differentiation" in connection with the Swedish school reform. I dealt with this in a series of lectures at the University of Chicago in 1959 (Husén, 1962). The way researchers and policy-makers interacted in this case I dealt with in an AERA presentation (Husén, 1965). I shall therefore confine myself to pointing out the strong political pressure in Sweden for a common 9-year comprehensive school catering for all children of the age range 7–16. The core issue was when and how differentiation according to academic ability and/or achievement should take place. On the basis of legislation passed in 1950, the government launched a large-scale 10-year pilot program of comprehensive schooling, the outcomes of which would in the long run "determine" how the comprehensive schools should look in terms of structure and curriculum. After some years, in 1956, the Parliament decided that no differentiation should take place until after the 6th grade. Prior to that, transfer to the selective university-preparing secondary school could take place after the 4th grade in primary school. Almost simultaneously a Government Commission, on which the political parties were represented by their leading educational experts and members of Parliament, was appointed. Among the Commission members there was a majority for a relatively undifferentiated, comprehensive school. The Commission sponsored a study of how the children in Stockholm developed from grade 4 through grade 9 in terms of achievements in basic school subjects. In the northern half of the city, the traditional system with transfer of the "academically-bound" from grade 4 in primary school to lower secondary school was still for a short time in operation, whereas the City Council decided to introduce the comprehensive system without transfer in the southern half.

The outcomes (Svensson, 1962) of the Stockholm study for the first 3 years only were available when the Commission had to make up its mind about how to resolve the differentiation issue. The conservative party and a fraction in the liberal party, together with a majority of secondary school teachers, were for early differentiation. On the whole, the findings seemed to indicate that a comprehensive milieu was particularly favourable to able children from lower class homes, and that *ceteris paribus* the able students did not significantly suffer from being taught together with their more slow-learning classmates.

The report coming out of the Stockholm study was subsequently subjected to criticism (Dahllöf, 1967) on methodological grounds. The issue was whether the indicators used in the study were adequate. By looking at other indicators, the critical review came up with results that tended to favour a more organisationally differentiated system.

The *fifth* model, the *tactical* one, simply refers to the frequent tendency to "bury" a controversial problem in research in order to have to defend procrastination or unwillingness to take immediate action.

The *sixth* is the *enlightenment model*, which Weiss thinks is the one through which "social science research most frequently enters the policy arena". This model refers to the way research is "permeating" the policy-making process. It does so not by any specific findings or specific projects, commissioned or not, but by its "generalisations and orientations percolating through informed publics and coming to shape the way in which people think about social issues".

Research without reference to any specific piece of evidence tends to "sensitise decision-makers to new issues and helps them to turn what were non-problems into policy problems".

The *seventh* model, finally, in Weiss's taxonomy could be called *research-as-part-of-the-intellectual-enterprise-of-society model*. Social science research is in this model simply regarded as a dependent variable along with other dependent variables, such as philosophy, history, journalism, etc. For instance, policy interest in a particular field stimulates research in it and helps to make funds available. Researchers thereby can contribute to widening the horizon of the general debate on certain issues and to reformulating the problems.

*   *   *

It appears that we can merge the above seven models into two major ones: the *enlightenment or "percolation" model* on the one hand and the *political model* on the other. The enlightenment model can easily be merged with the interactive one, and the political with the tactical one. The first two models, the "linear" one, from "pure" research to application, and the problem-solving one, do not appear to be particularly fruitful in analysing the relationship between researchers and policy-makers, because of making assumptions which seldom apply.

I shall in the following comment on each of the two merged models, particularly from the point of view of communication between researchers and policy-makers.

Michael Kirst, professor at Stanford University, when interviewed, pointed out that the problem of how educational research relates to policy-making has been "misconceived" and "overstructured" by the researchers themselves. They have been caught in rational and elaborate "knowledge-driven" models. The models that seem to have been successful in technology and medicine do not apply in social practice, such as the art of education.

Kirst cited the school finance equalisation issue, that initially was raised in the state of California and then "exploded" all over the United States in the late 1960s, as an interesting and typical example of enlightenment. Research played an important role in making certain facts and ideas "percolate" through the educational system. This made people, particularly many policy-makers, reconceptualise the problem and view it in a new perspective. The attempts on the part of researchers to measure equity in educational finance were of great importance in influencing the perceptions of many people.

The "percolation" process is a very subtle and intangible one. The direct contact, either face to face or by reading scholarly reports with all the paraphernalia of technical jargon, seems to play little role. The role of "middle-men" should be carefully studied, because it appears to be a key one. One can identify entire "informal networks" of intermediate linking mechanisms. Newspapers, journals with popularised versions of research findings, close friends of the politicians, and their staff members play important roles. Certain research-promoting, private bodies can also play an important role in spreading information.

Kirst points out that given the above background social science researchers should not be too apologetic about their inability to stick to timetables laid down in proposals and research budgets. Their influence is one *in the long run* and is not exercised by any specific project at any particular point in time. Research that in the long run has an impact, does not yield such tangible products as curriculum development materials to be used in the classroom. Its important "products" help reshape and formulate overriding problems related to school policies.

*   *   *

Carol Weiss (1980) has pointed out that there is a need to reformulate not only how research is "utilised" but how policy "decisions" are taken as well. Both researchers and policy-makers like to think that since research is the "pursuit of truth" it should be an integral "part of the decision-making process" (Shellard *et al.,* 1979). The quotation is from a speech by the then Australian Minister of Education, J.L. Carrick, at a conference on educational research for policy-making in Australia. He made a plea for more relevancy and better "application of research findings to current issues".

Weiss makes the point that policy actions are not "decided" upon in the sense that people with authority sit down and ponder various options, weigh them against each other, consider relevant facts and then choose one of the options. In reality, policies are decided upon in a much more diffuse way. The best way to characterise the process is by talking about "decision accretion". In the complicated dynamic play between interest groups, arguments advanced, and administrative considerations, including the inertia of the system, guide-lines for action slowly begin to emerge.

Certainly, in spite of all the misgivings about research being "useless" and contributing nothing to policies and practice, research "creeps" into policy deliberations. As Weiss puts it: the influence of research "is exercised in a more subtle way than the word 'utilisation' suggests" (Weiss, 1980). She interviewed 155 people with high level positions in mental health organisations in the U.S. federal government about their perceptions of the usefulness of social science research for their work. The main question put to them was their "conscious" use of research. This is different from the "circuitous percolation of research ideas into people's construction of social reality" (*op cit.,* p. 3).

The interesting thing was that 57 per cent of the respondents said that they "used" social science research, but only 7 per cent gave *specific* illustrations by referring to a particular type of research or to a particular study. The inter-pretation was that research to many policy-makers was a kind of "continuing education", a "medium of communication", and a way of "keeping up with the field". Research is integrated into the overall perspective that decision-makers get on a problem. Much of their information is obtained from news-papers, popular articles on scientific research, and books.

Given the way decision-makers and policy-makers "use" research one could distinguish between *conscious use in general* (considering the research ideas that through many channels have "percolated" to the decision-makers) and the *active search* for what "research has to say" which may or may not lead to commissioning of a particular research project.

Research according to the "enlightenment" or "percolation" model can best be described as a "mode of communication and persuasion in the public arena". It has become fashionable to refer to "what research has to say". Research findings often are a kind of "overlay" or "decoration" that is added to the recommendation of certain policy actions. It has become ritualistic to refer to social science documentation. In that respect "social science research has become a necessary language of discourse in the public arena" (Weiss, 1980, p. 18). Research provides "proof" for a proposed action and is referred to as giving evidence on the pay-off of this action.

*   *   *

In studying the role played by social scientists in policy-making I have become more interested in how educational researchers relate to policy-makers than to find out to what extent social science research *in abstracto* is actually "utilised" in policy formulation.

Quite a lot of valuable theoretical and empirical groundwork has recently been done in providing knowledge about the utilisation problem. I have made extensive reference to Carol Weiss's (1980) taxonomy of utilisation which I have found extremely useful. Both she and others, who have conducted empirical studies, have limited these to policy-makers' perceptions of how social science research is utilised. Most students in this field have, however, not tried to do the same mapping of how researchers perceive the use of research. This is a pity, because there are many clues that suggest a "two-culture" hypothesis about how the two partners relate to each other.

In their study of 204 policy-makers at the upper level of the executive branch of the U.S. federal government Kaplan *et al.* (1975) tried to test three hypotheses that related to why research was used, or, rather, not used. They found that what they call the "two-community theory" was supported by their data. Twice as much of the variance of utilisation was accounted for by the "two-community factor" as by what they call "knowledge-specific" or "policy-maker constraint" factors. They conclude:

> The implication of this analysis is that theories of under-utilisation with the greatest degree of explanatory power are those which emphasise the existence of a gap between social scientists and policy makers due to differences in values, languages, reward systems and social and professional affiliations. (*op.cit.,* p. 27).

Social science research utilisation has, as pointed out above, traditionally been conceived by both researchers and policy-makers in rather simplistic terms. The overall conception is the "linear" one of moving from knowledge to action. Policy-makers tend to extend the R & D model developed in the physical sciences and technology to the social domain.

This simplistic conception of how research is "utilised" or how it "affects" policies has prevailed until recently, when in the wake of research on research and with a newly awakened interest among social scientists themselves, one has begun to analyse what social science research does, if anything. Empirical studies, such as those by Weiss (1980) and Kaplan (1975), have shown that there is seldom a clearcut relationship on a one-to-one basis between a particular piece of research or a particular study and, say, preparation of a piece of legislation or taking of a particular decision. It has also become increasingly clear that there is ample reason to talk about "diffusion" instead of "dissemination" of research, the latter having been the preferred expression among both researchers and policy-makers.

From the above analyses we conclude that the relationship between policy and research is much more diffuse and hard to pinpoint than hitherto conceived. Scholarship in general, and in some instances particular programs of projects of research, contribute to putting certain issues on the agenda of public debate and to inspiring demands for political action. Research, not least through critical analysis, is an instrument of generating ideas more than specific "facts" or general "knowledge". In some instances research contributes to the reinterpretation of an issue by drawing attention to aspects or problems which have gone unnoticed. It also tends to affect the belief-systems among the general public. A good example of this from quite another field is the research on smoking and cancer.

Research can contribute to achieving consensus about an issue. Political decisions are taken within a context of accommodation. The decision is not clear-cut but is an attempt to arrive at resolutions that can accommodate a maximum of interests represented by groups and individuals who want to influence the decision- or policy-making process. As David Krathwohl put it in the interview with him, it is a process of "balancing the goodies so that everyone feels satisfied". This is quite different from decisions taken within the "context of command" which is the classical one in the military or which characterises decisions about production in a business firm.

Sixten Marklund in his contribution to the Symposium (p. 179) suggests a taxonomy of how research and policy-making according to his experience relate. He advances a two-by-two table by distinguishing between "free" and "commissioned" research and between "policy-making" and "policy-execution". He can claim quite a lot of experience, since not only has he been heading the R & D Bureau at the Swedish National Board of Education for quite some time, but brings perceptions also from the other side of the fence as a university researcher and a professor.

A major thesis for which I have quite a lot of support in the interviews is that the expectations held during the "golden years" about what educational research would achieve were extremely unrealistic. I happened once in the mid-1970s to travel between Madrid and Bonn with the former German Minister of Education, who had a background as a mining engineer and had been professor at one of the leading technical institutes in Germany. He apparently expected educational research to follow the example of metallurgy with a straightforward improvement of the production process and bitterly aired his misgivings about the dismal outcomes of all the resources given to educational researchers. This inspired me to contemplate the difference between "utilisation" of findings of social sciences as compared to those of the natural sciences.

Issues Emerging from Interviews, Questionnaires and Invited Papers

The relationship between social science research in general and between policy-makers and researchers as human beings of flesh and blood in particular was for a long time conceived to be relatively unproblematic in terms of the substance of their transaction, namely "research findings". Policy-makers, decision-makers, and practitioners simply "used" whatever "research" had to offer. The relationship was, however, felt to be problematic in terms of human contacts which often were perceived as a clash between two sets of values, between on the one hand the academic ethos, and what solemnly is preached as the long-range pursuit of truth, and on the other short-range political expediency and pragmatism. Frequently policy-makers were blamed for not using what the researchers had to offer them, whereas policy-makers accused researchers of coming up with irrelevant findings or doing something different from what they were supposed to do.

Several of the questionnaire and interview respondents have dealt with the relationship between basic and applied research, or to use another terminology between fundamental and policy-oriented research. A case is made for providing sufficient resources to fundamental research, since this has to constitute the fertile ground for applied research and development. In many cases fundamental studies without an eye on specific applications provide "spin-off" effects which turn out to be highly important and to have unexpected implications. John B. Carroll refers to his model of school learning (Carroll, 1963). When it was advanced, it went for some time almost unnoticed, but was picked up by Benjamin Bloom for his mastery learning concept (Bloom, 1968, 1981) and turned out to have a strong impact not only on instructional theory but on classroom practices as well.

Carroll in his reply also illustrates the process of influence. By 1960, partly as a result of the National Defense Education Act, there was on the part of the authorities a strong interest in foreign language teaching, although the Defense Department, the Peace Corps or the State Department had not then commissioned any studies. Instead private foundations, such as the Ford Foundation, gave the initial boost. Public agencies which were interested in specific answers from the research community to their problems then began to make funds available.

Friedrich Edding, retired from the Max Planck Institute for Educational Research and a member of the German *Bildungsrat*, refers to the policy-makers as "our beloved enemies". He goes on to say: "We need them but I had also continuously to defend research autonomy." Sometimes he has had the impression that policy-makers wanted to "buy" results pretending that these results were produced by "independent experts". Policy-makers by the very nature of their tasks tend to hold obligations to political power, whereas researchers tend to be obligated in the first place to the professional community.

Dahllöff in the paper prepared for this Symposium (p. 143) takes the Swedish school reform as a point of departure in discussing the role of research in policy-making. He, quite rightly, raises questions about the comparability of the four countries from which information about how researchers and policy-makers relate has been drawn. Quite naturally, the Swedish comprehensive school reform plays an important part in his analysis. What he has to say about social criticism as compared to systems criticism deserves to be seriously contemplated not only by instant reformers of education but also by those ready to take the time and trouble needed to go to the roots of the problems.

The setting up of the German *Bildungsrat* (Education Council) in the 1960s offers an interesting example of direct contact between policy-makers at the national, and in this case the federal, level and university scholars. Hellmut Becker, Director of the Max Planck Institute for Educational Research, was a member of the Council and its vice-chairman. The Council was established to plan the public school system in Germany within a long-range and long-term objectives' perspective. The outcomes of its deliberations to a large extent went into the *Bildungsbericht '70*, the report with a planning perspective on German education that was prepared by the Brandt government in 1970.

The *Bildungsbericht '70* was the central document in the review of educational policies in the Federal Republic of Germany conducted under OECD auspices in 1971. My personal copy is inscribed by Hildegard Hamm-Brücher, then State Secretary in the newly-established Federal Ministry of Education. The *Bericht* has a special chapter on educational research that begins with the following statement: "The causes behind the failings of the present educational system and the consequences of new structures and contents can be identified and analysed only by scientific research. Thereby educational research becomes an essential prerequisite for educational reform." (p. 135). The main recommendation is: "In the public budgets (federal and state) considerably increased funds have to be made available for educational research." (p. 138).

The Council provides a highly interesting case of institutionalised contacts or liaisons for a limited period between researchers and policy-makers. It resembles the Royal Commissions in the UK or the Government Commissions in Sweden, although in the two latter cases academics, and particularly professors, played a less prominent role than they did in Germany. Becker points out that the Council gives an example of the enlightenment model. The Council had a time-limited mandate and could therefore not wait for investigations which, if they had been commissioned, would have been completed long after the decisions in the Council were taken. Therefore it had instead to commission a series of the state-of-the-arts reports. These contributed to "smoothing the way" for certain of the Council's recommendations. One report contributed to the discard of the widespread idea of a limited reserve of ability. The major issue in German educational policy, as was the case in several other West European countries, was how to structure the upper part of the mandatory school. To what extent should it be comprehensive and how much selectivity should be allowed? Since one could not wait for original German studies, the problem arose to what extent studies conducted on grouping and differentiation in, for instance, Sweden and England were applicable in Germany.

It is interesting to note that, depending upon the political affiliation, research findings on school structure in a given country were used both as arguments for and against the comprehensive model in other countries. Swedish findings were by German Social Democrats and Liberals interpreted as support for the *Gesamtschule*, and by the Christian Democrats as confirming that comprehensiveness would lower the standards. The same happened in England. In the mid-1960s I was invited by Anthony Crosland, who was then Minister of Education in the Labour government, to discuss with him the issue of comprehensiveness and report on our studies on the social and pedagogical effects of comprehensive schooling (Husén, 1983). A few years later, in the so-called Black Papers issued by right-wing conservatives, I was, somewhat inconsistently, portrayed both as the "demon king" of the Swedish reform and as an extremely naive person.

The problem of transfer of research findings from one country to another also applies to problems of teaching objectives and curriculum.

Becker also gives us illustrations (p. 103 ff.) of the irritation among researchers being called upon to study problems that reflected immediate needs among policy-makers. Some researchers, who felt that reforms were badly needed, cheerfully played the role of evangelists and provided intellectual ammunition for reform, whereas others felt that commissioned research by the Council interfered with their research endeavours which were conducted within a longer time perspective and were more basic or conclusion-oriented in nature.

I met with similar problems during the time I was closely associated with the 1957 Commission that drew up the blue-print for the 1962 comprehensive education reform in Sweden. I have never belonged to any political party and have considered it an important matter of principle to avoid compromising my integrity and credibility as a researcher by having to observe the restraints that go with membership of a party. But my views on grouping came to be identified with the overall political position of the Social Democrats. I have found this to be the case, even with foreign observers. In England I have come to be regarded, particularly through my contacts with Anthony Crosland, as a representative of socialist education policies. Stuart Maclure, editor of the

Times Educational Supplement, reviewing my book *The School in Question*, questioned that I could be so critical of something I had played a part in creating through my work with Social Democrat educational politicians. But in good liberal tradition, equality of educational opportunity was for me a central aspect of the school reform, and this was a matter that was not so obvious in the 1940s as it is now. My studies during the late forties on the "reserve of talent" gave me a strong impression of the imbalance that prevailed between the various social classes in access to higher education, from upper secondary school to university. I therefore felt a strong personal commitment on matters concerning educational equality. In the preface to my book *The School in a Changing Society* (*Skolan i ett föränderligt samhälle*) (1961) I pointed out:

> Over the past decade I have had two spheres of activity in the work of school reform, partly as an educational researcher and partly as a teacher, including a period at a School of Education. At the beginning of this period, my attitude to school reform was fairly lukewarm. Together with the majority of academics, I was somewhat sceptical about a school system that did not select for special training at an early stage those pupils who obviously had an aptitude for study. But the more I have sought to understand the social function of the school, and its duty to realise the potential of the individual pupil, the more convinced I have become of the necessity for school reform as one part of the democratic transformation of society.
>
> To the extent that this book deals with central aspects of school reform, it should be regarded as a contribution to discussion. I am arguing *for* school reform. The book adduces facts from time to time from my own research and from that of others. An example is the analysis of the price paid by the selective school for the high standard attained by the group who reach the final examinations. However, I would not in any way pretend that the material published here is either comprehensive or always objective, any more than that it represents educational research. I am probably too strongly committed for that. My commitment is not so strong, however, that it prevents my having a clear understanding of the drawbacks of the process of reform, and particularly of the difficulties during the pilot period.

Alain Bienaymé, who has served as adviser to several ministers of education or higher education in France, has conducted a survey among politicians and colleagues. He points out (p. 121) that the very process of scientific inquiry prevents it from having a direct bearing on policy-making. He quotes Karl Popper saying that research is more a means of discarding bad ideas than of identifying fruitful or good ones.

Bienaymé points out that there are uninvestigated problems which in a way serve as "untouchables". He mentions student satisfaction in France. If he had been in Sweden, he could have mentioned cost development, attendance and truancy rates in schools.

There has in recent years been some talk about the credibility of the social sciences in providing a knowledge base for policies of social intervention. In a review of Jencks' (1972) book on equality of educational opportunity, Henry Levin even talked about a "credibility gap". Two circumstances have allegedly put credibility in jeopardy. In the first place, there has been a tendency to overstate the validity of findings for whatever policies under consideration. Studies that often have been cited as causing a credibility gap are those on the relative importance of school and home background for student achievement.

During the 1960s, in a series of national and international sample surveys, attempts were made, among other things by means of sophisticated multivariate analyses, to assess how much formal schooling "contributes" to student achievement. The technique aimed at finding out how much of the between-student variance that was accounted for by schooling. In spite of the fact that in studies by, for instance, Jencks (1972) only some 15–20 per cent of the total variance was explained by *all* the variables under control, sweeping statements were made about schooling not making much difference – or any difference at all. The other reason for credibility problems is that social scientists have tended to be politically radical to the extent that in some countries sociologist and militant leftist have become synonymous. Young researchers of various neo-marxist persuasions, convinced that Marxism is *the* scientific solution of social problems, have tended to reject the value of empirical studies.

There has been a growing feeling among academics that one needs to establish "enclaves" for "independent intellectual inquiry", which would balance the tendency towards excessive policy-orientation. In most instances universities are, of course, such enclaves. But government agencies and in some instances parliaments realise the value of having access to researchers and scientific advisors within their own organisation. Such advisors are able to work on long-range problems and can, freed of the urgencies of the daily time-table and of the necessities of immediate action, work out alternative solutions. They can even take a critical position *vis-á-vis* policies and actions of the agency they serve.

James Coleman raises in his paper (p. 131 ff.) the important question of how policy-oriented research should be institutionalised. How well considered are the existing institutional structures for the initiation of such research? He underlines that it is not proper for an institution in charge of the implementation of a program to be in charge of its evaluation as well. In addition to the self-evaluation there should be at least one evaulation conducted by an outside agency. Thus, Coleman recommends "institutional separation" and methodological pluralism for both implementation and evaluation. He contemplates several alternatives for achieving such a pluralism which are complementary and not mutually exclusive. In the first place, studies with the purpose of elucidating the same policy issue could be commissioned at two or more institutions independent of each other. Separate evaluations have already been mentioned. In order to secure greatest possible impartiality in assessing the scientific validity of the findings one could contemplate the establishment of some kind of "science court" where methodological and technical issues can be dealt with by competent and interested parties. Finally, pluralism in the dissemination of findings should also be considered.

Referring to his own bruises, Coleman takes up the "use" of social policy research in a situation of political controversy. He cites his 1966 survey on equality of educational opportunity as an example (Coleman *et al.,* 1966). The study was commissioned by the U.S. Congress which wanted information relevant to the civil rights legislation. But as Harold Howe, at that time U.S. Commissioner of Education, points out in the interview with me, "the report was never used by the federal agencies". The rightly asked themselves what policies were implied in the findings. These were, at the time when they were published, usually interpreted as supporting desegregation. But "the Feds" asked themselves in Howe's words: "What the hell should we do with this report!" Coleman points out that the results, instead of being used by the decision-making bureaucrats, were used by the advocates on both sides of the controversial desegregation issues. Coleman's experience is that social policy research tends to be "used" when there is intensive conflict over policy and mostly by those who are not in formal decision-making positions and who tend to challenge the policies decided upon by those in authority. He could thereby point at his survey on public and private education (Coleman *et al.,* 1981) when the findings got into the thicket of political controversy even before they were fully available to the public. I discussed his predicament in an article entitled "Coleman II – Another Case of Politics and the Professors" (Husén, 1981b).

James Perkins (p. 187 ff.) grossly simplifies his role by calling himself an academic bureaucrat. He brings more than that to the theme of the Symposium. He has served as Vice-President of the Carnegie Corporation which once set an example for private foundations in supporting education in general and research in particular. Furthermore, he has been instrumental in promoting educational research internationally, particularly on higher education. Finally, as a member of the Carnegie Commission and (later) Council on Higher Education he has participated in inquiries instrumental for framing policy. In a separate report, "Sponsored Research of the Carnegie Commission on Higher Education" (McGraw-Hill, New York 1975), an impressive series of investigations pertaining to major policy issues are summed up.

In analysing the situation in the United States Perkins points out that there are no real policy-making power centres in education at the national level, something that James Conant found to be lacking and therefore contributed to the establishment of a consortium of the American states (Conant, 1964). The support system for educational research is indeed pluralistic, with resources coming from federal, state, and private sources, whereas in the other three countries resources almost exclusively come from central, government, sources. The private bodies in the United States have played a role both in sponsoring studies and in framing policy. The Carnegie Commission on Higher Education could be cited as one example. The study of the American high school conducted by a task force chaired by James B. Conant (1959) is perhaps the most outstanding one in the past.

Comparisons Between Countries

Each of the four countries studied with regard to how researchers and policy-makers relate shows particular arrangements, usually institutional ones.

The sheer size of the United States defies comparisons with a country of the size of Sweden. In the latter the opportunities of establishing direct, personal and informal contacts between researchers and decision-makers in government or in parliament were, and still are, far more favourable. In Sweden both decision-makers and researchers are few in number. Consider that in the 1950s there were in Sweden just half a dozen professors of education who could be drawn upon by, for instance, Royal Commissions to conduct research on policy issues. By the early 1970s, there were still only some 30. In the United States they amount to several thousand, and the relevant research community is defined by the membership of the American Educational Research Association (AERA). Apart from a couple of White House Conferences on education, it was not until about 1970 that arrangements were made in United States for closer contacts. AERA set up a Legislative and Planning Committee which tried to rally support from various interest groups for the establishment of a National Institute of Education. The Committee was also involved in pushing and testifying for various pieces of legislation by talking to members of Congress.

Taking country by country, I shall begin with the United States, which has been in the lead with regard both to the volume of research and the amount of financial support it has enjoyed.

An important, catalytic role in the United States in bringing educational research to bear on crucial issues has, as mentioned above, been played by the private foundations, such as the Carnegie Corporation and the Ford Foundation. Not only have foundations, by providing initial grants to promising projects or innovations, given researchers an opportunity to tackle neglected problems. They have also been instrumental in building up support for educational reforms by influencing public opinion, for instance about equality of educational opportunity. It is possible to identify several problem areas where the foundations have taken initiatives which have subsequently been followed by support on the part of the federal government. The Carnegie Council on Higher Education, which sponsored an impressive volume of research, was deliberately set up in order to influence public policy in higher education.

Another feature of the relationship is the role played by private research firms, such as Stanford Research Institute and Abt Associates. When requests for proposals are announced, these firms tend to outbid the universities simply because they can concentrate entirely on their task as research agencies and are not tied down by teaching obligations or by social caretaking.

Requests For Proposals, RFP, is a third characteristic which is seldom found in the other three countries.

An example of successful educational research in the United States has been the way some universities in the 1950s and 1960s began to draw upon the resources offered by the whole range of social sciences. Earlier education departments suffered from a kind of solipsism with a focus on didactic problems and processes only. They were ready to take some help from psychology departments, but had little or no contact with other social science departments. Institutions, such as the University of Chicago and Stanford University, in the 1950s began to make joint appointments in the graduate school of education for outstanding sociologists, psychologists and political scientists. This substantially contributed to raising the quality and prestige of educational research.

Liaison between educational researchers and policy-makers in the United Kingdom and Sweden has in most cases been established by the so-called Royal Commissions, or, in the less royal Sweden, by Government Commissions (Husén, 1965). These can either commission state-of-the-art reports or sponsor original studies on key policy issues. Cases in point are the extensive survey conducted by the Plowden Commission (HMSO, 1967) on the influence of school and home on school achievements or studies sponsored by the Swedish 1957 School Commission on ability grouping and its social implications (Svensson, 1962). My colleague Kjell Härnqvist served as Research Secretary of the latter commission. In response to my questionnaire he writes: "There (i.e. in the Commission) I all the time found myself in a double role, partly as the contact man with external researchers and partly working with in-house researchers". But in both these roles it was his experience that the Commission was rather unspecific with regard to the focus of the research it supported. Therefore, the initiative was all the time with the researchers, who were able to operate within a wide scope. Härnqvist and I had similar experiences with the 1960 Commission on Upper Secondary Education (The *Gymnasium* Commission). There we both belonged to a reference group for the entire research program launched by the Commission. We participated in several sessions of the entire Commission, either giving testimony on investigations we were involved in or discussing other studies sponsored by the Commission.

Mrs. Rodhe presents in her paper (p. 241 ff.) her background as an educator in various capacities, among them the one of being responsible for an Educational Development Center. During the 1960s there was still little evaluation with "scientific methods" of the various local development projects. The picture she gives of the interaction between research and policy-making at the local level is a familiar one. The development projects were too crude and diffuse to be "neatly researchable". Development, however, had to go on, and so had decision-making, and the research reports, for instance on individualised teaching, tended to come with a considerable time lag. As Minister of Education she makes the observation that few "policy-makers at the cabinet level have much time for reading and thinking through problems on their own. They tend to be dependent on what input of new and constructive thought their staff and advisers can give them. They are lucky if they come to their office with a well-established network of friends and colleagues who are used to providing them with reviews, summaries and articles pertinent to the problems which they face in their political activity''. Issues which were on the political agenda during her time in office, such as the comprehensive school curriculum, the education of 16–19-year-olds and the system of school marks, involved educational researchers.

*   *   *

Third World countries offer a special case for at least two reasons. In the first place, education is expected to contribute the manpower resources that will bring about an economic take-off, with subsequent development. Secondly, research is expected to help substantially in coming to grips with the main problems that beset education in these countries, such as quality of instruction, attrition in schools, and relevance of curricula.

Mats Hultin of the World Bank and Neville Postlethwaite, Chairman of IEA and consultant on educational programs in Southeast Asia, have from somewhat different vantage points been able to study what research can contribute to policy-making in less developed countries. The World Bank serves, as Hultin puts it, "as a catalyst for research and as a middle-man between researchers and policy-makers in the developing countries". Those representing aid agencies are trying to serve as a kind of broker of educational know-how and research. This is often achieved by technical assistance within the framework of loan agreements.

The role of educational research in shaping educational policies in developing countries is strongly emphasised in the Bank's extremely carefully prepared educational policy paper. A research component has in recent years routinely gone into the loan agreements in education.

Neville Postlethwaite sketches half a dozen cases based on personal experiences, some of which certainly are not uncommon. Take, for instance, the Director-General for whom a problem existed only if it had been raised as a problem in the national assembly! His example about ethnocentrism which effectively hampers what to outsiders would seem to be badly needed reforms in education is a familiar one.

Postlethwaite discusses how links can be forged between policy-makers and researchers during the entire research process so as to bring home to those in power what the "facts" are. What he has to say on the setting up of reference groups or national research committees is a contribution to the list of suggestions of how to institutionalise research with policy implications. He also points out that planners and policy-makers usually are very unfamiliar with the language and basic methods of educational research. If ethnocentrism is added to these impediments, one can expect quite a lot of resistance against educational change.

The Dissemination Problem

Several of my interlocutors are convinced that dissemination of information is a key problem in establishing better relationships between research and policy-making. A policy debate brings up issues which might challenge researchers who can then contribute to the conceptualisation and clarification of the problems as well as to the conscientialisation of the general public. The fact that "state-of-the-art" studies in many instances have proved to have a strong impact on the public debate and on the policy-making process shows the importance of dissemination. Hellmut Becker cites as one example the big report by Erich Roth (1969) and others prepared for the *Bildungsrat* on ability and learning (*Begabung und Lernen*). It sold almost 200 thousand copies, and had a tremendous influence on the intellectual climate in which the debate in Germany on comprehensivisation was conducted.

Michael Kirst and his co-workers are convinced that dissemination is *the* answer to better communication between researchers and policy-makers. He points out that most people have a wrong concept of research utilisation. They tend to look for *direct*, instrumental uses of research in educational policy and to overlook the myriads of different ways in which social science research influences policy formulation. Research is just *one* element in the complex mix of experience, conventional wisdom and political accommodation that enters into decision-making.

Sixten Marklund on the basis of his experiences from the Swedish National Board of Education recommends that any grant-giving agency should require that dissemination be part of the planning of a project.

Postlethwaite takes up the jargon and the excruciatingly difficult language in which researchers sometimes tend to report their studies. But technical reports, readable or unreadable are seldom, if at all, read by policy-makers.

Some Overriding Issues

From the briefs I prepared in connection with the interviews and from the replies to the questionnaires 3 broad categories of tasks and issues emerge: 1. Studies, descriptive and/or analytical, of how the two partners relate; 2. Steps taken to improve this relationship and to facilitate communication, e.g. what could be done in terms of institutionalising better communication?; 3. Ways and means of institutionalising policy-oriented research in order to enhance its integrity and thereby its validity and credibility.

1. Is there any justification for saying that policy-makers and researchers represent two different "cultures" with different values and different professional ethos? Obviously, the policy-maker is obligated to political power, or at least to pay considerable attention to it. Equally obvious, the academic likes to think of himself as being guided by an ethos of seeking the truth.

2. If we agree that, given the conditions under which the two partners operate, there are "two cultures" between which there by necessity is always a certain tension, what steps should be taken in order to achieve a better "dialogue" or "liaison" between the two partners? What arrangements could be made to facilitate an improved two-way communication? What experiences have been derived from high level advisory panels, parliamentary hearings, participation in government commissions? Are there other steps which could be contemplated to achieve the same goal?

Can a convincing case be made for a "free sector" of research which could attract creative talent in the social sciences and extend the frontiers of fundamental knowledge which could in the long run benefit policy-making by broadening its knowledge basis? Why is research unhampered by immediate needs in the long-range interest of a pluralistic, democratic society?

3. The way publicly supported, policy-oriented research is institutionalised largely determines the validity of its products and the credibility of its producers. Presently, policy-oriented research in education is conducted in 3 different institutional settings:

1. University institutes which contract research with government agencies or with research councils where the academics themselves decide on research funds once they have been granted.

2. Research units which are part of public agencies and conduct studies which are expected to provide a knowledge base for decision-making, implementation and evaluation.

3. Private research establishments, profitmaking or non-profitmaking, which are on the market for research contracts.

One main issue here pertains to the balance between university and non-university research which basically is a problem of a proper balance between fundamental or conclusion-oriented studies on the one hand and applied or decision-oriented ones on the other. Another issue relates to the degree of independency between the researcher and various vested interests. Would "science courts", as proposed by James Coleman, be a viable instrument in achieving impartiality and in enhancing the credibility of the research findings?

There will always be tensions and communication difficulties between the two partners whose relationships will be analysed by the participants in the present Symposium. Researchers will always look upon those who provide them with their means of existence as their "beloved enemies" and policy-makers will always suspect researchers of doing their own thing instead of helping to solve immediate and urgent problems.

References

Aaron, Henry (1978) *Politics and the Professors: The Great Society in Perspective.* The Brookings Institution, Washington, D.C.

Bildungsbericht '70: Bericht der Bundesregierung zur Bildungspolitik. (1970). Der Bundes-minister für Bildung und Wissenschaft, Bonn.

Bloom, B. S. (1968) Learning for Mastery. UCLA/CSEIP, *Evaluation Comment,* 1, 2.

Bloom, B. S. (1981) *All Our Children Learning: A Primer for Parents, Teachers, and Other Educators.* McGraw-Hill, New York.

Carroll, John B. (1963) A Model of School Learning. *Teachers College Record,* 64, 8.

Cohen, David K. (1975) Reforming Educational Policy with Applied Social Research. *Harvard Educational Review,* 45, 1, February.

Coleman, James S. *et al.* (1966) *Equality of Educational Opportunity.* Department of Health, Education and Welfare, Washington, D.C.

Coleman, James S. *et al.* (1981) *Public and Private Schools.* Report prepared for the NCES, Washington, D.C.

Conant, James B. (1959) *The American High School Today.* McGraw-Hill, New York.

Conant, James B. (1964) *Shaping Educational Policy.* McGraw-Hill, New York.

Dahllöf, Urban (1967) *Skoldifferentiering och undervisningsförlopp* (School Differentiation and Teaching Processes). Almqvist and Wiksell, Stockholm.

Dahllöf, Urban (1971) *Ability Grouping, Content Validity and Curriculum Process Analysis.* Teachers College Press, New York.

Dooley, P. A. *et al.* (1981) *Survey of Educational Researchers in Britain.* Department of Educational Enquiry, University of Aston in Birmingham.

Ekman, Gösta (1951) Skolformer och begåvningsfördelning (School Types and Distribution of Size of the Reserve of Ability). *Pedagogisk Tidskrift,* No. 7-8.

Ekman, Gösta (1951) Skolformer och begåvningsördelning (School Types and Distribution of Ability), *Pedagogisk Tidskrift,* No. 1-2.

Halsey, A. H. (Ed.) (1961) *Ability and Educational Opportunity.* OECD, Paris.

Halsey, A. H. (1970) Social Science and Government. *Times Literary Supplement,* March 5.

Halsey, A. H. (1976) Priorities and Decision Making in DES. *British Parliament: Education, Arts and Home Office Sub-Committee.* Monday, 9th February.

HMSO (1967) *Children and Their Primary Schools.* A Report of the Central Advisory Council for Education (England) (Plowden Report) II: Research and Surveys. Her Majesty's Stationery Office, London.

HMSO (1971) *The Organisation and Management of Government R and D* (The Rothschild Report). Her Majesty's Stationery Office, London.

House, Ernest *et al.* (1978) No Simple Answer: Critique of the Follow Through Evaluation. *Harvard Educational Review,* 48, 2.

Husén, Torsten (1946) Intelligenskrav på olika skolutbildningsstadier (Ability Requirements at Various Levels of Formal Education). *Skola och samhälle,* 27, 1.

Husén, Torsten (1947) Begåvningsurvalet och de högre skolorna (Selection According to Ability for Higher Education). *Folkskolan-Svensk Lärartidning,* I, 4.

Husén, Torsten (1948) *Begåvning och miljö* (Ability and Social Environment). Almqvist & Wiksell, Stockholm.

Husén, Torsten (1962) *Problems of Differentiation in Swedish Compulsory Schooling.* Svenska Bokförlaget, Scandinavian University Press, Stockholm.

Husén, Torsten (1965) A Case-Study in Policy-Oriented Research: The Swedish School Reform. *The School Review,* 73 (No. 3), 206-225.

Husén, Torsten (Ed.) (1967) *International Study of Achievement in Mathematics. A Comparison of Twelve Countries.* Vol. I-II. Almqvist & Wiksell and John Wiley, Stockholm & New York.

Husén, Torsten (1968) Educational Research and Policy-Making. In: W. D. Wall and T. Husén, *Educational Research and the State,* National Foundation for Educational Research in England and Wales, 13-22, London.

Husén, Torsten (1978) Educational Research and Educational Reform: A Case Study of Sweden. In: Patrick Suppes (Ed.), *Impact of Research on Education: Some Case Studies,* National Academy of Education, Washington, D.C.

Husén, Torsten (1981a) Evaluating Compensatory Education. In: *Proceedings of the National Academy of Education,* Vol. 6. National Academy of Education, Washington, D.C.

Husén, Torsten (1981b) Coleman II – Another Case of Politics and the Professors. *Change,* 13, 6, (September, 1981, 11-12).

Husén, Torsten (1983) *An Incurable Academic: Memoirs of a Professor*. Pergamon Press, Oxford.

Husén, Torsten and Gunnar Boalt (1968) *Educational Research and Educational Change: The Case of Sweden*. Almqvist & Wiksell, Stockholm.

Härnqvist, Kjell (1958) *Reserverna för högre utbildning: Beräkningar och metoddiskussion* (Reserves for Higher Education: Estimations and Methodological Discussion). 1955 års universitetsutredning III. Stockholm: Statens Offentliga Utredningar (Government Printing Office) No. 11.

Härnqvist, Kjell (1960) *Individuella differenser och skoldifferentiering* (Individual Differences and School Differentiation). 1957 års skolberedning II, SOU 1960:13. Government Printing Office, Stockholm.

Jencks, Christopher *et al.* (1972) *Inequality: A Reassessment of the Effect of Family and Schooling in America*. Basic Books, New York and London.

Kaplan, Nathan *et al.* (1975) *The Use of Social Science Knowledge in Policy Decisions at the National Level*. University of Michigan, Institute for Social Research, Ann Arbor, Michigan.

Keppel, Francis (1966) *The Necessary Revolution in American Education*. Harper & Row, New York and London.

Kogan, Maurice (1973) *The Politics of Education*. Penguin, London.

Kogan, Maurice *et al.* (1980) *Government's Commissioning of Research: A Case Study*. Department of Government, Brunel University, England.

Kosse, G. B. (Ed.) (1982) *Social Science Research and Public Policy Making*. NFER-Nelson Publishing Company, London.

Levin, Henry (1978) Why Isn't Educational Research More Useful?. *Prospects*, **VIII** (No. 2), 157–166.

OECD (1971) *Reviews of National Policies for Education: France*. OECD, Paris.

OECD (1972) *Reviews of National Policies for Education: Germany*. OECD, Paris.

OECD (1980) *Reviews of National Policies for Education: The United States*. OECD, Paris.

Roth, Heinrich (Ed.) (1969) *Begabung und Lernen: Ergebnisse und Folgerungen neuer Forschungen*. Klett, Stuttgart.

Shellard, John S. (Ed.) (1979) *Educational Research for Policy Making in Australia*. Australian Council for Educational Research, Hawthorn, Victoria.

Svensson, Nils-Eric (1962) *Ability Grouping and Scholastic Achievement*. Almqvist & Wiksell, Stockholm.

Walker, David (1976) *The IEA Six Subject Survey: An Empirical Study of Education in Twenty-One Countries*. Almqvist & Wiksell and Wiley, Stockholm and New York.

Weiss, Carol H. (1979) The Many Meanings of Research Utilization. *Public Administration Review*, September–October, 426–431.

Weiss, Carol H. (1980) Knowledge Creep and Decision Accretion. *Knowledge: Creation Diffusion, Utilization*, **1**, 3.

Weiss, Carol H. (1982) Policy Research in the Context of Diffuse Decision Making. In: Kosse, G. B. (Ed.), *Social Science Research and Public Policy Making*. NFER-Nelson Publishing Company, London.

Questionnaire

on the relationship between educational research and educational policy-making.

1. How, in your view, are most research projects in education, which have important implications for educational policies, initiated?

   By policy-makers and/or planners?

   By researchers themselves?

   By both parts?

   In your experience, how does the initiation process in most cases occur?

2. In your experience, in what way have most of the research findings with important implications for educational planning policy in your country come about?

They have been derived from research that has been specifically policy-oriented.

They have been "spin-off" effects of research on fundamental problems.

3. What kind of contacts with policy-making bodies in your country, e.g. ministry of education, planning commission, parliamentary committees etc., have you had?

Invited to prepare a paper on a particular problem?

Commissioned to conduct a study on an important problem in policy-making?

Summoned to testify before such bodies?

Other contacts?

4. If commissioned to conduct research, with what kind of persons did you have direct contact?

Politicians on a parliamentary committee?

Staff members in a ministry or similar central agency, with or without background in educational research?

Staff members on parliamentary committees and/or ministerial committees, with and/or without background in educational research?

Others?

5. If asked to prepare a proposal on a research project, with what kind of persons did you discuss the proposal?

Politicians?

Staff members without background in educational research?

Staff members with background in educational research?

Others?

6. What kind of expectations about the outcomes of your research did those who commissioned you express?

They wanted answers to specific policy issues, such as . . .

They wanted me to provide part of the knowledge basis for planning and/or policy-making.

Other?

7. What were your own expectations about the outcomes of your research?

To what extent did you anticipate that your project would yield results that would contribute to fundamental research?

8. What kind of contacts did you have with the body that commissioned research during the execution of your projects?

   Only written progress reports. To whom?

   Only oral progress reports. To whom?

   How frequently were progress reports requested?

9. What is your general impression about the accuracy of the time-table set up for commissioned research proposals?

   Are most projects reported according to the time-table, or are most of them overdue?

10. What kind of direct personal contact did you, as a rule, have with those who commissioned your research?

11. In case you initiated a research project by submitting a research proposal to a public agency, with what kind of persons did you have direct personal contacts?

12. Were you asked to testify before a parliamentary committee or a group of top staff people in a ministry about the implications of your research for a certain policy issue?

13. In your view, what should be done in order to improve communications between researchers and policy-makers in education?

   Are the communications satisfactory?

   How could the researchers help to "sell" their products more effectively?

Report of Proceedings

BY PROFESSOR MAURICE KOGAN

Preface

A group of distinguished policy-makers, practitioners and academics in the field of educational policy-making and research came together in Sweden in June, 1982 to do honour to Torsten Husén on his retirement from the Chair of International Education at the University of Stockholm. The Bank of Sweden Tercentenary Fund and the National Boards of Universities and Colleges and of Education made it possible for the Symposium to be held. Participants contributed papers on a range of subjects which became the basis of discussion in the Symposium.

Whilst Husén's retirement lent a particular distinction to the event, the Symposium also strongly reflected some of his own interests in its subject area. For 2 years Husén has been conducting a study of how researchers in the social sciences relate to educational policy-makers in four countries: Sweden, the United Kingdom, the Federal Republic of Germany and the United States of America. In the 1960s he had collaborated (Husén and Boalt, 1968) in a study of educational research and educational change in Sweden. He was thus celebrating his interest in a theme which has, indeed, engaged much of his professional energies for some four decades of Swedish educational history. Torsten Husén is an academic whose research and writing has directly affected Swedish policy, particularly in the creation and evaluation of comprehensive schools from the 1950's, and in the world-wide debate about the structure and content of secondary and upper secondary schooling. He has been prominent in the field as a practising researcher, as one who influences policy and, in the context of this Symposium, as a scholar of the political science of science.

The list of participants (Appendix I) shows the range of disciplines and of countries which they represented. By virtue of Husén's own wide networks of scholarly and practical acquaintanceships it was possible to draw together participants from, of course, first and primarily Sweden but also the United States of America, France, Germany, the United Kingdom and the World Bank. Even wider international representation was secured through the attendance and the participation at some of the sessions of Husén's graduate students from countries as far afield as Mauritius and Namibia.

The papers were contributed not only by those normally engaged in policy sciences but also, and indeed, primarily, by leading practitioners of the art of educational research who have enjoyed sustained opportunities to reflect on the impact of their work upon the development and reception of policy. Not all of the discussion, of course, relied directly upon the papers and because of this, and because of the differences of perspectives and style from which they have been written, it has been decided that this account of the conference should take full stock of both what was written and what was said by referring simultaneously to written and to spoken contributions.

The organisers of the conference wish to convey their grateful thanks to the Bank of Sweden Tercentenary Fund and to the National Board of Education and the National Board of the Colleges and Universities for their help, both material and otherwise, without which this publication would have been impossible.

A word might be in order from the Rapporteur about the style that he has chosen to adopt in this report. Papers presented at a symposium are inevitably selective, and contributions made in the course of discussion even more so. The Rapporteur must do his best to reflect the emphases engendered by the contributions of individual members, in both their written papers and as they emerge collectively through the flow and growth of debate and discussion. At the same time, both participants and readers would expect that a report will organise the material into some kind of synoptic and/or thematic order. Furthermore, whilst it is hoped that this report will respond to the interests and needs of many who are not familiar with the main arguments of discussion in this field, it also seems right to set the discussion lightly within the framework of discussions already published elsewhere. The report is by no means intended to be a textbook or a summation of the state of the art in this vital field of policy studies. The Rapporteur has, however, felt free to develop points that have emerged, according to his own understanding of their relevance and interest, and partly on the basis of his own research in this field, and to refer, where appropriate and possible, to a very limited number of discussions of the same themes that are well-known in the literature. He hopes that the interest and vitality of the deliberations at Wijk will come through these pages as will the testimony of gratitude, admiration and affection to Torsten Husén that are celebrated in the inaugural speech by Professor Olof Ruin and in the Foreword with which this volume opens.

Opening Speech

BY PROFESSOR OLOF RUIN, DEAN OF THE FACULTY OF SOCIAL SCIENCES, UNIVERSITY OF STOCKHOLM

In the absence of the Rector of the University of Stockholm, Professor Staffan Helmfrid, I have the great pleasure of extending to you the warmest expressions of welcome on behalf of the University of Stockholm. This Symposium is convened as a tribute to Professor Torsten Husén who is one of the most distinguished members of the Stockholm Faculty, and particularly of the Faculty of Social Sciences.

One might have expected to meet at this Symposium either "pure" researchers or "pure" policy-makers. But when we look at the list of participants, this seems not to be so. Most of us assembled here today have been both researchers and policy-makers. We seem to combine the two roles and to commute between two worlds. Because of this we do not behave in accordance with the traditional political science textbook descriptions of the political process.

In the textbooks that I read as a political science undergraduate in Lund, soon after Torsten Husén had finished his studies there on the problems of the psychology of adolescence, the main actors in the political system were usually assumed to have quite distinct roles. Politicians make policy decisions; the bureaucrats carry out the decisions reached by the politicians; the representatives of different interest groups look after their specific interests; the journalists record and illuminate; the researchers pursue their research in an unbiased manner.

These distinct textbook roles have been successively loosened and blurred in most societies. It is therefore not unique to be present at a conference where concurrently many researchers appear as policy-makers and many policy-makers appear as researchers. This Symposium assembles, however, in a society where blurring of traditional roles is particularly striking and somewhat far-reaching. Swedish politicians are seated on the boards of a number of administrative bodies; ex-politicians are appointed to high office within the administration. Civil servants engage in politics and can simultaneously be MPs, whilst playing a key role in advising on the formulation of policy. Representatives of the large interest organisations are active in both politics and administration; interest organisations concern themselves with questions far beyond their original areas of concern. Journalists orchestrate, to a large extent, the political debate and contribute to the determination of the political agenda.

The position of Swedish researchers in this boundary-crossing activity is of course of particular interest to us. They are often heavily involved in administrative work at the universities. Furthermore, many of them take part in politics and national administration outside the universities, as they do to some extent even in the work of interest organisations. Politicians, administrators and representatives of interest organizations influence for their part, the world of research by virtue of the fact that they are represented on a number of research-initiating bodies. Furthermore, many administrators, even when they confine themselves to their specific administrative entities, are involved in research-type activities, that is, gathering of data and analysis of different kinds.

The involvement of social science researchers, Swedish or non-Swedish, in the world outside Academia varies of course with disciplines. Economists, for instance, have often been in great demand. Another group, very visible at this conference, are professors of education. One explanation, I suppose, for the existing closeness between researchers in the field of educational policy-making is an organisational correspondence between a field of research and a sector of public policy. The academic field of education or pedagogy coincides, in its boundaries, largely with the sector of education.

Torsten Husén is a prototype of a professor of education who, at the same time as he has been professor, has been closely involved in policy-making in education. His type of involvement in Swedish affairs has had two interesting traits. One concerns the timing of this involvement, the other concerns the phase of national decision-making where he has been involved.

The time that Torsten Husén was most active as an expert in Swedish educational policy-making seems to have been, according to his memoirs[1], the first two decades of the post world war period. From the middle of the sixties his interests and activities shifted to the international stage. Today many of his distinguished international colleagues are here. Torsten Husén was by no means unique in his different activities as an expert in Swedish politics in the late 1940s, 50s and early 60s. He shared company with other Swedish researchers in education. Some of them are also present here today. He shared company, furthermore, with other social scientists; economists, political scientists, sociologists, etc.

Torsten Husén's activities remind us that so-called commissioned social science research already took place, and was fed into the decision-making processes, before the 60s. We are again and again reminded today how in the 60s and early 70s a substantial amount of money was allotted to social science research in many countries. and a growing part of this money came to be used

---

[1] *An Incurable Academic*, Pergamon Press, 1983.

for more or less clearly commissioned research. In Sweden for example, a so-called sectoral research policy was gradually established. That is: the different sectors of public policy are supposed to have at their disposal R & D resources as a means for developing their particular areas of responsibility. This expansion, in the 60s and early 70s, in social science research resources is in turn one of the reasons for the growing interest these days, across societies and disciplines, in the use or non-use of social science. This Symposium is one more example of this interest. But, my point is, much had happened already before the 60s.

The phase of national decision-making in which Torsten Husén, as well as many other social scientists, was particularly active during the first post-war decades is the phase before Cabinet and Parliament take their stand. This is the "input side" of politics.

Important programs to be enacted upon in Sweden by the Cabinet and Parliament have as a rule, as pointed out in several papers, been prepared by *ad hoc* commissions, appointed by the Cabinet. We used to call them "Royal Commissions". In Britain, for example, an appointment of a Royal Commission is regarded as a somewhat spectacular event emphasizing the importance of the problems to be looked into. In Sweden, it was, and still is, a very normal event. For decades, an average of more than 50 Royal Commissions per year have been appointed; the Ministry of Education has long been one of the ministries that tends to have a particularly large share of the reports published. The size of these commissions varies: from one-man inquiry up to inquiries consisting of as many as ten to fifteen people. The memberships of these large commissions might not only encompass politicians from different parties, representatives of interest organisations and bureaucrats, but often also experts from the research community. Furthermore, social science experts might be attached to the secretariats of these commissions. A great deal of the social science research commissioned by the governmental authorities before the expansion of the 60s just took the form of research initiated by royal commissions, not least those dealing with educational problems.

Parallel with the expansion of social science resources in the 60s and early 70s there occurred, certainly in Sweden but to some extent also in other societies, a shift of emphasis in the phases of national decision-making where social science and social scientists were involved: a shift from the input side of politics to what could be called the output side; how the administrative apparatus implemented decisions.

It was this apparatus that in Sweden was given increasing R & D resources as a part of the recently established sectoral research policy. The organisational arrangements varied. In some sectors the ministries themselves were given prime responsibility for the use of money available for research, in other sectors this responsibility was laid in the hands of national agencies or specially constituted entities directly under the Ministry. The National Board of Education as well as the National Board of Universities and Colleges are examples of central agencies with substantial and permanent resources for R & D. The bureaucrats and planners should in their daily work of implementing and evaluating different programs as well as of proposing changes have access to pertinent and up-to-date research results. This expansion of research, initiated by different administrative entities, made research commissioned by royal commissions less visible, but it did not vanish altogether.

In regard to tendencies in the use of social sciences, let me for a moment be autobiographical. Twice in my lifetime I have crossed the boundaries between Academia and national educational policy-making. The first time was in the early 60s when I was appointed head of the secretariat of a royal commission with the task of preparing new legislation concerning financial aid to students. The chairman of this commission was the then young politician, Olof Palme, who less than a decade later became Prime Minister. The second time was in the late 70s, when for a short period of time I served as Deputy Chancellor of Swedish Universities and Deputy Head of the National Board of Universities and Colleges. In this connection I was also appointed a member of three royal commissions dealing with university and research matters.

In my second experience I saw very little impact of social science research in decision-making, whereas in my first experience, at a time when Torsten Husén was very active on the Swedish stage, I could ascertain a "linear" relationship between knowledge and policy of the type whose existence many of us now tend to deny.

The Royal Commission chaired by Olof Palme started with the aim of proposing a far-reaching expansion of the existing system of stipends for students. Stipends were seen as the best means of overcoming obstacles of an economic, geographical or social nature in recruitment of students to higher education. Many members of the commission were under the impression that there was still a heavy, socio-economically and geographically correlated loss of talent at the transfer from *gymnasium* studies to the universities and equivalent educational institutions. Research was undertaken by the secretariat with the assistance of expertise in the field of education. Professor Kjell Härnqvist, among others, was involved. It turned out that the assumptions of many commission members had been exaggerated. The socio-economically and geographically correlated wastage or selection in the Swedish education system seemed to take place before the *gymnasium* level, not after it. These research findings, together with a few other factors, were central to the decision of Olof Palme and a majority of the commission members totally to reverse the original plans. It was proposed that state financial study aid at the *gymnasium* level be augmented considerably, whereas a new form of loans, not stipends, was to be introduced at the post-*gymnasium* level. The main points of the Commission proposals were accepted by the Cabinet and by a large majority in Parliament.

This is at least one concrete example from Swedish educational policy, although now almost twenty years old, of close relationship between social science research and the framing of government policy.

Today, at the same time as we have seen an increase in R & D resources available to governmental authorities and a shift of emphasis from the initiating stages of the decision-making process to the implementing, administrative phases, we have an intensified discussion about the limits and difficulties in infusing systematised knowledge into policy-making. The papers prepared for this Symposium bear witness of this. Earlier, with less money available for R & D in social sciences and with a different emphasis on decision-making, this malaise seemed to be less developed. It is tempting to formulate a hypothesis: the more R & D money available and R & D undertaken and inspired by the administrative side of the decision-making, the less use there seems to be of R & D results. The empirical evidence supporting such a loose and absurd hypothesis is, however, very shaky, to say the least! For a long time a policy style of consensus and innovative capacity was said to be particularly characteristic of Swedish political life. Foreign observers, especially, were prone to emphasise this. The style was very visible in the policy sector that interests us most at this Symposium: education. Gradually a system was built up at all levels – at the levels of the nine-year basic school, *gymnasium* and *post-gymnasium* – which has been characterised by comprehensiveness and broad accessibility. The far-reaching reforms have as a rule been decided upon by large majorities in Parliament. It is wrong to say that the processes preceding these decisions have equalled intellectual and technological processes. Continuous bargaining has been involved between a series of well-articulated interests. But my point is that a close connection has existed between knowledge and politics.

Many contend today that national policy-making is getting more and more difficult, in Sweden as well as in other Western countries. The tensions and disagreements between all actors involved seem to be increasing; the capacity to be innovative and anticipatory, to plan for the future, seems to be decreasing. A variety of explanations are given as to this state of affairs.

National agendas are overcrowded with issues; many issues have been more difficult to solve; the rhythm of politics has speeded up with great outside world "spill over" into the individual countries; special interests pressing for their points of view have gained in strength; the political parties have been weakened and the confidence in politicians diminished; the bulging bureaucracies have had paralysing effects, etc. Behind everything else loom drastically deteriorated economies. This, I am afraid, is the context in which a discussion has to be pursued on the relations between knowledge and policy-making, if the discussion is to be oriented towards the present and the future. In these introductory remarks I have been slightly nostalgic and parochial in tone by lingering on the past, and on the Swedish reality. This, however, was the stage on which Torsten Husén was for many decades active, as a professor and as a contributor to educational policy-making.

Let me end by saying that this perspective in our discussions which is oriented towards comparisons across nations and towards the future is, of course, most congruent with the personality of Torsten Husén. He has this Spring retired from his chair after decades of service to Swedish university life, but the Professor Emeritus is as active as ever and I hope that we can keep step with him both during these days here at Lidingö and in future encounters and joint ventures.

The Main Issues

In asking the question *"Researchers and Policy-Makers in Education: How Do They Relate?"* we invite discussion of several vexingly difficult issues at once. We must first ask what have been the impacts of research on policy-making. There is then the equally difficult evaluative issue of how policy-making has affected research. Once we have some sense of what the mutual and reciprocal impacts have been – a formidable chore involving many micro histories and case studies – we must move on to seek explanatory models of the relationships between research and policy-making. In so doing we incidentally encounter considerable confusion in the literature between what ought to be and what is, and between analytic conceptualisation and sometimes subjective summations of what now happens. In order, then, to advance the arguments about relationships between the two entities we need to analyse their components. What are the characteristics of research as they affect policy? What are the characteristics of policy-making as they affect research? Are there "two cultures" which can be bridged through discernible arrangements for science-policy dialogue and liaison?

On the basis of its discussion of impacts, relationships and the methods by which policy-oriented research is or can be institutionalised, the Symposium considered policies that it wished to endorse. And throughout, it was possible to relate conceptualisations to the actual cases of the role of research in Sweden, the USA, France, Germany, the UK and the developing countries.

In the account of the discussions that follows, individual participants are not named except where a point was made *in extenso*, but written contributions are referred to as appropriate and denoted by the placing of the contributor's name in brackets.

How do Educational Research and Policy-making affect each other?

In this report we cannot avoid the word "impact" although it is not a good metaphor to describe such effects of research on policy-making as can be established. It assumes definable objects being moved by definable forces. The relationship is held by most observers to be insidious, subtle and non-linear rather than direct and decisive. There is no simple and clear movement from cause to effect. The simplest models which assume that knowledge directly affects policy do not help to explain what happens in most of the cases of which we have convincing accounts, although they might be useful for managerial and prescriptive purposes. Having said this, however, we shall use the word "impact" because of its brevity and vividness but with awareness that it does not really serve well to describe the phenomenon that we seek to analyse.

Evidence of Impact

The Symposium, in both its papers and its oral contributions, sought to exemplify and conceptualise the evidence of impact. In this section and the next, the evidence will be summarised and then stratified into such generalisations as it yields. All were agreed that the influence of research upon educational policy-making and practice is most often not direct. Both the written papers and our discussion were mainly silent about the reverse process, namely, the influence of policy-making on the development of research, and that is an issue which has to be elaborated more from speculation rather than from evidence. Then it is clear that the mutual interpenetration of research and policy varies according to different contextual factors. In giving the empirical accounts that follow, we will try to bring out examples of different contexts which affect the different cases.

There are many accounts[1] in American and European literature of the impact

---

[1]These have been well-analysed in John Nisbet and Patricia Broadfoot, *The Impact of Research on Policy and Practice in Education,* Aberdeen University Press, 1980.

of research on policy-making including several statements of doubt and even scepticism. In this section we do not attempt to cover all of the examples and all of the arguments that have been stated in previous writing but add to the stock of discussion from statements made for and during our Symposium.

Sweden

We begin with the statements provided by the host country, Sweden. At the beginning of the Symposium, as the reader will have already noted, it was stated by Olof Ruin that interaction is greatly enhanced in Sweden because the traditional roles of researcher and policy-maker have become increasingly blurred. Swedish researchers are often heavily involved not only in administrative work in universities but many also take part in politics and administration outside the university, including the work of interest organisations. Politicians, administrators and representatives of different organisations influence the world of research by virtue of the fact that they are represented on a number of research and associated bodies. Many administrators are involved in research type activities by gathering data and analysis. Here, then, is our first contextual factor: the degree of assumed consensus underlying the research activity in order for interchange between government and their potential critics to be feasible. When researchers accept the social objectives underlying the educational policies that are promoted by governments, the relationships between them and their sponsors, and the very nature of the work being undertaken, are affected.

Ruin went on to note how the involvement of social science researchers, and not just in Sweden, varies with the disciplines. Economists have been in particular demand. The frequent use made of their special skills says something about the extent to which economic paradigms fit comfortably with the paradigms that policy-makers often feel it necessary and desirable to use, particularly when dealing with problems of macro economics.

Sweden, together with the USA, is an example of the maximum interaction of policy and research, although the two countries are very different in context and therefore in the ways in which research findings and speculations enter the policy bloodstream. No country has been more assiduous than Sweden in attempting to commission and use research and to use disciplined enquiry in its evaluation of existing policies and its plans for educational reform. In the USA there has been a massive amount of research on policy-related questions both because of the size of the academic and governmental enterprise in education and also in response to massive, if spasmodic, efforts at the political level to cause social change through education, such as in the Great Society programmes. Multiple and often conflicting federal agencies have sponsored research, each wave of which responds to the policy fashions and impulses of the time only to be succeeded by new policy and research initiatives. The private foundations, too, add to the rich profusion of work which may contribute to change and debate but does not become part of a deliberately accretive process of social engineering. The USA presents a market model of research in which public authorities may or may not be the major customers.

By contrast, Sweden has been the home of systematic application of knowledge in which the national authorities have been the most important movers. That application has gone through different stages. Swedish social science was most active in the first post-war decade on the "input" side of politics. Policy development has traditionally been prepared through the use of *ad hoc* commissions appointed by the Cabinet. During the 1950s and 1960s an average of 75 commissions were set up each year (Premfors, 1982 (b)). The Ministry of Education has tended to generate a particularly large share of the reports published. Social scientists are members of the commissions themselves or of their secretariats. Much social science research commissioned by the government before higher education expanded in 1960 was initiated by the Royal Commissions (Ruin and Husén.)

As reforms begin to take effect, and as research itself began to extend the range of its interests, Ruin recounts that there was a shift from input to the output side of politics. This latter stage entailed work for, and about, the administrative process and the apparatus for the implementation of policy. As officials and planners implement and evaluate programmes already established, they draw upon the resources of relevant research on policy outcomes. Our second generalisation might be, then, that the nature of the research contributions change with the evolution of the policies being illuminated.

The implications of this point deserve a little more elaboration. The research used on the input side of policy will be concerned primarily with examining existing educational and social states and ways of improving them. There have been important studies of existing curriculum and its organisation, and its effects on teaching and learning. There have been important studies of the access of different social and gender groups to different phases of educational opportunity. There have been the now classic studies of Husén himself and his students, Svensson and Dahllöf, of the pilot schemes in comprehensive education at the secondary level in matched schools in the Stockholm area. There were data collection and analytic exercises as well as evaluation exercises. The questions underlying such research could be raised either by the social scientists, or the policy analyst, the politician or the senior administrator. In Sweden, connections between the main groups who might raise questions are strong and institutionalised which make it easier for these questions to be raised and answered. Once, however, research moves onto the output side it is dealing with far more complex issues. Here it might approach questions of impact and implementation. In these, the assessment of process is as important as assessment of product so that the evaluation of more definable gains and losses should be combined with evaluation of impact, affect and sentience. Just as first generation educational planning, largely based upon estimates of manpower needs and the contribution of education to their satisfaction, became complemented by second generation planning in which political and psychological considerations were increasingly brought into the argument, so did Swedish researchers increasingly concern themselves with the political, and institutional impacts of change (Premfors). Thus both policy and research evolve from concentration on relatively straight-forward issues of fact and conceptualisation to far more comprehensive and complex patterns.

Ruin also gave an example of impact of research on policy. The Royal Commission on student aid chaired by Olof Palme was concerned with enlarging the system of stipends for students. Research undertaken by the secretariat with the assistance of statistical expertise showed that the socio-economic and geographical correlations with wastage in the Swedish education system were more powerful before the *gymnasium* level (at the age of 16) than after it. This research finding contributed to the decision of the commission members to reverse their original plans. They decided to augment state grants at the *gymnasium* level and they proposed a new form of loan rather than stipends at the post-*gymnasium* level. This is at least one concrete example from Swedish educational policy, although now almost twenty-years-old, of close collaboration between the results of social science research and the framing of government policy. All countries will certainly be able to produce such examples.

Another contribution to the seminar (Premfors) contained in a paper without the author's oral contribution, because he was called for military service at the time of the conference, evaluated the impact of research on policy-making in Swedish higher education. Premfors' paper was an important attempt to deal systematically with the issues before the Symposium and is therefore exploited at length in this report.

Premfors singled out five dimensions of higher educational policy: quantitative planning of higher education; social recruitment of students; regionalisation of institutions; governance and teaching and learning. Following these main themes, he recounts how in quantitative planning isolated efforts associated with the work of *ad hoc* commissions in the 1930s and 1940s developed into a "plethora" of projects in the 1970s and early 1980s. The early efforts were primarily focused on the inputs (recruitment of students) and later on the output (number of graduates and their absorption into the labour market) aspects. Research successively came to bear on almost every aspect of higher education. In the 1970s there was a shift from study of the educational process, that is to say, pedagogy, towards the examination of the social processes and structures in higher education. These included a growing interest in the research function of the system in the late 1970s. Statistical and psychological-pedagogical approaches used to be predominant. They have been absorbed in the whole range of social and behavioural sciences. The Swedish example is thus the best for those concerned with considering a full natural history of research commissioning because of the way in which it evolved alongside the changing preoccupations of the policy-makers.

At the same time, however, as the range of research increased, the pattern of funding did not greatly change. Most of the research was initiated from centrally funded R & D programmes rather than general university funds or the research councils. It was not, then, that the sources became more various but that government funders became increasingly eclectic in their range of interests.

If, in Sweden, the use of research has been both impressive and systematic, that does not answer the question of what impact it had. On quantitative planning first, research relating higher education to economic development was used by the majority of policy-makers to support the expansion of the 1950s and 1960s. This was, as Premfors relates, "a nice illustration of partisan use of research". A further example comes from the area of forecasting of the manpower needs for specific professions. Research was also used to develop the methodology of forecasting. At first, manpower planning, based on the work of Wicksell-Jerneman in the 1930s, was seen as feasible, but in the late 1960s the limits of manpower planning methodology became clear; at the same time there were challenges to the underlying value assumptions of the rate-of-return approach. So the decision in 1975 to adopt a system-wide *numerus clausus* and thus reduce the role of private demand was the result of a complex political process. A political decision will lead to closure on an issue. Research findings add to, rather than reduce, uncertainty for decision-makers. The interplay between decision-making which must be authoritative and firm and the questioning and generation of uncertainty implicit in the research is an important phenomenon. It leads to a central policy question: can national authorities sponsor the generation of uncertainty?

Swedish research relevant to the issue of social equality in higher education "clearly added to our knowledge and understanding of the issues involved". In the 1940s and 1950s studies of the reservoir of talent "strengthened the expansionist coalition". Social equality was thus added to economic growth as a major benefit resulting from the overall expansion of higher education. Research also played a part in pointing to the inadequacy of formal merit as a predictor of performance and thus eventually influenced admission policy. Then followed studies of the form of implementation and impact which fitted the growing pessimism about the possibility of changing the social composition of higher education.

Research underlies some of the decisions to "regionalise" higher education in Sweden. Here Premfors asks "if contrary research evidence and cautionary remarks were not largely absent from research on regional problems in Sweden at that time". He thus reads into the literature a strong ideological commitment to decentralisation not only among policy-makers but also among researchers.

The role of research in policy development on governance is among the more interesting of Premfors' examples because it shows how different models of higher education governance – the professorial as against the rationalistic and managerial models provided by some consultants to commissions – came into conflict. From the 1970s university based researchers, mainly from political science and business economics, conducted several projects on higher education organisation and decision-making which supported the managerial model. More recent research may, however, feed the growing assumption in Sweden that higher education has become heavily bureaucraticised – a study from Umeå has shown that while the number of students and researchers has grown only slowly in the 1970s this is not true of teachers and, even less so, of administrators.

Premfors uses the example of studies of governance to make a generalisation. It is not so much the research studies as the more general intellectual activity connected with them which might have affected attitudes. "The major channel of influence has probably been the plethora of conferences, advisory groups and the like which have been an integral part of the R & D activity of the National Board. Here researchers have been allowed to teach their post-rationalist message directly to policy-makers and their staff. And there is scattered evidence that it has 'percolated' much according to the 'enlightenment model', into policy deliberations."

Finally, there are examples of the impact of research on developments in teaching and learning. Dahllöf, for example, reanalysed the data on the output of university graduates. This had been assumed to be a relatively reliable measure of the "efficiency" of the universities. That measure became less reliable if the stated objectives of the students were taken into account. Current attempts to reform the study organisation of the universities may have resulted from such findings. There is the example of how research and public debate applied critique to the educational technology paradigm in favour of the need to tailor teacher and learning strategies with the variable character of the individual disciplines. But as Premfors implies, there can be no certainty that either policy documents or research reports cause change in practice. "Much has changed but much has also stayed the same in the private life of Swedish higher education, unaffected by any paradigm or other kinds of shift occurring in the public life."

Research, then, has been heavily "used" in policy-making in Sweden. But "I am prepared to argue that the use in policy making in Swedish higher education has been relatively marginal. . . . I have observed no major instance of policy change where research made a difference, an instance where similar policy measures could not or would not have been taken in the absence of research". And the outsider might then wonder if this is so of Sweden how much more so will it be true of other countries.

Premfors follows Lindblom (1977), Lindblom and Cohen (1979) and Wildavsky (1979) in assuming that policy change comes both from social interaction and the operations of the market. This might lead us to the conclusion that research concerned with policy would have to act actively rather than passively with social interaction by esconsing itself with both confidence and freedom within a political context by addressing itself to the issues, and with the style, that will enhance its active role. At the same time, however, social science should not undersell itself, its practitioners must argue. Policy-makers may foreclose on issues too quickly; social science can help keep open the space between the dissemination of ideas which might lead to policy changes and their enforcement through social engineering. It can help define, and extend, and challenge the agenda for social action.

The case of Swedish higher education provides overwhelming support of the thesis that "research in policy-making is mainly used as partisan analysis or political ammunition", a point advanced by James Coleman, too. Where research knowledge has been viewed as "authoritative" it has concerned minor aspects of policy or simple fact gathering exercises. Research in the form of methodological development was important in the area of quantitative planning and it can cause reinterpretation of what was widely held to be a fact. There is convincing evidence that the Swedish researchers had an impact on policy making in line with the "enlightenment model" discussion of which will be attempted later in this report. Research on policy-making and organisation spread the message of post-rationalism: if programmes are defined and implemented mechanistically, they are likely to fail. Great care must be taken about the process of implementation and its unintended consequences. The examples which Premfors examines of enlightenment "were better at description and criticism than at prescription. Their main function has been to discourage simple solutions to policy problems in higher education".

This finding is consistent with Marklund's reflection (quoting the Swedish Government *Report on Educational Research and Development,* Skolforskning, 1980) that basic research appears to have quite tangible effects on educational policy, greater perhaps than the effects of what has been regarded as applied research.

The Swedish cases illustrate how political and social contexts are more important than the scientific quality or theoretical results of what is produced. Birgit Rodhe was expressing the same assumption in contrasting research to development. She was not advancing the need for Research-and-Development in the fixed combination in which it is often stated. She wanted development to be promoted as an independent and parallel activity to research. Both were necessary preconditions for policy-making. For example, research commissioned by Swedish school reformers on the issue of differentiation has played an important role for the policy-makers. But the model on which the reformed upper level was based was taken from spontaneous development work in one of the experimental schools, Österåker. When, as in educational technology, research has been expected to include development and to have a ready-made product, the results have been strikingly limited. But where either research or development goes beyond technological objectives where ample scope has been given schools to work independently, results have been much more useful for policy-making and will probably last longer.

Finally, and the seminar could make no exhaustive analysis of the impact of research on Swedish policy-making, we return to Husén himself. In his earliest researches he related test scores and information on formal education for twenty-year-olds then registering for military service. In doing this, he estimated how many with the requisite ability did not proceed to upper and higher secondary education; these studies were reported by two Royal Commissions and were quoted in the Educational Bill of 1950 which presented a blueprint for a pilot programme of comprehensive education. The 1957 Commission tried to analyse the outcomes of the pilot programme and in the evaluation of competence imparted by school education in comprehensive and selective schools the issue of differentiation at lower secondary level (age 13 to 16) was the key issue.

Other Examples

We now turn, more briefly, to evidence presented in the Symposium of the impact of research on policy-making in other countries.

Postlethwaite gave six examples from his international experience of impact research on policy-making. He recounts how after the IEA Six Subject Survey, of the twenty-one countries taking part, impact in terms of legislation, curricula guidelines or policy actions had happened in fifteen of them and nothing had happened in the other six. "My general assessment of the reasons for this dichotomy was that in the countries where nothing had happened the researchers had no links with policy-makers and had also made no attempts to forge such links." In one of the countries, the minister identified one subject area in which the country was below the international mean and school inspectors then discovered that certain aspects of the curriculum in that subject area had not been adequately covered. Legislation was then enacted to ensure better coverage. In others among his six examples, however, there was no impact at all likely or intended by policy-makers.

Germany

In the case of Germany (Becker) the Education Commission of the German Educational Council (*Bildungsrat*) established by the Federal Government included experts in educational research, scientists with general interests in education and representatives from public life. It was charged with drawing up requisite and development plans for German education, for making suggestions on the structure and on its longterm planning for the different levels. Becker sees the effect of research as having a place within the general process of

enlightenment. "In individual cases the problems facing the Education
Councils would have indeed stimulated new research, but in these very cases it
was scarcely able to use the results. It mostly made use of the available level of
knowledge and, in the few very important cases, the Council drew on research
which had been available for a long time and, by a critical development of this,
made it applicable in a special way." Here Becker is implicitly pointing to the
importance of scholarship as such – of the reordering of concepts and of
findings that might come from the established body of research rather than of
the direct applicability of research specifically commissioned for policy purposes.
Although the Education Commission has a precarious legitimacy because of its
mode of appointment its work proved to be a strong legitimate foundation for
the Overall Educational Plan of the Federation-State Commission for Educational Planning.

Husén comments that the Council provides an illuminating case of institutionalised contacts or liaisons, at least for a limited period, between researchers
and policy-makers. He also recalls a case of the impact of research studies on
policy formation in Germany. An OECD study in the early 1960s had predicted
a severe shortage of teachers to the extent that even if all upper secondary school
graduates enrolled in teacher training they would not cover the needs. This
created a panic and talk about "educational catastrophe". In the wake of this
the Federal Ministry of Education with the prerogative to plan was set up.

The Council used its findings for its proposals to the Commission on stages,
entrance age to school and the extension of the Kindergarten. There were
contradictory scientific evidences on many of the issues but the structural plan
of the Council took account of the variations in methods, findings and the
ensuing policy options. In another case, a study on intellectual ability by Erich
Roth, previous scientific work was updated to become background material for
the work of the Educational Council. Becker also gives other examples of work
directly feeding into policy.

There were examples of how previous studies can be drawn on. Again, the
case of Germany illustrates how research contributions work in parallel with
policy development. During the 1950s there was hostility to planning but the
1960s were "a period of euphoric planning", . . . "which turned into planning
nostalgia in the 1970s". In the 1950s research was undertaken quietly and had
no effect on the development of educational policy. Germany was still in the
period of "non-reform". At the beginning of the work of the Educational
Council in 1966 there was knowledge available that the Educational Council
was able to draw directly on, and to use it as a form of enlightenment that
might affect political decisions. Between 1970 and 1974, when it was discontinued, the Educational Council's work became more detailed and had to cover
ground with uncertain scientific backing. As with Swedish research, therefore,
a period of input to policy based on fairly confident research work gave way to
less certain contributions as the policy process itself moved forward.

France

Based on the French experience, Alain Bienaymé concludes that the direct influence of scientific research is probably weak, that the indirect influence is a little more substantial but hard to assess and that the potential influence might be improved. Almost no decision on French educational policy can be credited unquestionably as a precise and unique result of a scientific research. On specific occasions ministers have benefited from commissioned research. Bienaymé quotes the case of researchers consulted about the problems of youth transition into professional life. Reforms in the fund allocating process between the universities were introduced in 1975. Research had been launched about it, but the minister left office a few weeks after the report was handed to him. His successor preferred to rely on recommendations of an internal body appointed by him. Researchers must expect to have their contributions treated as in any other kind of policy input. A research centre under the aegis of the Ministry of Education and Universities was producing first hand information on how young people coped with their careers but the researchers felt that the research contributed weakly to the design of new policies in higher education. All the same, many policy-makers feel the need to use reliable data and research has been commissioned on several important issues over the last 15 years. Researchers either deny or underestimate their contribution but they do not know whether it has been followed up and they are uncertain themselves about the nature of the policy-making process.

USA

The American contributions to the Symposium went beyond assessments of impact and into the institutional relationships affecting it. Perkins noted that the Carnegie Commission on Higher Education Reports were often ignored by the professoriate, yet attentively studied by government officers, legislators and administrators. Stated policies came from the experiences of the Carnegie Commission, and later, the Carnegie Council on Higher Education. "It would be fruitless to try to disentangle the effect of Carnegie deliberations and publications from the effect of the social impulses then at work . . . The Carnegie enterprise rode the tide of an increasing public concern for social justice in higher education and a preoccupation with financial and social stability within its institutions." Yet it should be noted that the President of the Commission, Clark Kerr, was unable to point to substantial impacts that the report had made and he attributed much of its success to the quality of data and concepts formulated by the many research studies as well as to the Commission's deliberate attempts to ensure impact. (Kerr, 1979). Martin Trow was concerned, as we will see later, with the creation of new kinds of "brokerage" roles that would enhance the impact of analysis upon policy-making and execution.

Coleman, in a contribution to the normative development of our subject area, was primarily concerned with the institutionalisation of social policy research. He recorded that it is a common complaint that social policy research is not used but left to gather dust on the shelf. Yet it is often used in ways that are not intended. It is used in conditions where there is extensive conflict over policy and in a way not anticipated by the researchers. "So *Equality of Educational Opportunity,* prepared by the U.S. Office of Education under the Civil Rights Act and published in 1968, was never used by federal agencies in formulating civil rights policy but was widely used in local conflicts over school desegregation. Social policy research is most widely used where there is extensive conflict over policy and is often used by those without direct control over policy, who challenge the policy of those in positions of authority." Coleman goes on to challenge the use of research, and particularly evaluative research, by those who have promoted a policy. There is then a conflict of interest and an inability on the part of the scholarly community involved in the research efforts, to apply proper critical standards. We shall return to Coleman's critique and ideas later.

We can extend the points made by the contributors from the USA by looking at some of the systematically recorded evidence of the impact of research upon American policy and practice.

There is plenty of room for scepticism and criticism and for believing that research findings are either wrongly based or wrongly used. But Nisbet and Broadfoot quote historical analysis, such as those of Travers (1978) who believes that "there is overwhelming evidence" of the impact of research on educational practice and policy at least up to 1950. The areas where research has had the greatest impact are: reading material, age placement and sequencing of subject matter; testing, studies of learning and the psychology of school subjects; classroom climate, the teacher's role, moral education, attitudes and values; and evaluation studies. It has not produced "cook book solutions to problems" but it can provide general principles. The impact of research is not necessarily beneficial, particularly when it is conducted within the context of a somewhat unreflecting positivism. Geraldine Clifford (1973), quoted by Nisbet and Broadfoot, reviews development in the seven decades since 1918 of the impact of research on teaching. The main impact of research was not in the direct form envisaged by the scientific movement but rather through a process of "cultural diffusion", influencing ways of thinking among other effects. A report of the National Academy of Sciences (1977), *Fundamental Research in the Process of Education* refers to the "glacial advance of human understanding" in the creation of more humane attitudes in readiness to treat each learner with greater dignity. "Systematic, disciplined enquiry has helped in the transformation over the century."

UK

Educational policy in the UK (Kogan, oral contribution) again provides varied examples of impact. For example, three major policy moves in Britain have been: the creation of selection for secondary education at 11; the demolition of selection at 11 in favour of comprehensive education; and the quadrupling of access to higher education from 1945 until the 1970s. The introduction of selection at 11 was based on the work of educational psychologists, such as Cyril Burt whose studies in differential psychology were in the tradition of Francis Galton. Their findings were mediated through reports of the pre-war Consultative Committee on Education and formed the foundation for work on educational testing which became universally applied by local education authorities throughout the country. But, equally, it was the work of educational psychologists such as Vernon and Husén, and educational sociologists such as Halsey, Floud and Martin, who showed the unreliability of selection decisions made at 11 and the ways in which the use of selective secondary organisation distributed educational benefits to those already relatively well off and reinforced existing expectations of performance. It was within the climate created by such findings that many local authorities began to introduce comprehensive education. For this to happen, the research, and the knowledge of teachers about the effects of selection, had to become politically salient so that eventually a Labour government in 1965 began the process of dismantling the selective system.

In the case of higher education, as in Sweden, work undertaken by researchers such as J. W. B. Douglas and, later, a research team led by Claus Moser, dismantled the notion of a fixed "reservoir of talent" and thus provided the intellectual underpinning for the Robbins Report which recommended that places should be made available for all of those qualified to enter higher education. It is interesting to notice how the concept of the fixed reservoir was attacked in both Sweden and the UK. Whether this was the result of cultural transfer or the indigenous development of ideas based on separate national experiences, or both, is a matter for speculation. Certainly such ideas were being disseminated among researchers and policy-makers as at the Kungälv conference in Sweden convened by the OECD in 1961 (Halsey 1961).

Again, therefore, we can see how the social and political context determined the policies which research findings might have initiated and then reinforced. So the direct pressure for the ending of selection at 11 came from parents, 60 per cent of whom wanted their children to be educated in selective grammar schools whilst only 25 per cent were to be offered places, from teachers who observed the effects, and ultimately from politicians. The pressure on the higher education system began to build up as the schools produced an increasing number of adequately qualified pupils, and at a time when economic development seemed to reinforce the need for more skilled manpower as well as heightening the appetite for the good life which higher education seemed to make available to those who participated in it.

Apart from major policy movements, research played a part in the discussion of changing educational practice. Research in the UK dating from the 1940s, beginning with Elizabeth Fraser (1959) and reaching its climax in the research for the Plowden Committee on primary education, pointed to the importance of engaging parental commitment to education as one of the components of better educational performance. It was, perhaps, these research findings, together with the increased middle-class insistence on a place in the conduct of their children's school, that eventually led to the policy proposals for changing the composition and functioning of school governing bodies made in the Taylor Report (1977). Again, progressive primary education which has been an internationally notable feature of British schooling has recently come under attack as likely to lead to a weak emphasis on skill training. It is said that this movement, which has certainly become important in the politics of education, was reinforced by the publication of Neville Bennett's work (1976) which showed that the more informal methods of teaching in primary education were less efficient as measured by certain criteria for certain groups of children. And, again, but not so well documented, it could be argued that developments in the sociology of knowledge, less a matter of empirical research than of speculative conceptualisation, built up the arguments about the ways in which knowledge and its production were socially determined. This probably helped undermine the authority of academic institutions and those holding power in them and vitally affected the relationships of students and teachers in higher education and perhaps in the society at large. (Kogan, 1978).

British educational policy, however, also provides dramatic examples of how research takes a subordinate place in the face of determined political action. The arguments for the increase of access to higher education, for greater equality in schooling, are placed at total discount when a government decides to turn the clock back, as has happened since 1979 in both the advance of comprehensive education, particularly in its post-16 emanations, and in the reduction of access to higher education.

Third World and World Bank

Finally, the symposium was able to consider the example of the Third World as seen through the eyes of a middle man, the World Bank. The World Bank is the largest agency making educational loans to developing countries. It appraises education project proposals and tries to do so knowing the state of the art and the appropriate technologies in education. (Hultin) "To do it properly, bank staff have to stay abreast of educational research. They must understand what findings would be relevant to a specific country situation. Bank operators may talk about academic research, with a slightly negative connotation but, nevertheless, use the findings in their work. The bank serves as a catalyst for research and as a middle man between researchers and policy-makers in developing countries. It is urged to transfer 'know how'."

The impact of educational research on the bank is direct. The World Bank considers support for education to be an important part of its work for economic development. It believes this to be justified by research evidence. The Bank was able to establish a strong correlation between economic growth and literacy rates in the non oil exporting nations in the 1960s and 1970s. Circumstantial evidence seemed to show that there was a cause and effect relationship between literacy and growth. The social rate of return for investment was relatively high compared with many investments of physical aspects in developing societies. Research indicates that educated workers produce more than the uneducated. It is higher than the correlation between life expectancy and any other nine important basic indicators. So the Bank began its loans policies primarily on manpower grounds. But in the early 1970s one began to see education in a wider development perspective. Macro-economic reasons for general support of human resource development began to be accepted. The reduction of poverty and promotion of equality became the important concern in educational finance and unequal access to school and low educational policies began to be reasons for lending.

The Bank, then, adopts the optimistic social engineering view, dominant in Western Europe until recently. Its research and development programmes match its policy perspectives. Once projects are achieved, evaluation is undertaken. In fact, there is always an evaluation component in every project. Research knowledge and skills are important in this work. Evaluation requires base line data and must be institutionalised at the time of the project's conception. But it has been used not primarily as an assessment of past activities but rather as a management tool in order to identify new priorities. Student achievement measures, school resources surveys and tracer studies are seen as future-oriented operations.

The 1980 Policy Paper on education issued by the Bank has drawn upon research and discusses educational research and research needs. It draws attention to the restricted scope of research in developing countries and its lack of relationship to policy. It is hampered by the lack of qualified personnel and the failure to accept it as part of the policy-making process. It is also inadequately financed. It urges that research should be pursued into education as a social force interacting with society and the economy as part of the developmental process and as an individual learning process concerned with the determinants of learning, application of skills, retention. Developing countries should also participate in the international research networks, such as the IEA (International Association for the Evaluation of Educational Achievement) projects. The annual allocation of educational research funds averaged $800,000 during the last few years. The Bank's own research programme has resulted in about 100 papers published by staff and consultants between 1974 and 1981. And the Bank's projects contain research and other analyses. Thus a project in Columbia drew upon the IEA type study conducted in Colombia by a research group. The use of studies facilitated the formulation of concrete proposals affecting policy practice. The research played an important part in the Tanzania project designed to improve primary education and systematic performance evaluation. The Ministry of Education is organising itself to promote the use of research, evaluation and monitoring. In the Philippines, frequent references were made to findings from Filipino international research and the government has shown interest in the use of education research in the formulation of its policies.

To many present at the Symposium the perspectives of the World Bank and the discussion about the role of research in developing countries provided useful contrasts against which to analyse the experiences of the more affluent countries.

Generalisations Derived from Empirical Cases Discussed in the Symposium

The general inferences to be drawn from the country cases discussed at the Symposium reinforce the generalisation that the knowledge-policy relationship is indeterminate and unsystematic. In Sweden, cases could certainly be found where policy had been reinforced, illuminated or even changed as a result of research findings but we must respect Premfors' general conclusion that other processes, those of the larger social ideology, of political negotiation and of the "pull of the market", often are more important. Research may trigger off or legitimise those policies but is not the strongest determinant of them. The same general conclusion, that the relationship is uncertain and indeterminate and unpredictable, can be drawn from all of the western European and American examples, although major exceptions can always be found.

The case of the developing countries is somewhat different. Here the example given at the Symposium is of the World Bank acting as a stimulator in countries which were seeking development and would therefore be the more eager to understand and evaluate the conditions by which educational progress could be achieved. The developing countries therefore exemplify the major tautology of our subject, namely, that the relationship between research and policy will be strongest when policy-makers feel the need for data, conceptualisation, and evaluation of developments that they themselves desire. We return to the question of stages of research-policy connections later in this section.

A second generalisation is that the impact of research is strongly conditioned by several contextual factors. To those we now return, first by expanding the discussion of how research might evolve through different stages constructed by policy demand.

In the cases of both Sweden and Germany research has gone through different stages. In the Swedish case there were, as pointed out above, first an emphasis on the input side (for example, student recruitment to higher education) giving way to an emphasis on the output side (numbers of graduates and their employment and evaluation of reforms) (Ruin) and in Germany three stages were depicted in which a lack of commitment to planning gave way first to euphoria and then to nostalgia (Becker). These stages seemed to correspond in style to developments in planning. The harder certainties associated with manpower planning, based on the optimism that educational development would lead to a growth in the economy, gave way to the uncertainties about the role of education in the economy and in social relationships. There was then an emphasis on the need to take account of political and negotiative aspects of the planning process. The World Bank example may also be generalised. It was emphasised in the Symposium that a simple model of development, where "developing" countries were expected to move from simple categories of involvement to more complex states, did not explain the histories of these countries. Many of them had highly sophisticated political administrative leadership from the beginning and their ambitions for education were further complicated by the dual inheritance of indigenous culture and the infrastructure of political ambitions a.nd school systems of former colonial powers. Nevertheless, it is likely to do no violence to the complexity of the problems, and the sophistication of attempts to deal with them, to say that where a country has a low literacy rate and a shortage of trained manpower and is setting up new or greatly reformed educational systems, the learning gains from research and development efforts are likely to be far larger than in the more developed countries. Establishing data bases and surveying the characteristics of the system and of education population, for example, are far more rewarding in countries where facts have simply not been gathered or analysed.

Moreover, the "enlightenment" function of research must be more potent when analytic and prescriptive formulations of the present state and the desired states of an educational system are being worked through a policy system for the first time. Because the use to which knowledge is put depends so strongly on the receptivity of the user it would be surprising if the very novelty of the research-policy dialogue were not to enhance the usefulness of disciplined enquiry in the policy-practice fields. Conversely, as an educational system moves into a period of turbulence and uncertainty following a period of development and confidence, the role of research becomes far more precarious. The quest for equality of educational opportunity in the USA is a case in point. If it must no longer concern itself with analysis of restrictions of access but instead begin to unravel the enormously complex consequences of wider access, of new forms of education installed over decades, of new patterns of governance and participation, it is into some tricky arguments, many of which require sensitive qualitative judgements not easily accommodated in classical research patterns. The participants in the Symposium felt that there was indeed a major research to be conducted on the stages of the research-policy dialogue reached in different countries to see whether generalisations could be made about stages of evolution. A glimpse of a fascinating terrain was experienced. Here it would be appropriate to refer to "finalisation" theory (Mussachia, 1979) which is concerned with the extent to which research is more or less susceptible to sponsors' steerage according to the paradigmatic stage reached.

There were several references to the political context in which research was being conducted and used. Participants in the Symposium, including students speaking about countries other than those directly represented, pointed out that the progress and use of research could be strongly conditioned by political intervention. This phenomenon has been generalised in one of Carol Weiss' models (1980) of policy-research interaction, namely, the political or partisan model where research is used, or neglected, according to the political opportunism of those in power or those opposing those in power. It is a nice question whether political stability enhances or reduces receptivity to research. Partisanship may mean that research findings are overstated and illegitimately sharpened or even distorted, to gain a political point. Or it may mean that the findings are simply ignored or rejected. Or official sponsors of research may use them selectively (Coleman). Yet strong consensus and stability, whilst making it more certain that results are not directly abused or research over-prescribed in its formulation, may mean that research critical of the system is less well-encouraged. There are, perhaps, traces – we should not say more than that – in earlier Swedish educational research history. It has been remarked that educational research has preponderantly been financed by the national authorities. Those national authorities have been remarkably supportive and wide ranging in the research which they have sanctioned and promoted. We have also noted cases of counter analysis (for example, Dahllöf's assessment of criteria of higher education's effectiveness), but the "counter analytic" mode has not developed too strongly. Another variation of political turbulence is that of overloading of government when many different groups with many different value perspectives are simultaneously putting pressure on. At such a time, too, the intellectual noise in society might be great and ideas being pushed hard, and it is not too clear that education research necessarily finds an easy passage through such competition. Its essentially long term and reflective nature might have to make concessions to the demands for short order analyses and quick answers on big questions.

Other political factors are that policy-makers have their sacred cows (Bienaymé) and that in France turmoil has seemed to get in the way of science. There seem to be some research "untouchables" or at least neglected research topics: student satisfaction in France, cost development, attendance and truancy rates in schools in Sweden (Husén). And Bienaymé, as well, notes a similar point to that made above, namely, that as the issues being evaluated become more complicated and tackled by multivariate analyses, this leads to complex conclusions which are not easily assimilated in the political system.

Indirect impacts need time for absorption. Yet another political factor was the extent to which research was credible to the politicians and administrators who were supposed to "receive" it. Social science cannot evade its role of critical analysis. Politicians might complain that this sometimes becomes confused with biassed radicalism.

Closely associated with political characteristics, such as stability, turbulence and openness, were thought to be the formal political structures. As Husén notes, two of the countries represented, Germany and the United States, have federal constitutions which bestow educational prerogatives on the states or the Länder. In all four cases, however, whatever the influence on educational policy in general, the national authorities have taken the lead role in providing funds for educational research. The reception and use of research are, however, affected by the arrangements for the administration and finance of education, and by the extent of private interest in it. For example, federal and unitary systems present distinct differences in the promotion of research, policy research-making and the relationship between them (Perkins) – a point also made by Weiss. Plainly, the distribution of responsibility and funding between different levels of the system, and the presence or non-presence of the private sector of higher education or schools affect the propensity of national authorities to promote and receive research. In highly-centralised states research might be commissioned and its reception presupposed. Authority would be placed behind the use of research linked with prearranged plans for implementation. When, however, important institutions are private, as are many leading universities in the USA, or when power is diffused to different levels of government, clear and simple impacts should not be expected.

In the USA, for example, commissioned research in higher education was undertaken and presented for the enlightenment of those who felt they needed it. A case in point was the Carnegie Commission on Higher Education with its mixed "constituency". Its use in policy-making depended almost entirely on the initiative of the government or authority concerned with the problem. Academic institutions had their own policies and practice and might or might not follow the recommendations derived from the research put into studies such as that of the Carnegie Commission (Perkins). Not only contextual conditions and structure but ideologies also affect use. Socialist countries are likely to give more attention to utility than to research and improved understanding. Democratic and pluralistic systems are more likely to give increased weight to findings that concerned individuals or small group justice. Perkins' assumptions could be further developed. The stronger the government and the more prescriptive its styles, the more research would be devoted to shaping the system and the less on the impact of policies.

It is reasonable to hypothesise that a relatively high degree of centralisation would strengthen efforts to mobilise research for decision-making (Premfors). Centralisation might determine the nature of the research undertaken; it would be largely tailored to the needs of central decision-makers. In the case of Swedish higher education, decentralisation had not been so decisive as to change the central authorities' capability of using research. But as the institutions become stronger it can be predicted that the demand for "institutional research" (as opposed to central government sponsored research) will increase in Sweden.

Yet another contextual factor is the presence of research networks. We have already raised the question of how far research findings on the "reservoir of talent" affected national policy in Sweden and the UK on access to higher education. Michael Kirst (quoted by Husén) relates how in the USA legislation on the equalisation of school finance and minimum competency testing spread rather rapidly through the states. "How did it happen that, for instance, minimum competency testing in three years was legislated in 32 states?" Kirst hypothesises that certain cross-state networks of various interest groups were operating and had disseminated effectively. In Germany, too, because the government could not wait for the results of German studies on the structuring of the upper part of the mandatory school system, they had to consider how far studies of grouping and differentiation in Sweden and England were applicable in Germany. The issue of policy and practice transfer is one that is now engaging the minds of comparativists and would be a useful contribution to policy studies.

Impact varies, too, according to the areas being studied. Rodhe's concern that development should be encouraged relatively independently and alongside research also contains a plea for more attention to institutional self-development. Unless knowledge is connected with practitioner development, its chances of being taken up were small. Others (Marklund) shared the views of some of the American authorities (e.g. Getzels) that the more fundamental work stood a better chance of being accepted, that the disciplinary base of research certainly had an impact. As we have noted above, economic formulations go directly to the concerns of policy-makers and if convincing research conducted by economists is more likely to be taken up than the findings of, say, political science, sociology or social psychology.

Bergendal argued that non-scientific knowledge has an unacknowledged place in the improvement of education. For example, practitioners' day-to-day knowledge of the conditions under which children learn, or what Lindblom and Cohen (1979) call Ordinary Knowledge, being the knowledge available to journalists or politicians or laymen, could take their place alongside the products of academically-created science.

Contextual factors featured prominently in Dahllöf's paper. He maintained that there were contextual conditions on different societal levels, which all may exert an influence on the part played by school reforms in social and educational changes. They also affect the extent to which reform will succeed. Fundamental economic and social structure conditions determine the extent to which educational reforms take effect in relationship to other reform strategies. As with Perkins and Premfors he considered that degrees of centralisation determine the type of planning process and what kind of experts will play a role. In Sweden the small number of suitable people as leaders of commissioned research may also be taken as a contextual restrictive condition on the supply side. He provided a matrix to illustrate this point, reproduced below, in Table 1.

TABLE 1.

Hypotheses about some crucial contextual conditions concerning reform demands and probabilities in some selected countries

| Country | Fundamental conditions of society at large | | Educational system | | Research community in social and educational sciences Supply |
	Social change demand	Room and probabilities for educational reforms	Reform demand	Reform probability	
France	High	Low	High	High	Moderate
W. Germany	,,	,,	,,	Moderate	,,
England	,,	,,	,,	Low	High
USA	High*/Low	Low	Low	Low	High
Sweden about 1950	Moderate	High	High	High	Low

*For certain specific strata, otherwise low.

Dahllöff explains his matrix as showing that in the European group of countries social and economic stratification is so deep that educational reforms have a low probability of working effectively for social change even though the educational systems as such "could be ascribed a high reform demand". Within the group of countries there is considerable variation in the forms of educational administration, the likelihood of reforms being implemented in it, and in the supply of researchers.

Dahllöf, together with other Swedish commentators, referred to the importance of certain institutional factors. The role of the Government Commission in Sweden was obviously important. (Premfors, 1982(b)). So, too, was that in the UK and, to a lesser extent, the Presidential Commission in the USA. (Dahllöf, Husén and Ruin; Kogan and Atkin, 1982). The existence of commissions is not only a contextual factor instrumental in providing evidence, which might lead to action, but is itself a product of interaction and liaison. The use made of commissions by government and the use made by commissions or research are factors embodying attitudes towards research. If a government does not believe in using research, the commissions will not become channels for research to impact on policy.

So far, therefore, we have noted some of the empirical evidences of the research-policy relationship and examined some of the factors affecting that relationship. The inputs are variable according to the political, ideological and structural context in which the research-policy interaction takes place. The evidence is patchy and inconclusive on the actual impacts. Diffusion and enlightenment are the dominant metaphors rather than "impact" or "cause and effect". It is now time to consider some of the models that were referred to at the symposium and elaborated in the course of the discussion. It will then be possible to begin to strip down some of the components in models of interaction, namely, the knowledge and policy systems and their characteristics.

Models of Interaction

The Symposium was mainly concerned with bringing the experience of different countries to bear upon the problem of how educational research affected policy-making. It was not concerned to create a range of formal models which might either explain or predict relationships. Inevitably, however, modelling was implicit in the attempts to make sense of observed experience. There were several references to models that already existed. Those discussed in this section include those which attempt to show the *components* of the interaction and which, by emphasising the need (a normative consideration) for effective linkage, take on a consensual and linear mode (Marklund, Postlethwaite). An associated model, arising from the work of the World Bank described earlier, was not necessarily linear but was designed to enhance *brokerage* and *managerial* activities (Hultin). Somewhat different models were implicitly concerned with advancing the notion of *interaction*, multi-dimensionality and strong reference to contexts (Dahllöf, Rodhe, Kogan, Perkins). Another strain emphasised the discard or falsification function of research (Trow, Bienaymé). A further discussion was concerned with the dichotomy between technocratic and cybernetic models and pluralistic models (Coleman, Wittrock). Running through the discussion was frequent reference to the useful taxonomy of models suggested in the work of Carol Weiss (1977).

Much of the discussion was concerned with linkages between different kinds of knowledge as they come into the field of policy and practitioner action – the relationship between, for example, fundamental and applied research and the conversion of such knowledge into policies. At the same time, however, models were discussed that implied institutional and role relationships – the relationships between researchers, government and the precipitation of multiple and complex roles within and between the worlds of knowledge generation and policy creation (Trow, Coleman, Kogan, Postlethwaite, Ruin). The emphasis of the discussion reflected the state of research in this field. There is a great deal of work on the characteristics of science institutions. There is much reflection on relationships between science and government, if largely at a normative level – a concern with what ought to be rather than with what is. There has been little concern, however, with the nature of government as a knowledge seeking and using system (Marklund, Dahlstrom, 1979 and Kogan *et al*, 1980 and 1981, Baehr and Wittrock, 1981). This section will attempt to depict the kinds of models implied or overt in the Symposium and also note the extent to which they relate to some of the more important statements in the literature as summarised by Carol Weiss.[1]

Husén usefully merged the seven Weiss models into two: the enlightenment or "percolation" model itself merged with the interaction model and the political model which included the tactical model, although the political use of research is, in fact, interactive as well as tactical. Weiss' two basic ideas are (Husén) that research is not utilised in a linear way in policy formulation and administrative decision making. It affects policies diffusely and indirectly by heightening awareness of certain problems and reshaping others, or by contributing certain facts that provide new perspectives on existing problems. Decision-making is more like an accommodation or "accretion" process than a clearly identifiable set of decisions made here or now. Weiss' perspective is, of course, shared by many other students of policy.

In considering the models produced at the symposium, the reader should note how each model does itself attempt to emphasise different necessities that different groups, with different orientations, hope to see satisfied in research. Thus the linear and consensual models (Marklund, Postlethwaite) rely upon certain premises. Marklund was concerned to redress the balance between concentration on the problems of the researcher and those of the policy-maker. He thought of educational policy as shaped at two levels, namely, government and politicians, and the administrators and executors of educational policy. The first are "policy-makers" and the others are "policy-executors". Once the policy-makers have stated their goals the administrative and executive apparatus must interpret the aims, adopt a position on aims conflict, and set priorities between them. Thus educational R & D has to find instruments to realise the aims and objectives of politically stated guidelines. Research produces effects by arousing interest among policy-makers and executors,

---

[1]In *Using Social Research in Public Policy-Making,* 1977 Carol Weiss offered seven models of research impact. The *classical, linear model* deriving from the political sciences assumes that basic will lead to applied research; this will then lead to development and application. Fundamental knowledge bears on particular practical problems. The *problem solving model* is in Husén's words the "classical philosopher king" conception. Missing knowledge is identified. Social science is either acquired or collated. The research findings are interpreted in the context of decision options. Policy is then chosen. The third is the *interactive model.* It assumes "a disorderly interconnection" and dialogue between policy-makers and researchers, sometimes directly and sometimes intermediary. The *political model* assumes that research findings become ammunition for the client of a political debate which finds the research conclusion congenial. The *tactical model* allows for the burying of a controversial problem by allowing research in order to justify a delay in decision-making. The *enlightenment model* is one through which "social science research most frequently enters the policy arena". It allows for permeation of the policy-making process, not by specific findings or projects but by its "generalisations and orientations percolating through informed publics and can shape the way in which people think about social issues". The seventh model is research as part of the *intellectual enterprise of society model.* In this, social science research is merely one of many dependent variables in policy development.

influences their judgement and attitudes, gives rise to suggestions for new organisational structures, influences curriculum, contributes new methods and produces new teaching aids, etc.

The effect of a given research may be negative – demonstrating difficulty rather than feasibility. Marklund also sees a relationship between the functioning or research and the political system. He thinks a good balance is in fact struck between "free" and "commissioned" research. In general, the Marklund model reflects some of the prevailing assumptions of educational research policy in Sweden: consensus, convergence and accumulations of wisdom capable of being "used" in the policy system. It can be criticised on several grounds: it makes no provision for contributions to policy through practitioner development. Husén also lists the policy-makers but does not allow for the aggregation of the experience of practitioners into the policy process. Marklund divides policy creation from policy execution. It is a linear model which perhaps too comfortably assumes that policy-makers state objectives, that researchers take them up in a search for fundamental knowledge and concepts, and that the results of their research are then applied.

One point which became clear from the Symposium and which could have benefited from closer analysis was that the experience – at least of Sweden – of research on school systems differed from the experience of research on higher education which seems to work more independently and openly. "To begin with, it was regarded as part of the central decision-making organisation of higher education, its task being to improve the input documentation used for planning and control. Now the object is to serve all higher education interests more openly and independently by contributing towards more coherent and, at the same time, deeper knowledge concerning the tasks of higher education, its internal life and its role in society." (Björklund, 1982).

Postlethwaite advanced a more elaborate version of the linear model which was concerned primarily with linkage. The unit of analysis was the research project. The main components of the model are given on the next page.

The model assumes that when research has an impact on policy it is the result of clamour or the noise made by groups in the general political environment. Research is then undertaken and must be presented persuasively and by mobilisation of political forces and funds in order to lead to action. Again, this assumes a somewhat linear process, although the model may only work when commissioned research can rely on political consensus. It does not, however, allow for Husén's "percolation" or Weiss' "partisan", "interaction" or "enlightenment" applications.

Hultin's model (page 73) of the relationship between education research and policy-makers – programme execution – is a three dimensional matrix for analysing relationships. The Z axis shows the political and decision-making mode of responsibility. The Y axis shows the subjects and topics which should be researched, developed and executed; the X axis shows the actions to be taken

The Beginnings of a Model
(Neville Postlethwaite)

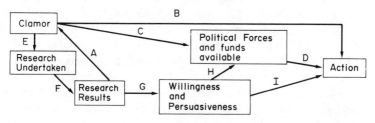

Figure 1.

In this model the unit of analysis is, as mentioned above, research projects. They can *either* be many different types of research projects in different countries or within a country *or* the same project (as in IEA) but in different countries. For example, the Second Science Project has some 40 countries participating in it.

<u>Definition of Terms</u> (constructs)

ACTION =
action occurs/does not occur;
intensity of action;
direction of action (e.g. perceived or as progressive or conservative).
Each could in itself be taken as a separate dependent variable or a composite could be created.

CLAMOR =
Frequency and amount of noise from
– parliament
– teachers' unions
– pressure groups other than teachers' union
– media.

RESEARCH UNDERTAKEN = Number and size of research studies initiated as a result of clamor. (The research could be undertaken anywhere within the nation).

RESEARCH RESULTS =
– existence/nonexistence of research results;
– similarity/dissimilarity of findings;
– strength of methodological criticisms from academic community.
The research could come from anywhere in the nation.

WILLINGNESS AND
PERSUASIVENESS =
(within the major agency
– typically the Ministry of
Education)
– existence of permanent channel of communication of research results to policy-makers;
– number of such channels;
– existence of key persons in agency able to understand research reports;
– research reports written in easily communicable language;
– existence of mechanism for sifting good from bad research;
– intensity of belief of agency's top personnel in utility of research;
– to help policy-making;
– the level of persuasiveness of key persons within the agency in their dealings with policy-makers and the treasury (Ministry of Finance).

POLITICAL FORCES AND
FUNDS AVAILABLE =
– strength of acceptance or rejection of proposal for reform by by key persons (or Parliament) in authority;
– strength of willingness to allocate (extra) funds required.

Before proceeding to the links, two points should be mentioned:
(i) the variables making up the constructs should be thought of as manifest variables although

through the R & D interaction process. Although stated in a linear form, the author explained how actions may "jump about" among the three axes and along the different stage of each axis. This model might be a useful beginning for stating the components that must be accounted for by those who wish to make use of R & D in policy-making. It is not intended to depict the components on each axis as variables although the formula is algebraic.

In contrast to the linear and managerial models there were several attempts to state components of interactive and multi-dimensional models. These added up perhaps less to model building than to statements of the need for interaction.

Husén pointed out that the relationship is much more diffuse and hard to pinpoint than had been hitherto conceived. Scholarship contributes by putting certain issues on the agenda of public debate and by inspiring demands for political action. Research, particularly through critical analysis, often generates ideas more than specific facts or knowledge. It contributes to reinterpreting an issue by drawing attention to aspects that have gone unnoticed. It might affect the belief systems of the general public. It can contribute to achieving consensus about an issue. Political decisions are made within a context of accommodation. The decision is not clear cut but is an attempt to arrive at resolutions that can accommodate a maximum of interests represented by groups and individuals who want to influence the decision or policy-making process.

---

their operationalisation may require indicators. In this case, the indicators would become the manifest variables and their compositing would mean that the variable would then be a latent variable.

(ii) the model should have a hierarchical structure. Thus, to take "Willingness and Persuasiveness", I suspect the model would be:

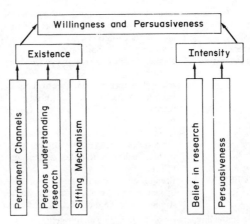

Figure 1a.

RELATIONSHIP – EDUCATION RESEARCH AND POLICY-MAKERS –
PROGRAMME EXECUTIONERS.

Three dimensional matrix for analysing relationships between researchers, research topics and policy and decision-makers. (A comprehensive review of the research-policy link requires an analysis of the managerial structure and the relation between each item (item by item) on the X – Y – Z axes).

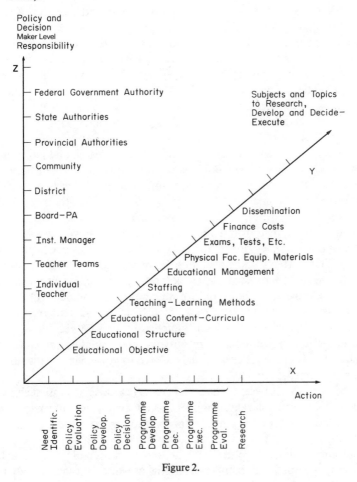

Figure 2.

Such assumptions about political process and the place of research in it are echoed in the assumption about the nature of educational development that underlies the interactive models. Rodhe described how practitioners hoped that science would provide them with answers but, in effect, were themselves the prime movers in searching for both the definition of problem and its solution. Another starting point was pluralism (Coleman) which assumed that there will be many centres of thought and development from which policy was derived and against which policy will be tested.

Perkins urged that "for the development of policy making there must be a recognised need, the sense of priority in the presence of thoughtful administrators, civil servants and politicians who also emphasise the ways in which particular institutions take the initiative in promoting and selecting their own reflective thinking". Research and policy-making, and the relationship between the two, are affected by the cultural and constitutional backgrounds in which this process takes place. In higher education, for example, if research is to be digested and policy-making accepted, the participation of the university community and particularly the faculty is necessary. This touches on the theme of reflexiveness, advanced by Dahllöf, that different social values and systems of governance require that research should be in tune with the style and philosophy of the policy-making.

Moreover, it is too easy to assume that both the research and policy-making take place at single levels. Dahllöf was at pains to point out that both sets of functions might derive from and have an impact at several levels. Research and Government are not single entities. Different levels of institutions and different groups in the whole research–government complex have their own knowledge systems, their own reference groups, their own values and their own interests to pursue. They pursue them with different styles and with different intensities. This affects implementation because: "implementation structures exist in the sense of interested parties before implementation proper . . . they might well be active in defining and forming a programme that will later reach the implementation stage". (Wittrock, Lindström and Zetterberg, 1981.) The "results" of the research-policy encounter are therefore exceedingly complicated and varied because so many groups and other variables come into it, and the kind of result, if any, is also strongly related to movements in the polity and society at the time.

The dichotomy between what Coleman characterised as technocratic-cybernetic as against pluralistic models could be further understood in the following terms. Those responsible for promoting policy and practice – the systems managers, the politicians, the heads of professional groups – must take decisions and elaborate policies. So at one level we might have a linear, managerial, cybernetic or technocratic model at work. But increasingly policy-makers might recognise that the research enterprise works best when it works interactively rather than in a linear fashion. In so doing, they might work best in the managerial interest when, as has become the case in government sponsored R & D for Swedish higher education, "it is the interaction between researchers and practitioners that is seen as the means whereby new studies are initiated". (Björklund, 1982).

It follows that while rationalistic and linear planning attempts to control and define the processes necessary for social action it need not be devoid of creativity and interaction. Politicians and administrators who are expected to act on behalf of all the groups in society attempt to incorporate legitimate fantasies about society's future through rationalistic planning. The fantasy is necessary even if it might never be achieved. This is not, however, a reason for not making it succeed. It *is* reasonable to hope that a problem can be tackled by the use of fundamental research which will then feed into applied research, development, dissemination and implementation. That is precisely the way in which anybody responsible for introducing reforms has to work – see Hultin's matrices as they apply to World Bank planning. So there needs to be reconciliation between models of perfection, in which reform is engineered with the help of disciplined enquiry, and pluralistic interaction which is allowed its full and natural place in the way in which matters actually proceed. Wittrock criticised Coleman's dichotomy in some such terms. Are the cybernetic, technocratic and pluralistic ways really dichotomous? If policy-makers do no more than accept the fact of pluralism will we ever be able to tackle complex problems with any commitment or sense of purpose? He might have added that by allowing for pluralism we might then institutionalise it. Attempts to bring all of the many interest groups into the policy process – the institutionalisation of the anti-bodies – can become as tired as attempts based on the linear model. Is that not, perhaps, the lesson of attempts to introduce co-determination into many areas of Swedish life? Who wins when interaction between interest groups replaces politically directed bureaucracy? Most countries surely try to secure mixtures of both.

Other interesting aspects of the linear multi-dimensional conflict were introduced into the discussion by Trow and Bienaymé. Bienaymé quoted a French minister who had showed all of his Cartesian teeth by philosophising the issue; was there not a process of Popperian falsification at work? Was it not the role of research to falsify leading propositions as they emanated from both the knowledge and the policy systems? This resounded well with Trow's notion that politicians and administrators must learn to live with failure instigated by research. They must accept that research could delimit the potential for success in policy initiatives as well as enhance it.

A similar point was that the concept of "system" needed to be used with caution. Some argued that the emphasis must be on interactive processes rather than structures and products. Yet the Symposium was concerned with the way in which authority, power, resources, legitimacy and knowledge linked together and interacted. Processes become regularised as structure ("structure is process in slow motion"). When structure becomes hardened and immobile processes are adversely affected. That hardly, however, makes the case for avoiding analysis of structure.

The models of interaction implicit in the discussions reflected the extent to which interpenetration between research and policy varied enormously between countries. In Sweden particularly, but also in the USA, researchers and policy-makers are in and out of each other's domains, changing roles as they go, and, as a result, research consciousness, relating to the enlightenment model, may be heightened (Dahllöf). This does not, of itself, dispense with the problems of the relationship between policy and research. They do retain different cultures, reference groups, knowledge systems and functions. The criteria for success and implementation of each are different.

The second and perhaps more important point concerns the role of research in social engineering or planned social intervention. It is one thing to say that we can find examples of research having an impact on policy, and of how research "percolates" or enlightens or indirectly raises consciousness. But it is another thing to assume that impacts can be engineered. We have observed that there is a likely cycle of development for research and that learning gains from it are highest when policies are first being adumbrated and subsequently implemented. Even then, however, research effects might come from zones of thought and institutions well away from government commissioned work. The most conscientious attempts to co-opt researchers into the formulation of policy related research and to devise programmes on joint thinking have produced enormously difficult problems in the few cases where they have been documented (see the case of the British Department of Health and Social Security (Kogan, Korman and Henkel, 1980)). Action can certainly be influenced by knowledge. But the best systematic attempts to cause action to be affected by knowledge are often frustrated.

Before going on to consider the characteristics of knowledge and of the policy sides of the relationship, it will be as well to briefly note some of the purposes assumed for the relationship. Research, it is thought, can clarify issues for the policy system. It can thus either constitute conscious policy analysis, with relevant role structuring for the purpose (Trow) or can, by a process of more diffuse enlightenment, add to the "noise" and consciousness that issues need to be taken up by the policy system (Postlethwaite). Once issues are raised researchers may evaluate existing states-of-the-art, or attempt projective work on desirable developments, as in the curriculum or educational technology or organisational structuring. But research can raise consciousness in the wider society as well as in the policy system. It can create space in which policies can be discussed and tested before they are put into action. There were examples quoted from the USA, the UK, Sweden and developing countries, of the "partisan", or "political" uses of research; these could be analytic statements of justifications for normative shifts in policy. And, obviously, research can directly cause shifts in policy and practice, whether or not it is commissioned for the purpose, when it "discovered" that, for example, selection at different stages of access to education has certain effects as was the case of Sweden with regard to the issue of comprehensive education. It can also evaluate the impact of policies. All of these functions are within the domain of research as it interacts with policy and practice. But the Symposium could not find its way to prescribing systematic arrangements by which all of this could happen to the satisfaction of all of the main stake holders in educational planning and practice.

SECTION V

Knowledge

The Symposium throughout its discussions touched upon the characteristics of knowledge and its institutions as they impinged upon policy. The issues that were raised could be organised into the following questions: What knowledge base is needed for educational policy and practice?; What institutional conditions will favour which kinds of knowledge and with what other results?; What perceptions of roles and role relationships between policy and science can be derived from what can be conceptualised of the nature of knowledge?

What knowledge is needed by policy-makers and practitioners in education? Again, the Symposium made no systematic assessment, but a range of desiderata could be derived from the discussion. First, it was taken for granted that *basic research,* about the nature of social and psychological states, about the teaching and learning processes and the nature of the social and other systems within which they take place, was necessary. Indeed, as has been observed above, some contributors considered that it was studies of a fundamental nature that made the most important changes in policy, if at some long and new remove. One contributor (Noonan) differentiated between studies of the state of the art, by which was meant pedagogical studies such as those of curriculum, curriculum development and system, which would be studies of the institutions which made possible teaching and learning. Basic research could figure in either of these but so would other elements and styles of knowledge.

Basic research is often thought of as being highly theoretical. But another meaning of basic research is that of the *collection of data.* Thus in all of the countries represented knowledge about the socio-economic status of students and of their performance is quite basic to conceptualisations about how performance relates to socio-economic backgrounds. So data collection is certainly an important part of the research and intelligence function.

Again, not in conflict with the previous two categories, but of somewhat different order, is the *ordering of concepts* and *analysis of existing knowledge.* This is sometimes noted as "scholarship" as against "research". (Becher and Kogan, 1980). Practitioners must order concepts and relate them to the existing knowledge base whenever they determine on new curriculum. Within social science at large some of the more important moves forward have figured as scholarship, or the reordering of concepts, rather than discovery of new facts, for example, the works of Daniel Bell or Thomas Kuhn. The reordering and exploitation of concepts may be a strictly academic exercise. But it seems, as well, to underpin the work of applied analysis as in the policy analysis described by Trow. There are then studies of the state of the art as well as studies of the state of the system which we have already mentioned.

A further function for disciplined enquiry is *critique of existing systems* which leads to analysis of policies and prescription for change. And, finally, there is the work of *development*. We have seen how practitioners may cry out for help from scientists but, essentially, development work is concerned with taking the state of the art, formulating desirable changes, and building up analytic sequences and substantive contents which will lead to desired change.

It is, perhaps, too easy to move from categorisation of knowledge that is needed – and these categories must themselves overlap with each other – into the different institutional and other contexts that different kinds of knowledge imply. Nonetheless, some kind of classification is necessary, particularly since the Symposium benefited from quite sustained challenges to the notion of academically based knowledge (Bergendal). Thus it would be possible to take the kind of knowledge needed and then recategorise it into the following types: classical science; applied science and development; non-scientific knowledge and learning; policy analysis and critique. It should be noted that each of these strands can be found written throughout the cases that were considered. The case of higher education in Sweden, for example, (Premfors) shows how a succession of issues did call upon different types of knowledge in aid of policy and practice.

Classical science has values and epistemologies which might be typified as both "objective", and based on clear-cut academic disciplines. Its institutional characteristics are that it is "internalist" and free of control. In principle it need not be permeable and can be quite aloof from policy and practice needs. Policy-makers may commission research in the classic style. But more often they ask for applied science and development which have values and epistemologies concerned with "relevance". They are rooted in the political and social context and the needs of practitioners, and they move away from disciplines towards problem centred "domains" which may draw on several disciplines (Trist, 1972). Policy-related research is in its institutional nature interactive and interdependent. It is highly permeable. It has, of course, strong connections with policy and practice and its reference groups are both those of the scientific peers of the researchers and of the client groups in the larger society. Further along the spectrum is non-scientific knowledge and learning advanced by Bergendal in the Symposium and also promoted as Ordinary Knowledge in a well-known paper by Lindblom and Cohen (1979). This concept argues the case for knowledge deriving from practice, from the feelings of clients who may be ordinary people, needing, certainly, ways into the policy system, but unauthoritative of its nature and the sentiments and knowledge that might be mediated as well through journalists or through statements of politically active people as from the academies. It may share some of the institutional characteristics of applied science and development.

Finally, there is the growing realm of policy studies and policy critique. (Trow). Its values are also strongly based on relevance and context but it claims to be objective and not stating the views of some partisans only but taking account of all partisan views as it works out future lines of action and critiques of existing lines of action. It is interactive and interdependent and highly permeable.

With some such classifications as these in mind it is possible to take account of some of the problems that the various characteristics of knowledge produce in its relationship to policy. It was a commonplace of the Symposium that a great deal of policy-related research is simply not used. When used it sometimes has unintended consequences. When government consciously initiates research, there might be a narrow definition of its objectives and it is too closely tied up with programmes created by policy-makers (Coleman) instead of with the curiosity and analytic motivations of the researchers themselves. At the same time, however, it was urged that a certain institutional separation between research and policy was essential. If research was too closely tied to the chariot wheels of the state, there might be no institutional means of challenge of the result, no review before release and therefore no true legitimacy of knowledge as such rather than as reflections of the authoritative demands of the political system (Coleman).

It is thus difficult to get it right. Come too close and research is socialised and dominated by policy. Be too far away and nothing will happen. In practice, as we have alrady remarked, there can be, in some countries, a culture of mobility between researchers and policy makers (Perkins, Dahllöf). There are professional and social networks and diffusion of similar talents in both areas of activity.

In any event, it is important not to oversimplify the knowledge landscape (Bergendal). It is too glibly assumed that only universities can give a certificate of "good" knowledge and there now needed to be a shift of norms to plurality and with it a shift of power. Such developments as computerisation imply a new balance of power in which the academics might give way to other holders of knowledge and techniques. There is far more than scientific rationality in the truth that society needs. New epistemologies in the social sciences have emerged in recent years, such as hermenetics and phenomenology with a more humanistic than scientific approach. Artistic as well as scientific norms have to be observed by practitioners who need to know how to do things and to think about them as well as to make theories about them. This point of view was contested by Wittrock[1] who said that it was unfair to assume that policy makers and researchers working with them embraced a single epistemology. No

---

[1] These comments are now written up.

"correct" notion of knowledge was being implied. It may be, however, that "profiles" of knowledge were being assumed and, as with all profiles, some features were more prominent than others. At the same time, it was noted that in most of the countries there was no high risk university centre where research and scholarship concerned with policy but not tied to policy-makers could be freely advanced. And the Symposium noted generally that disciplinary based research had higher status than that of problem solving and there was still too much emphasis on impact rather than enlightenment.

There was a particularly interesting discussion on the knowledge needs of developing countries. The formulation of what knowledge was most worth was strongly conditioned by environmental factors, such as the scarcity of resources and political domination of the research commissioning process. The research needs are dominated by immediate demands for basic data. The discussion on the developing countries raised the problem of how knowledge would be controlled, and of cultural imperialism. Researchers share cosmopolitan ethics of research even though they might be constrained by the politicians who commission them. The question of prescription arose not only when national government was involved but could also result from pressure from brokers who might impose their sense of what was most right and relevant. Yet in developing countries it was important to avoid the "closed circuit syndrome". At the same time, it was obvious that the impact of research could be terrifying. Where the knowledge base was frugal and the goals of the policy system were being asserted strongly by single-minded politicians, they might be tempted to draw large conclusions from small scale or even poorly conducted researches.

What were the institutional conditions by which knowledge would be encouraged or discouraged? Policy practitioners (Orehag) could state these clearly. Government certainly needed to get knowledge. But knowledge generated too prescriptively and with limited and instrumental ends would not help them. They need free researchers who can devote themselves to problems that directly concern policy-makers. Researchers in formulating their areas of study and in formulating their results also need to be realistic about what could be usable to politicians, administrators and practitioners. Other commentators on the Swedish scene (Marklund) thought that commissioned and "free" research spontaneously concerned themselves with similar issues and used similar methods. Against this (Lövgren) made the factual point that research work commissioned by the Swedish government at least implicitly assumed that certain political objectives were elaborated and that commissioned research would assist the pursuit of those objectives rather than alternative political policies. As has already been implied, many participants were concerned that research should include practitioners' aspirations for development and that institutional arrangements for research should take account of them.

Two of the more important discussions of institutionalisations came from the USA. Coleman was concerned that social policy research was used in ways that were not intended. He was concerned with the process by which central authorities initiated social policy research through requests for proposals (RFPs). He doubted whether RFPs invited research that could be used by all of the interests surrounding a given policy, including those opposed to the agency's interest. There was doubt whether the contractor was sufficiently independent to design and carry out the research that might provide information inimical to the agency's interests. If the results did not support the agency's interests, would the agency use and make known the results? "The answer to all these questions is sometimes toward narrowly defined RFPs contracted for by captive or subservient research organisations which design, execute and analyse their research in ways that will be most flattering to their clients and resulting in reports that are buried if they would harm the agency's interests and used only if they aid that interest." At the same time, unsolicited research proposals may simply embody the motivation of academic social scientists who want publication in academic journals and who do not care about the "relevancy" of their research.

Coleman maintained that, at least in the USA, there was no satisfactory institutionalised separation between bureaucratic interests and the interests of those finding out about its functioning of effects. A conflict of interest might be built into the setting up of a research contract. As a result, members of Congress were often suspicious of the result. Research which evaluates social programmes is used to provide feedback to those responsible for them or to provide those higher in the institutional structures with information relevant for major modification. But research must also provide information relevant to the broader concerns voiced by those outside bureaucracy. In spite of these different kinds of evaluation, research is often funded from a single point within the agency close to the bureaucratic interests of maintaining or expanding a programme. Nor is there any means by which there can be challenge to the research results before they become public. Such behaviour destroys the credibility of social research for the public as well as neutralising its impact.

For this reason, Coleman believed more thought needed to be given to creating "science courts" where there could be challenge of results by groups who had legitimate interests in opposing the results. There could also be simultaneous initiation of more than one research project. And, in a more controversial suggestion, Coleman thought that policy-related research should be funded by Congress or other legislative bodies rather than by the governmental agencies.

Coleman's proposals aroused much interest. The American context is different from that of other countries in two ways. Legislatures have their own analytic capabilities, for example, the Congressional Budget Office and the General Accounting Office, both of which are able to launch analyses of policies with the help of policy analysts. These form part of the critique of the Executive's proposals. To many of the participants in the Symposium, such developments seemed entirely desirable in themselves but did not reduce the need for bureaucracies to commission research and, at the same time, to be held responsible for making their commissioned research subject to adequate academic critique outside itself. Indeed, in many countries, such as Britain, commissioned research is criticised by other scientists. The work of units wholly funded by government departments is held up for criticism by visiting groups of scientists in much the same way as is work commissioned by research councils. (Henkel and Kogan, 1981). The complaint is then quite different from Coleman's: that scientists follow their own narrow scientific criteria instead of the broader criteria that should be applied to policy-related research.

Coleman's contribution also substantiated a generalisation about the institutionalisation of knowledge. It is an important fact of the American culture that there is resistance to and suspicion of government, particularly federal government. In such a context, research inevitably and perhaps rightly takes on a strong stance of criticism. Attempts to use research to instantiate, implement and evaluate policy developments are treated with suspicion and resistance. This is in strong contrast to the Swedish pattern where the use of Royal Commissions and of commissioned research has been legitimised by the fact that there has been far stronger political consensus and a belief that the government acts, on the whole, for the benefit of the various groups in society. (This feeling may have been reduced since the mid-1970s but is still far stronger than in other countries). So the political culture affects the role of research and its "acceptability".

A further American example of kinds of knowledge and institutionalisation was given in Trow's paper on the *policy analyst*. He referred to the development of a dozen graduate schools of public policy within the USA producing graduates who were taken up for employment by policy institutions. Trow based his analysis on the percolation model "since it is the way through which research actually has an influence on policy". In such a model, the role of the "middle man" becomes important. He follows Premfors (1982) in suggesting that "analysis" research on the one hand and social interaction on the other are not alternative forms of reaching decisions but are complementary. And if both are needed, new roles might be precipitated to ensure that both are used. Therefore, according to Trow, "an analyst is sometimes very much like a researcher, defining a problem, doing analysis and gathering and interpreting the data; sometimes a 'middle man', bringing together and interpreting for decision makers the findings of research by others; and sometimes himself a decision maker". In the United States this neo-profession emerges "expressly designed to narrow the gap between the research and the policy-maker, and to bring systematic knowledge together more directly, more quickly and more relevantly on the issues of public policy". The training is interdisciplinary because that is the way that problems present themselves to decision-makers. He is trained to formulate problems from the perspective not of the academic disciplines but of the decision-maker. He accepts the contraints of the actor. He is taught, however, by academic social scientists trained in social science disciplines or what James Q. Wilson has called "policy intellectuals" while the students Trow describes are policy analysts. Analysts work in government rather than research institutions. The paradigms of research that they acquire emphasise the importance of "serving the client". The reputation is not made in an academic setting and he is subject to the mechanisms of information "drift" and "creep" as with "percolation", through a small but active community of analysts in government agencies, on legislative staffs, in think tanks and special interest organisations who know of his work and its quality. They are not necessarily concerned with developing new knowledge but with exploiting and recording existing knowledge.

The role of policy analysis has thrown up some problems. Because policy analysis often makes little use of ethnographic field methods it might be captive to existing and official statistics. By contrast, university researchers are more likely to question the quality of research data. The phenomena and variables taken into account are constrained by the analyst's position within the bureaucratic setting. There is the danger, therefore, of indulging in oversimplification.

This important and interesting development contains paradoxes. A country which is "anti-government" nonetheless can be quite profuse in creating thought related to policy action. Moreover, it seems able to proliferate a range of roles from the most rigorous of academic researchers to the most interactive and opportunistic of policy analysts. In so doing, they might come near to Bergendal's category of "non-scientific" knowledge or Lindblom and Cohen's Ordinary Knowledge although they must seek to be analytic even if they are not concerned with producing fundamental categories of knowledge.

Trow's account of the precipitation of the new role accords with other notions of "middle men". There is evidence of brokers developing not only within the academic community or between the policy and science communities but also within the policy systems. Research management is distinct from policy creation and execution within government agencies and the research manager must be a middle man between his policy-making colleagues and the researchers with whom he must relate in both controlling and in an encouraging relationship. The role may be "patronal" but must also take a fairly neutral brokerage role between policy-makers who need the research and researchers who provide knowledge. (Kogan, Korman and Henkel, 1980)

These considerations lead us to our next section which is concerned with some characteristics of the policy system.

Policy Systems

For the most part, the Symposium was concerned with characteristics of research and interaction with policy. There was not much discussion about policy-makers as "receptors" for research, or of the different modes through which research might be commissioned. In the literature, government and the policy system are often taken to be aggregates whereas they are themselves tribal and multi-modal. Within government departments there are many different groupings consisting of policy-makers, planners, professional advisers and research managers. Nor are the functions of government in relationship to research simple and unitary. Government is both a primary and a proxy or secondary customer for research. As a primary customer, government is concerned with generating knowledge and data about the issues which it itself must solve. As a secondary or proxy customer it acts on behalf of the wider world of policy-making and of practice. The policy system operates at several levels, particularly if the practitioner is included (Dahllöf, Marklund, Rodhe and Perkins). So a national ministry or board of education will commission work on curriculum development or on organisational forms which will help practitioners and administrators in the field authorities or in the schools themselves.

A further dimension of the same issue is that policy-making is increasingly connected with policy implementation. Policy-making has to take account of how it will be implemented, who will implement it, and who will be recruited and motivated to help in its implementation. The policy-maker who fails to think about the impact on clients or the likely response of practitioners in the field will not be making policy that will work. (Richardson and Jordan, 1979). Hence the need for parallel thinking about Research and Development and about the multi-level interaction required for both (Rhode and Dahllöf). Moreover, although policy is determined by central politicians and policy-makers, it is also an aggregate of developments in the field. The problem of policy aggregation and disaggregation from the centre could affect the kind and style of knowledge which policy systems will seek to secure, although there is not much evidence that central authorities have grappled with this point.

If there are multiple roles within government which are concerned with research commissioning, and if government is both a primary and secondary customer, the same issue can be converted into analysis of the style of functions at the centre. Government has to be authoritative and convergent. It must, in the terms of David Easton, "reduce interests". At the same time, however, in a democratic society it encourages pluralism and does not pre-empt the normative developments of many thousands of institutions and of individual practitioners and clients whose voices ought to be heard. Government sponsored research must therefore not only help the policy-makers in their attempts to produce authoritative and workable policies but must also encourage divergent and creative thinking. If government must analyse existing situations and produce solutions, research and other disciplined enquiry can test government's assumptions and working. They can scan wider ranges of interests and options and are not under pressure to rush to quick conclusions. Research can thus be the basis of alternative and counter analysis.

These considerations lead to a range of potential relationships which government might sponsor with the world of disciplined enquiry. (Kogan and Henkel, forthcoming.) Some governments have in-house research units whose objectives and ways of working are set within the prescriptive bounds of government itself. Such research is set up within a managerial mode. At the other end of the spectrum, there is the mode of free grant. In this mode, government may donate capital and blanket grants to freestanding institutions on the assumption that they will contribute to the knowledge that society and policy-makers need by themselves listening to the problems that society presents and that their contributions are made from the base of their own curiosity and motivation. Such has been the underlying assumption of wide discretion given to universities in Britain through the device of the quinquennial grants until the economic blizzards and change of sentiments in the early 1970s caused a change of the formulas, and it largely underlies government support for universities in all free countries.

The third kind of relationship is that of negotiation. This is best described in terms of exchange theory. The government may provide resources, institutional legitimacy and access to the field of work. In return it gets the knowledge that it needs. Government cannot do without knowledge, so there is an exchange of knowledge for resources and legitimacy. But certain conditions are necessary for the exchange to be sustained without a pathological imbalance of power. For one thing, exchange assumes that institutions will be strong enough to enter into the relationship as free negotiators and will not be largely or wholly captive to the government for their existence. Such conditions might exist while tenurial patterns are strong and underpin the groups who conduct commissioned research. But where government relies largely on short life units, or teams or projects on "soft" money the pattern is nearer the managerial. It might rely on a system of piece work rather than that of negotiated give and take. In Britain, the customer-contractor relationship enunciated by the Rothschild Report (1971) was too glib a metaphor. In most instances the contractor (the researcher) is not able to go on to the open market for alternative work if a monopoly customer (government) decides not to use him.

These three relationships (free grant, managerial and negotiation) are primarily concerned with patterns of accountability and funding. Other dimensions of the government-science relationship concern the modes of functioning. Thus there is a question of how far implementation is in the hands of government alone or whether, as well, "implementation structures exist in the sense of informal networks of interested parties before implementation proper". (Wittrock *et al,* 1980). We noted earlier how researchers on higher education (Premfors) influenced policy through advocating points of view based on their studies of higher education. Research spontaneity and responsiveness to social needs may, but need not be, in conflict, but very different kinds of research are generated according to the mode and source of its generation. The full democratic model of research commissioning would want to secure several things at once. It would want the best minds to engage freely, from their own spontaneous interest and curiosity, in problems of social importance. To do so, it has been assumed in the past, government will, through its core grants to institutions and through relatively freestanding research councils encourage excellent and spontaneous application for monies. At the same time, it requires high quality work which is devoted to bounded problems arising from policy and practice. To some extent, it can rely upon those whom it funds to be free and responsive – senior and tenured academics – to lead such projects. But there is always danger, and it seems to increase in most countries, that the terms of reference for such researches will not import a sufficient degree of freedom to ensure that the work is genuinely conditioned by curiosity, freedom to establish the researcher's own research methods, and freedom in the nature of presentation and dissemination of the results. (Coleman, Husén and oral contributions about developing countries).

Government might encourage and sponsor research work. What does it do with the knowledge that it sponsors? What can be said about its receptor role? The Symposium hardly touched on this issue. How does government respond to knowledge generated either from research commissioned by itself or from research created by freestanding centres? Some varied examples were given. They did not, however, expose the full range of possibilities. In Sweden, the use of commissions was an important way in which government acted as a receptor. Government appointed commissions to elucidate and make recommendations on policy issues arising from politically led initiatives. The commissions could include researchers as members, or could commission research. Both the commissioning of the research and the formulation of conclusions by the commission ensured that government would receive the results of research and make use of them. The case studies are fairly clear that this happened although Premfors, it will be recalled, attributes to other factors a stronger part in the policy conclusion.

At the other end of the spectrum we have an account of government in the USA acting arbitrarily in its partisan use of research, using it to legitimise policies already endorsed politically rather than as a critical and reformulating source of knowledge.

Other studies (Kogan, Korman and Henkel, 1980) note what happened within a British government department (Health and Social Security) when strenuous attempts were made to create a system in which researchers helped policy-makers formulate objectives and analyse the results of them. For one thing, the process of joint formulation of research objectives was said to raise the consciousness of the receptor, or the policy-maker. They became more aware of the kinds of knowledge that could help them. The process of formulating research objectives strengthened the process of formulating policy objectives. Examples can be found of work that helped create, or apply science to policies.

Contributions to the Symposium responded to the difficulties of government getting the knowledge it needed without enforcing narrowly instrumental prescriptions on to the researcher. Björklund said that there are many special problems in the educational sector which are not best treated by university research but better dealt with by the administration's own study groups or task forces. Björklund quoted Lord Rothschild's recent report on British social science (1982). In a controversial and not well-substantiated statement, Lord Rothschild suggests that the customer-contractor principle cannot be safely applied to the social sciences which ought to be funded in a freer way by research councils. "Customer demand should be held back; this principle has little application in the social sciences". Lord Rothschild's caution should itself be treated with caution. It does not accord to the evidence now accumulating about the need to strengthen rather than weaken the customer voice or the successful attempts to engage scientists in helping customers to state their needs. (Kogan, Korman and Henkel, 1980). The other caution about the too strong, and narrowly dominant customer, expressed by Coleman and Trow have already been noted earlier. Relationships between two major sets of institutions such as the scientific community and government will always be complicated and difficult to manage. It is for this reason that it can be argued that it is important for both sides to be strong in their demands, strong in their freedom to argue and to negotiate.

Björklund also maintained that more long term, independent research should be funded from central funds given to research councils, the R & D resources should be allocated to the state authorities as stated recently in a Swedish Research Policy Bill. And Björklund and Lars Ekholm maintained that national authorities should encourage studies of the very issues here, of the relationship between researchers and policy-makers. Comparisons should be made internationally about the ways in which research into education has been used for policy-making and which qualities of the decision-making process account for the use of research.

Husén refers to a study in the USA by Caplan *et al* (1976) who tested three hypotheses that related to why research was used, or not used. In studying 240 Federal government policy-makers they elaborated the "two-community theory" and found that twice as much of the variance of utilisation was accounted for by the existence of a gap between social scientists and policy-makers due to differences in values, languages, reward systems and social and professional affiliation than by what they called "knowledge-specific" or "policy-maker-constraint factors". An earlier study (Williams, 1971) of the way in which social science research techniques may be used by policy-makers in federal social agencies to improve anti-poverty and equal opportunity programmes, concluded that social science research studies were seldom relevant to major policy decisions in federal social agencies and the results were often peripheral to the most crucial policy questions. The social policy agencies were not successful in building ties with the social science community or in specifying their urgent needs for high level and challenging research. The severe problems of implementing complex new programmes were given relatively little attention in social agency operating offices. Williams is pointing to the lack of suitable institutional links rather than to the cultural and values gaps implied by Caplan.

The seminar did not fully explore these issues. There is also a lack of published studies and research on research needs to go far more deeply into a far wider range of government departments, covering a fuller span of subject areas and of political cultures. Such work is presently being conducted by Wittrock and Premfors in Sweden as well as by Kogan and Henkel in Britain.

Policy Proposals

Many of the papers and contributions were concerned, rightly, with what ought to be. For the most part, the Symposium sympathised with the needs of government and of practitioners but also sponsored the need for scientific pluralism which was not only best for science in the long run but would also make sure that government benefited from a wider range of knowledge.

How might these objectives be reconciled? It may be that the objectives of commissioned research must be set by customers. But the objectives set by the customers could well be sharpened and reformulated by stronger interaction with researchers; and, in any event, the methods should largely be in the hands of the researchers.

Educational researchers are in a good position to test value assumptions in their collaboration with policy-makers. Equally, whilst the researcher should be able to engage in methodological pluralism, and be free to choose his own methods, the method must be such as not to nullify the purposes of what was being attempted, or being evaluated, and those who were being researched also had rights to be respected. Both sides need to be strong in stating their needs and rights.

In these regards the rapporteur must note some unfairness. The Swedish policy-research relationship was criticised because it assumed consensus without much questioning of the value assumptions underlying educational policy. Yet interaction between policy and research and researcher critique of policy differs considerably between the zones of schools and higher education policy. Moreover, the risks arising from too cosy a consensus are likely to be higher in these systems where there are conscientious efforts to recruit the help of disciplined enquiry and not simply allow policies to develop without the benefit of external analysis.

The multiplicity of objectives in the science-government encounter is well reflected in the models of interaction (see Section III) produced for the Symposium. It was noted earlier how each model itself attempts to emphasise a different orientation that the groups hope to see pursued in research. Thus the linear models assume that research responds to a political system that can hope for consensus. Educational R & D will find instruments which will help the political system to realise the aims and objectives of politically laid down guidelines. Postlethwaite's model is, perhaps, less consensual but is equally linear. Hultin's model is the most overtly system-related of them all, because it shows the different processes through which research initiators must go if they are to successfully sponsor, manage and gain from research performed on their behalf.

In contrast to such models which specify the different groups who have a stake in research and the components of process are the interactive models which, again, start from different assumptions. They assume that good intellectual work may begin spontaneously from researchers or equally from policy-makers with a problem to solve. In education they may derive from the accretion of knowledge among practitioners or the clients of the educational system. One kind of interactive process might begin with the needs of teachers. Another kind of process might begin with freestanding institutions which pluralistically develop thinking about the nature of educational problems and their solution. Such models are obviously difficult to use predictively or prescriptively and those who manage education systems might well feel sceptically that any attempt that they make to encourage interaction will inevitably be regarded as an attempt to bureaucratise the sources of spontaneous and creative thought.

The Symposium, no more than any other group who have worked on these problems, did not find it easy to reconcile the two points of view. Government must govern and is remiss if it does not attempt to clarify its objectives and bring to its aid the work of academics outside itself. But when it resolutely commissions the production of knowledge its best efforts may be mocked by the fact that the most important ideas come from sources other than those which it sponsors and enter into the policy system through the processes of "enlightenment", political "turbulence", "noise", "percolation" and all of the other metaphors whose very use in this area of study denotes the lack of predictability and precision of the processes being described.

Because, however, government cannot turn its back upon its obligations to assess and evaluate the social conditions and to seek to use knowledge in taking action about it, but at the same time, must respect the intrinsic needs of science, it seems likely that some of the precepts derived from exchange theory would be the most realistic to follow. Whenever government enters any market it is not acting in the same way as any ordinary customer can act. It has the advantages of political legitimacy. It has the advantages of access to information which many researchers would like to share. It can give all manner of rewards, direct and indirect, to those who help it and, above all, its pursuits are not trivial: central government policy turns up many of the most important issues that the speculative and the curious might want to pursue. Moreover, it has the advantage of ultimately being almost a monopoly customer for educational policy research. Whilst it was argued in the Symposium that research should also be available to the many groups who might find themselves opposed to government, the fact of the matter is that it is government which will provide the money and the legitimacy, and researcher access to many of the more important research issues. But the disadvantages of government in its commissioning of science are, simply, that researchers are suspicious of research commissions which do not start from their own quest for knowledge and whose objectives might be conditioned by values and thought systems which are not their own. Policy research is not innocent research.

It is for this reason that some kind of analogy to a market relationship seems most appropriate. A modified exchange theory might therefore be the most productive to follow. Government needs to pay, in resources and in legitimacy and tenurial certainty if it is to have worthwhile research undertaken for its benefit. It must thus be willing to do several things at once. Freestanding institutions would provide the training base, the critical force, and the research enterprise based on intellectual curiosity that policy-making in a free society needs to encourage and to use. At the same time, government should not be defensive about stating its needs which could be met by seeking help from the intelligentsia in formulating its objectives and – not least – in clarifying them, and in putting them to the hardest test, through counter analysis. It should also be able to rely upon the academic enterprise for evaluation, data collection, formulation of notions of good practice and good systems management as well as for evaluation of impacts and products and processes. If it wanted these more instrumental functions performed on its behalf it does well to take account of the psychological and social make up of successful research which has to embody internally governed methodological rigour, individual curiosity and creativity, as well as responsibility to those who might pay for the research. Thus even the most instrumentally conceived research will have to embody within it the social and economic rewards of free time, freedom from the pressure of the sponsor and hope for continuation of work on fundamental problems. Research work that has no hope of accumulation of basic knowledge is frustrating and a poor deal.

It seems obvious that for such relationships to prosper, which demand strength on both sides, mechanisms for discussion and collaboration between policy-makers and researchers are necessary. For these to succeed, policy-makers must be willing to let researchers join in the discussion of the policy objectives which are being researched.

The symposium was, indeed, concerned with the problem of how government might produce its own critics and its own counter analysis. Nourishing its own "antibodies" calls for a liberal exercise of the power of governments, as the best political systems have done. Governments must, however, become explicit about ways of advancing democratic electicism in which policy discussion is based on the knowledge of many different networks including that of disciplined enquiry. This is difficult for politicians and administrators to achieve during a period of constraint when they themselves face turbulence, pressure and anxiety from their constituents and from strong interest groups, not least on the labour market. It would require governments to regard policy systems not only in terms of the pursuit of rational objectives and of hierarchical structures that can achieve policies but also in terms of the interconnecting networks of interest groups, politicians, administrators and intellectuals that already exist but are not fully endorsed and understood. Some such style as implicit in the role of the Swedish Secretariat for Future Studies whose "work has been characterised by an ambition to clearly spell out alternative courses of action and to promote a public debate on options and developments. Thereby, it has been able to influence Swedish policy formation, mainly in the field of energy, in ways that indicate alternatives to those envisaged by most rational models of policy analysis". (Baehr and Wittrock, 1981).

Husén's introductory paper raised the question of the extent to which there could be a free sector for research. It seems unlikely that public authorities in any country have systematically worked out the amount of free time for research which is embodied in tenured teachers' contracts and how the degrees of freedom already in the system are then capable of being related to the many means through which government institutionalises policy-oriented research: university institutes; research council grants; granting of contracts to private research establishments as well as the research units which are part of public agencies themselves.

One aspect of the institutionalisation of relationships is the way in which a range of roles necessary for good science-policy encounter have begun to develop. The role of the policy analyst, of the broker within and outside government, of the multiple roles that both policy-makers and researchers perform, is an area for development and for further study. As functions become more complex so do interactions, and so do the roles needed to ensure that the interactions happen and the functions are well-performed. Transfers across the career lines would also help interaction and sharing of assumptions although it was important not to slide relationships into cosy consensuses or into patterns inducing too strong a dependency of one group on another. Hybridity, however, becomes one of the names of the game. It is in the nature of academic intelligentsia to be sceptical and critical towards government and authorities. It is in the interest of democratic society that they are.

In this regard, James Perkins gave an illuminating account of how an academic finds himself increasingly involved in systems management as he becomes first a Dean, then a University President, and finally, Chancellor of a large system, an intellectual Rakes' Progress in reverse. There comes a point, however, when he is still protesting that he is primarily an academic in his values and functions but is nonetheless co-opted to the larger policy system. Kogan referred to the issue of the co-opted academic who still remains regarded as an academic within his own institution and within the "invisible college" but nonetheless enters into allocative duties as a member of a grants committee or of a research council. We can thus envisage, and broaden the application of the concept, the academic who is moving from primary academic tasks to systems maintenance. But the criterial breaking point is whether he is maintaining his *own* system or helping to maintain the system belonging to the politicians and the administrators. Many academics will try to do both at once in which case the role conflict has to be recognised.

Further issues concern ways of making research more relevant to the customer. Many papers and contributions spoke of the importance of bringing the research customer into closer relationship with the researchers. For the developing countries, the relevance of the customer needs was specially emphasised. Obviously, more developed countries find it easier for customer needs to be articulated and for the profusion of research to ensure that some time and somehow the problem will be taken up. Not all countries are fortunate enough to enjoy the same flow of resources. Even the most developed may have to rely on too few people to perform policy-related research (Dahllöf on Sweden).

In any event, the Symposium clearly showed that policy proposals and the models underlying them were strongly affected by the settings from which they derived. In the USA, conditions for research must offset the narrowness of bureaucracy and take account of prevailing suspicion of government. The American contributions thus assumed a conflict model. Other countries had assumed that consensus was more secure for benign government intervention in the education system although new forms of integration were observable. But at least there were coalitions of interests upon which consensus could be built, assuming that election results conferred legitimacy on governments to act. There might be value conflict between scientists and policy-makers. The knowledge systems, reference groups and bases of legitimacy are different. But the existence of different networks and cultures need not be a cause for despair. After all, it is because there are such value conflicts running throughout the whole of political and social life that democracies have established political processes in which conflict can be brought out into the open and mechanisms created by which collective decisions can be made. The lesson is, perhaps, that neither side should expect too much from the other. Science has, of course, no exclusive rights in determining the action of government. Government must allow the scientific system to follow its own ways while responding to the needs of society as represented by government.

The Symposium confirmed the belief of researchers and policy-makers that the research enterprise was worth improving and extending rather than reducing and restricting. Even if the impact could not be clearly denoted and if the processes were messy, that was also true of most good things in life. The over-riding problem was how institutions could be made free and strong and yet responsive to social need. For these reasons, the softer imagery of "percolation" of "enlightenment" and of negotiation took pride of place over the harder notions of managerialism, the definition and implementation of social objectives in a linear model of research, development and governance. Yet all models contained assumptions that could not be ignored or wished away.

References

Peter R. Baehr and Björn Wittrock (1981) *Policy Analysis and Policy Innovation. Patterns, Problems and Potentials,* Sage Publications.

Tony Becher and Maurice Kogan (1980) *Process and Structure in Higher Education,* Heinemann.

Eskil Björklund (forthcoming) *Research into Higher Education: An Overview,* R & D for Education, National Swedish Board for Universities and Colleges, *and* Communication in Guy Neave (July, 1982).

Nathan Caplan (1977) Social Research and National Policy: What Gets Used, By Whom, For What Purposes, and With What Effects?. *International Social Science Journal,* **28.**

The Carnegie Council on Policy Studies in Higher Education (1980) *A Summary of Reports and Recommendations,* Jossey-Bass Publishers.

Geraldine Clifford (1973) A History of the Impact of Research on Teaching, in Travers, R. M. W., *Second Handbook of Research on Teaching,* Rand McNally.

Edmund Dahlstrom (1979) Interactions between Practitioners and Social Scientists in Research and Development, in *Research into Higher Education: Processes and Structures,* Report from a Conference in June, 1978, Swedish National Board of Universities and Colleges.

Elizabeth Fraser (1959) *Home, Environment and the School,* University of London Press.

A. H. Halsey (1961) *Ability and Educational Opportunity,* OECD.

Mary Henkel and Maurice Kogan (1981) *The DHSS Funded Research Units: The Process of Review,* Department of Government, Brunel University.

Torsten Husén and Gunnar Boalt (1967) *Educational Research and Educational Change,* Almqvist & Wiksell, Stockholm.

Torsten Husén (1983) *An Incurable Academic: Memoirs of a Professor,* Pergamon Press, 1983.

Maurice Kogan (1982) *The Politics of Educational Change.* Fontana Books.

Maurice Kogan, Nancy Korman and Mary Henkel (1980) *Government's Commissioning of Research: A Case Study,* Department of Government, Brunel University.

Maurice Kogan and Myron J. Atkin (1982) *Legitimating Education Policy: The Use of Special Committees in Formulating Policies in the USA and UK,* The Institute for Research on Education and Finance in Government, Stanford University.

C. E. Lindblom (1977) *Politics and Markets,* Basic Books.

C. E. Lindblom and D. K. Cohen (1971) *Usable Knowledge,* Yale University Press.

M. M. Mussachia (1979) *Scientific Development: Theoretical Issues and Perspectives,* University of Gothenberg.

National Academy of Sciences (1977) *Fundamental Research and the Process of Education.*

John Nisbet and Patricia Broadfoot (1980) *The Impact of Research on Policy and Practice in Education,* Aberdeen University Press.

Rune Premfors (1982a) *Analysis and Politics: The Regionalisation of Swedish Higher Education,* Group for the Study of Higher Educational Research Policy, University of Stockholm.

Rune Premfors (1982b) *Social Research and Governmental Commissions in Sweden,* University of Stockholm, Group for the Study of Higher Education and Research Policy, Report No. 22.

Report on Educational Research and Development (1980) Stellforsking.

J. J. Richardson and A. G. Jordan (1979) *Governing Under Pressure: The Policy Process in a Post-Parliamentary Democracy,* Martin Robertson.

Rothschild Report (1981) *The Organisation and Management of Government R and D.,* Cmnd 4814, HMSO.

Rothschild Report (1982) *An Inquiry into the Social Science Research Council* by Lord Rothschild, Cmnd 8554, HMSO.

Taylor Report (1977) *A New Partnership for our Schools,* DES and Welsh Office, HMSO.

Travers (1978)

E. Trist (1972) *Types of Output Mix of Research Organisations and their Complementarity,* in A. B. Cherns *et al* (eds), *Social Science and Government: Policies and Problems,* Tavistock Publications.

U.S. Office of Education (1966) *Equality of Educational Opportunity.*

Carol Weiss (1977) *Using Social Research in Public Policy-Making,* Lexington Books.

Carol Weiss (1980) *Social Science Research and Decision Making,* Columbia University Press.

Aaron Wildavsky (1979) *Speaking Truth to Power,* Little, Brown.

Walter Williams (1971) *Social Policy Research and Analysis. The Experience in the Federal Social Agencies,* Elsevier.

Björn Wittrock, Stefan Lindström and Kent Zetterberg (May, 1981) *Implementation Beyond Hierarchy. Swedish Energy Research Policy,* Group for the Study of Higher Education and Research Policy, Report No. 13, University of Stockholm.

Papers presented at the Symposium

The Case of Germany: Experiences from the Education Council

BY HELLMUT BECKER

I

No political solution has been found in Germany to the problem of scientists acting as advisers to policy-makers. Indeed, no convincing answer has been found to this question in any other country. The unity of science and politics, as propounded by dogma in Socialist countries on the Soviet model, merely conceals the considerable tensions which exist between scientific-determined reality and the politically-desired objective. A close examination should be made of the extent to which science, in Western democracies, is mainly used to conceal the fact that a representative democracy no longer has an adequate, legitimate basis, and the extent to which, in individual cases, science and politics manage to achieve truly productive cooperation.

In the Federal Republic a symbolic example of the unresolved tension between practical politics and scientific advice for policy-makers was the well-known claim by the Social Democratic opposition, in the election campaign of 1964, that it was advised by 36 professors, and the grotesque reply from the CDU Federal Government that it was advised by 471, as if the number of professors was important! No less bizarre is the formulation in the law on the establishment of the Board of Experts for the evaluation of overall economic development; this law entrusts these experts with the analysis of overall economic development, but expressly forbids them to recommend specific economic or political measures. Both examples illustrate two dangers inherent in scientists giving advice to policy-makers: it could be misused as a kind of *carte blanche* or it could arouse fears in policy-makers that, because of the power of these experts, pressure could be brought to bear on them which is not politically legitimate but politically effective.

II

The aim of ensuring that the Scientific Council (*Wissenschaftsrat*) and the Education Council (*Bildungsrat*) would provide independent advice led to each

103

of them being organised differently. Both have a two-chamber system. In the Scientific Council the Chamber of Government Representatives (*Regierungs-kommission*) and the Chamber of Scientists (*Wissenschaftskommission*) decide together. In the Education Council the Commission of Experts (*Bildungs-kommission*) decided alone; it was, however, obliged to consult the Government Commission before taking any decisions. In this connection it is interesting to note that the experts responsible for evaluating overall, economic development are obliged to give the Federal Government 8 weeks to comment, before publishing their analyses. Three characteristic examples – the national economy, science and education – clearly demonstrate that scientific conclusions and political opinions can be combined in widely-differing ways.

The Education Council and the Scientific Council are not made up solely of experts. The Scientific Commission of the Scientific Council also includes six representatives from public life (e.g. from churches, trade unions, employers) in addition to the sixteen scientists appointed after being nominated by the German Society for the Promotion of Research, the Max Planck Society and the West German Conference of University Rectors respectively. The Education Commission of the German Education Council included experts in educational research, scientists with a general interest in education, and representatives from public life. There are no details as to their distribution among these groups. Unlike the experts responsible for evaluating overall economic development, the advisory service of the Education Council and Scientific Council is provided not only by experts but, as in a Royal Commission in England, by a combination of experts and representatives of public life. Nevertheless, this advice should also be viewed in the same light as scientific advice, as it is safe to assume that the representatives from public life are there to ensure that the connection between expert knowledge and politics takes place, as it were, in the public eye. In the practical work of both bodies, the representatives from public life often proved to be a link between science and politics.

III

The Education Commission was responsible for:
1. Drawing up requisite and development plans for German education, which correspond to the demands of the cultural, economic and social life and which take into account the future demand for trained people;
2. Making suggestions about the structure of the education system and calculating the costs;
3. Making recommendations for long-term planning at the different levels of the education system.

How can research affect a body of this kind? It is evident that the relationship between science, policy-oriented advice and practice does not take the form of the comparatively uncompleted model whereby practice wishes to know something, research undertakes an investigation, policy advisers recommend it and practice realises it. Research processes must be seen, to a far greater degree, within the framework of a general process of enlightenment, which influences practice in vastly differing ways. In particular cases the problems facing the Education Council did indeed stimulate new research, but in these few cases it was barely able to use the results. It mostly made use of the available stock of knowledge and, in a few, very important, cases, the Council drew on research which had been available for a long time and, by means of critical evaluation, made it applicable in special ways.

The Education Council was a body, set up to provide advice on policies, in which policy-makers, administrators and the appointed members of the Education Commission worked together in a planning process with long-term objectives. Target criteria were not given for the recommendations, unless one regards the Constitution as one such objective. The Education Commission therefore had to develop objectives and measures. In this context research cannot determine planning; scientists in the Education Commission had to take political decisions as well, when making recommendations. They did, however, introduce the enlightenment of science into the policy-making process and offer politics, through the long-term nature of their perspectives, a decision-making basis which is not possible in everyday political life.

Unlike the Board of Experts for the Evaluation of Overall Economic Development, the Education Commission could not claim a clear politically legitimate basis through the participation of experts. Such a basis was missing because the Commission was neither politically controlled nor elected, but was appointed by a politically very obscure procedure. Similarly to a Royal Commission in England, it could establish a legitimate basis only through its work. It is, therefore, all the more surprising that this work proved to be the strong legitimizing foundation for the Education Report (*Bildungsbericht*) of the Federal Government and for the Overall Education Plan (*Bildungsplan*) of the Federation-Laender (states) Commission for Educational Planning.

IV

During the 8 years when the Educational Council was active, it is possible to observe the influence of research on the policy-making process in various aspects and forms. They are discussed under the following points. The Education Council took the decision, at the beginning of its work, to oppose, by means of a more thorough study of the relationship between ability and learning, the belief which was widespread in Germany that reserves of ability were already exhausted and that there was a small number of highly-gifted, a larger number of averagely-gifted and a majority of less-gifted people. The Council did not initiate any new research but to a large extent used research findings which had been available for a long time, and subjected them to a critical review as the basis for a large-scale process of enlightenment. This enlightenment also affected the members of the Education Commission. As a result, ability was regarded in the structural plan not only as inherited but as something which could be developed, and that particular importance should be attached to the motivation of pupils.

In a similar way the research of Basil Bernstein, covered in the report by Ulrich Oevermann on class-specific forms of speech behaviour and their influences on the cognitive process, illustrated the differences in the early development of children and the extent to which these differences are dependent on the social class to which the child belongs, i.e. on the language the parents use. One could say that these findings constituted the scientific basis for all the Education Council's ideas on the admission age, the lowering of the school entrance age, the extension of kindergarten education etc. However, science could only illustrate the importance of this age level and of certain forms of class-specific treatment; the Education Council had to find the solution to this scientifically-defined situation. Science showed where the difficulties resided, but not what should be done to remedy the situation.

The Education Council received a quite different report from Scheuerl on the structure of German schools, and from Saul Robinsohn and Helga Thomas on the secondary school system. In this problem area scientists came to different conclusions. Robinsohn recommended the restructuring of the federal German tripartite school system into comprehensive schools; Scheuerl recommended a further development of the tripartite school system, with increased transfer possibilities, comprehensive schools as an exception and vertically-organised schools for the majority of pupils.

The authors of both reports had different scientific methods, differing motives for their interests, and divergent basic political options. Robinsohn based his approach on the international comparison of little-operationalised criteria; Scheuerl gave a historic, socially-immanent description of the development of schools in the Federal Republic of Germany. Robinsohn tried to simplify the school system through the construction of basic models. Scheuerl tried to maintain the given complexity of the federal German education system. Robinsohn believed it was possible to realise history and to implement fundamental decisions on school policy taken on the basis of functional considerations. Scheuerl's basis was historical individuality and he limited himself to the careful stimulation of the further development of this individuality. If one reads the structural plan, one can see how these contradictory methods and basic options influenced the make-up of this plan. The Education Council did not decide in favour of Robinsohn and against Scheuerl, nor vice versa. To be sure, both positions did not first come to the attention of the scientists in the Education Council through these reports. They remain a contradiction and were adopted as such into the structural plan, when the discussion in the first Education Commission slowly moved from Scheuerl to Robinsohn.

The book on intellectual ability by Heinrich Roth, the report by Oevermann and the reports by Scheuerl and Robinsohn have, in our opinion, one thing in common. We have selected them as an example of a case where scientific works updated the mainly general research background for the work of the Education Council. Robinsohn provided Germany with information about the international stock of research; Scheuerl actualised the traditional approach to education; Roth's report on intellectual ability and learning provided a stock of available, psychological knowledge; Oevermann illustrated the findings of his own and foreign research.

V

Some further examples should serve to show the way in which research was adopted into the recommendations by the Education Council. Let us take first the problem of early learning. In this area, the report by Hans Aebli on mental development as a function of talent, maturity, environment and conditions of education made a particular impact. The recent research findings from developmental psychology led to a realisation of the necessity for an experimental programme on pre-school education, and for a changed primary school. Aebli's basic notion that development is not a process of maturing, but learning, formed the foundation not only for this section but for the whole structural plan as well.

Here, research findings suggest changed functions of the education system. Institutions must offer learning opportunities at an earlier age than had previously been the case. Research had not, for the most part, given details about such possibilities, e.g. curricula and teaching strategies. Consequently, in its structural plan the Education Commission recommended an experimental programme. That learning at this age must be promoted by institutions is a scientifically-backed conclusion if one agrees at all with the objectives of an intense encouragement of the cognitive development of the individual. How this encouragement is to be achieved depends on the development of new teaching models. Practical imagination is a prerequisite for this and developmental-psychological research had only developed general target criteria. Science has only undertaken the evaluation of the findings of practical imagination drawn from the teaching of children from an early age. In fact, this recommendation of the Education Council was not only based on the direct influence of the work of Aebli, the background of whose report includes, to a large extent, the research findings of Bloom, Bruner and Piaget. Because Aebli covered their research it was thus included in the recommendation by the Education Commission.

A second example is the recommendation in the structural plan for curricular reform. This section of the structural plan is based not only on research findings but also on certain political necessities. What must be taken into account in this respect is that Robinsohn's well-known writings on "Educational reform as a review of the curriculum", which introduced international curriculum research into Germany, appeared in 1967. Thus, the members of the Education Commission knew of curricular problems mostly from Robinsohn's writings.

VI

The fundamental political decisions behind the structural plan aimed at bringing general and vocational learning processes closer together. In the structural plan this is not backed up by scientific arguments but is introduced as a fundamental objective of the Education Commission. Scientific reasons are, however, given for an extensive reform of the curriculum. They are based on research on learning processes in the traditional school system, which drew attention to the following three problems:

> In the school system so far the pupil is not sufficiently motivated by the opportunities for selection. Curricular development should, therefore, according to the recommendations of the structural plan, make possible a wider variety of subjects suited to individual needs, in addition to the general basic education.
>
> According to research undertaken so far, the traditional school does not make sufficient allowance for the different learning capacities and preconditions for learning of pupils. This led to the recommendation for the provision of increased opportunities for individual curricula to be developed which are suited to the needs of individual pupils.
>
> Existing research demonstrated that the transfer effect of learning processes cannot be achieved to any great degree in the traditional school. The structural plan therefore recommends that general teaching objectives, ways of thinking and modes of behaviour be favoured in further development of curricula.

The recommendations for curricular development were therefore based mainly on research findings from educational and motivational psychology. From their negative results, they formulate recommendations about the existing school system which indicate the direction of change, without specifics about the contents of this change. Thus, scientific criticism of the existing situation merely led to the very general direction being set for structural changes.

The widely divergent directions of American curricular research were not properly analysed in the structural plan. In German educational research such an analysis has only been undertaken in the subsequent years, so that it was still not considered in the structural plan. By contrast, a reflection of such an analysis is clearly to be seen in the recommendation by the Education Commission of November 1973 "for the promotion of practice-related curricular development". It is interesting that it was in the Seventies that the Education Commission itself first commissioned the writing of reports by experts on curricular development (e.g. K. H. Flechsig and Dieter Haller on "Decision-making processes in curricular development"). The decisions pertaining to curricular contents proved to be too complex, too normative and thus too controversial to be successfully processed by the Education Council, which was far removed from practice. Research could only provide guidance as to the procedures necessary for curricular development. Thus, if the Education Council limited itself to questions of procedure, this does not imply its resignation about questions of contents, but an adequate division of labour between policy-making and teaching practice.

The recommendations for setting or grouping – a third example – are based on clear, political evaluation criteria which, unlike other recommendations, are clearly stated. The aim is to reduce social selection in the school system and, if possible, actively to promote the cognitive development of all pupils. In this respect the recommendation had to fall back on investigations conducted in schools in other countries, the general application of which remains highly contestable. This is true for Anglo-Saxon grouping and setting investigations, which form the basis of the recommendation. On the one hand the Council, therefore, on the basis of existing research, comes to relatively concrete conclusions. However, it is forced to overinterpret these results as it simply ignores specific national variables which are relevant in this context. It was right that Robinsohn and Thomas, in their report on grouping in the secondary school, should draw on American and English grouping investigations, because corresponding German studies did not exist. Nevertheless, the reasons behind the policy recommendation of the Education Council were by necessity inadequate as they did not make sufficient allowance for problems of international comparison. With such a gap in educational research in Germany, the Education Commission had no other choice but to act as it did. The problems had to be solved quickly and it was not possible to wait for experiments to be carried out in German schools and for these then to be researched. The similarity in the problems suggested a similarity as to the answers, even if no scientific proof could be given for this.

Finally, the fourth example concerns the problem of teaching objectives and the control of their attainment. The recommendations in the corresponding section of the structural plan were based on a taxonomy of teaching objectives as developed in particular by Benjamin Bloom and Robert Gagné. Such taxonomies supposedly provided value-free classification systems. They were, however, not at all suited for the drawing up of recommendations. Thus by necessity the recommendations remain plausible but abstract. The Council recommended that more demanding teaching objectives be developed with an increased transfer effect and increased learning efficiency. The scientific taxonomies only determine, as it were, the geometrical location of teaching objectives.

Thus the structural plan recommends that, in contrast to the individual content of German curricula, deliberations about teaching objectives should be introduced into school practice. The school should thus be entrusted with a scientific discussion. However, scientifically-oriented educational planning sometimes proves not to be an aid, but rather an instigator of doubt. In contrast to a past which was marked by a naive belief in the rightness of a given set of traditional teaching contents, it was unavoidable that the structural plan should encourage teachers to think about teaching objectives. However, as it was unable to tell them what they should teach, the deficit in scientific development tended to be reflected in schools. Such recommendations leave the schools lacking and, if they provide general guidelines only, do not give them what they need. On the other hand, general guidelines have the disadvantage that they leave the reassessment of values to parents, too, who would like the school to provide their children with the image of an unscathed world, an image which they themselves can no longer believe in. That is why policy-makers are afraid of general guidelines. But they must find the courage to draw them up and enter into subsequent discussion. This is precisely what science cannot take away from policy-makers.

In many cases the Education Commission could fall back only on extensive research in its critical analysis of the existing tripartite school system. For its practical recommendations it was dependent on its constructive imagination, as well as on foreign research undertaken in a different cultural context and on the experiences of imaginative German practitioners. This already became clear in research on the language barrier, which emphasised the importance of education in early childhood and identified the dangers of class-oriented selection at the pre-school age. This research does not, however, say what concrete form compensatory schooling within, for instance, pre-school education should take.

The Education Commission was in a similar situation in the case of the recommendation for the comprehensive school. The existence of social inequality of opportunity in the traditional school system has been investigated and proved many times over. In this context international and German regional comparisons led to varied findings. Research had already laid the basis for a broad popularisation, and in this context one need only to mention the names of Friedrich Edding and Ralph Dahrendorf. However, only English studies on the comprehensive school could answer the question of what form the solution to the problem of unfair social advancement in the tripartite school system should take in the educational reform, and findings from these studies could simply not be applied to Germany. It was therefore no coincidence that the Education Commission appointed Walter Schäfer, the head of the Odenwald school, and Horst Mastmann, the head of a Berlin comprehensive school, to the subcommittee for the recommendation for the comprehensive school, in order that they might at least establish direct contact with the first practical experiments.

One could say that the Education Commission recommended the comprehensive school as an experimental programme because scientific information was clearly against the tripartite school system, but not sufficiently in favour of a general introduction of an integrated comprehensive school with the grouping system. Hence, the members of the Education Commission, who like myself politically support the comprehensive school, also decided on its experimental introduction. Only in this way, as a careful experiment in unexplored territory, did the establishment of the new school form seem a good idea. On the very question of grouping, which was so important for the comprehensive school, the research situation was so unclear that the recommendations had to be limited to careful basic statements. In particular, no one could know at the time how long it would take for teachers, parents and pupils to adjust to the new concepts of the comprehensive school system. For the first time the Education Commission involved science itself in the planning of comprehensive schools in that it suggested controlled scientific experiments and developed some individual cases. It is interesting to note that it was this which led to its failure. I do not wish to go into the general difficulties of accompanying school research (*begleitende Schulforschung*) here but would like to point out that joint scientific accompanying research for all federal *Laender* was not least a victim of growing political polarisation and the dislike by individual *Laender* of a joint external control procedure. In the comprehensive school issue one can see a typical illustration of the relationship between research and political decision-making. Science can provide a critical analysis of the actual problem or situation; it cannot, however, suggest any courses of action nor take over the practical testing. The investigations on grouping which were available when the comprehensive school was introduced in Germany, were like paths in a maze; they could not point, with any degree of certainty, to the right path to follow. To avoid any misunderstanding, it became clear too that accompanying research is also unable to indicate the right path. It can only ensure that the political decision which has to be taken is taken in an atmosphere of increased enlightenment.

VII

The transfer of specific scientific propositions to general educational recommendations constitutes a considerable difficulty. An interesting example of this is the report by Heinz Heckhausen on the promotion of learning motivation and intellectual skills. The report concentrates on the principle of the coordination of individual learning motivation with the degree of difficulty of the contents of certain teaching. A consequence of this principle of coordination is the demand for school organisation, which leads to grouping in certain subjects according to ability at the lower level of the secondary school.

In this case one scientific report comes to relatively precise conclusions on school organisation. This is possible because one specific factor, i.e. the learning motivation, drawn not from the school but from laboratory research, is regarded in isolation. Conclusions on the basis of the analysis of this factor are then drawn for schools. What is particularly questionable about this procedure, which derives school models directly from the findings of laboratory-based psychological research, is that from the very outset no analysis is made of all the possible side-effects of the suggested model of ability grouping in other areas (e.g. teacher behaviour, social consequences, interaction among pupils etc.). The psychological methods of investigation used by Heinz Heckhausen set out to isolate the connection between a few, precisely-defined variables. By contrast the recommendations for a new basic model deal with a highly complex social relationship. The derivation of the latter from the former by simply missing out stages of complexity brings with it the danger that when the recommended model is adopted into practice, it will have many unforeseen side-effects. Heckhausen's individual analysis as such is correct. The difficulty begins when the specific result is applied generally. It leads to an overevaluation of grouping according to performance and an underevaluation of social interaction in class, as well as of the emotional areas involved in the cognitive process.

VIII

In some sectors the Education Commission could hardly draw upon any research. It had, moreover, to take up these sectors urgently as they were relevant to educational policy. As research processes are lengthy, the Commission was unable to obtain a clear picture through short-term investigations. Such investigations can really only serve to update available research with certain aspects in mind. They can also of course initiate lengthy processes of research and processes of cognition, but the results of these by necessity came too late for the work of an advisory body like the Education Council.

An interesting example in this problem area is the sector of vocational training. In the recommendation for the training of apprentices, the Education Council could refer to the research of Wolfgang Lempert and Heinrich Ebel, among others, on length of apprenticeships, training systems and training success. Nevertheless, the scientific decision-making basis was narrow when the recommendation for apprentices was written. Furthermore, the narrowness of this decision-making basis was made obvious in later comprehensive investigations over the entire federal territory. On one important point the Education Commission was obliged to change direction on the basis of a single report – Dietrich Winterhager's study on criteria for the assessment of the quality of apprenticeships.

It is known that few works of the Education Commission met with so much solid resistance among the general public as the apprenticeship recommendation. This came about not only because of highly obvious and divergent economic interests, but also because research about vocational training had not yet reached the stage of broad scientific enlightenment. Hence the recommendations because of the limited scientific knowledge of this area had to be made without the back-up of such enlightenment.

This is not a criticism of the relevant recommendations. It does, however, illustrate that the importance of research, in connection with educational planning, lies not only in the scientific preparation of recommendations, but at least as much in the process of enlightenment which takes place before, during and after this preparation. The lack of research in vocational training is also partly connected to the fact that vocational training was regarded as less prestigious education and could only find a place with difficulty within the framework of arts-oriented pedagogics. It was only in connection with research involving the social sciences that vocational training could attain the position which such a general process of enlightenment could prepare for it. Moreover, in this case the access of researchers to their field of investigation is massively obstructed by economic interests too.

Similar things can be said of the recommendation and report by the Education Commission for the reform of the educational administration. Administrative theory and administrative research are not very highly developed in Germany. This is not because of economic interests, but because of problems of loyalty and discretion. The researcher quickly finds himself in the same situation as a journalist with background information; the question arises as to how far he can divulge this information. Moreover, there is the question of to what extent scientific analyses and models, which are drawn from specific social areas, can be transferred to concrete problems in a different social area. On the other hand, sufficient critical analyses were available about the tension between the form of educational administration up to that point and the tasks of educational reform. Once again the Education Commission had to proceed constructively, because of the scientifically-necessary critical analyses of the present situation, without being able to back up this constructive procedure scientifically in individual cases. Furthermore, the administration itself regards any change to its organisational principles as disruptive, whilst the general public has a resigned attitude towards the administration. In this respect it could only be hoped that the Education Commission's suggestions for the reform of the administration would stimulate further research.

IX

At the beginning of the work of the Educational Council there were still no state educational research institutes in the Federal Republic of Germany. Educational planning within the state ministries was still in its initial stages. As a result, the Education Council also initially had to undertake duties which should have been the work of an enlightened administration. In this connection mention should be made of the reports on the estimation of public expenditure on education between 1965 and 1970 or the estimation of the national product, public budgets and educational expenditure up to 1975. The more administration bears in mind the scientific tradition which it had in the early nineteenth century, the more it remembers that the administration was originally responsible not only for order but also for enlightenment, the more it will itself undertake this survey research or accept a commission to do so. In this respect, the administration must learn that even "unpleasant" findings can be of importance for it.

In some cases it was the task of research to smooth the way for the introduction of recommendations. Two typical examples in this context are the reports by Horst Harnischfeger, Gerhard Heimann and Peter Siewert on legal issues of the comprehensive school, on teaching and space requirements of the comprehensive school or the report by Recum on the financial requirements of an extended pre-school system. Here political decisions by the Education Commission were regarded as the beginning of specific, scientific issues. The legal issues, in terms of organisation and of the individual, the new position of the teacher in the comprehensive school, could only be investigated once the political decision had been taken to introduce the comprehensive school, at least on an experimental basis. On the other hand such investigations were necessary; without them it would have been difficult for the administration to come to terms with the introduction of the comprehensive school.

X

One difficulty, that of translating research into recommendations for action, became very apparent when the Education Commission, at the suggestion of Heinrich Roth, undertook an experiment, involving a committee of experts led by him, aiming to introduce order into the wider sector of educational research. A large number of experts put together a collection of reports which illustrated the various fields of educational research with their problems and research strategies. Every larger research area could make good use of such a collection, but it must be quite clear that it cannot use this as a basis for setting its own priorities. There are limits to the extent to which science can steer its own course. Reports on research priorities within the educational research can only be prepared for very specific problems. The setting of priorities between areas could not be justified.

Nevertheless, the recommendations put forward various, specific research strategies with wide perspectives. It has, in the enlightened framework provided by the reports, determined the boundaries. As far as the setting of priorities is concerned, a necessity in the light of research capacity, it could not pursue the path which it had followed for individual recommendations: i.e. where political decisions are taken in a situation enlightened by research. The Education Commission felt it was not capable of this in respect of the research on which it was building.

XI

What effect did a body such as the Education Council, sandwiched between scientific enlightenment and the political preparation of decisions, have on a large institute for educational research? In the Max Planck Institute for Educational Research in Berlin, we have been faced with this question for a long time. Mr. Edding and myself chaired committees of the Education Council. I was a member of the Education Council for 9 years, chairing the committees for the experimental programme, full-day and comprehensive schools, organisation and administration and the committee for the report on the orientation stage and the lower stage of secondary education; and for 5 years I was the Vice-Chairman of the Council. Many colleagues in the Max Planck Institute for Educational Research participated in investigations or prepared studies, sections of studies and reports. In this connection the Institute only accepted assignments from the Education Council for areas in which it was already involved, or where Max Planck researchers had special knowledge which was not available elsewhere. The main work covered by the Institute ranged from international comparisons, matters of financing, questions of vocational training, issues of grouping and the comprehensive school, matters of curricular research to various problems in specific subjects, pre-school, legal and financial questions, matters of the administration reform and problems of further training. This led to a broad spectrum of contributions, without which the work of the Education Council, at least in the first 4 years, would certainly not have been possible. Through this work the Institute was constantly confronted with topical questions of reform.

In the Institute the Education Council was popular as a stimulator by raising questions, but unpopular because it interfered with individual research work. As many scientists pursue their activities from political motivation, without being able to introduce this political motivation into their individual research work, they sometimes welcome an opportunity to give advice to policy-makers. On the whole, however, it must be said that advice on policies, with its mixture of scientific considerations, political decisions, untested hypotheses and added elements of general knowledge, remains a doubtful enterprise for a scientist but an enterprise which must not, in my opinion, be abandoned in spite of these misgivings.

Saul Robinsohn described the years 1945 to 1965, i.e. the years before the beginning of the work of the German Education Council, as the "two decades of non-reform" in a paper which has since become renowned. It could also be said that the Fifties – the years in which there was a hostility to planning – were followed by the Sixties – a period of euphoric planning – which turned into planning nostalgia in the Seventies. What place does research have in this development of educational policy? In the Fifties research was undertaken quietly and had no effect on the development of educational policy. At the beginning of the work of the Educational Council in 1966, there was thus a considerable stock of knowledge available, part of which the Education Council was able to draw directly on. Hence it was able to disseminate scientific knowledge as a form of enlightenment in its reports, and was thus able to prepare enlightened political decisions in its recommendations. In the second period of the Education Council, from 1970 to 1974, its work became more concrete and detailed. The recommendations of the Education Commission increasingly had to cover ground which had no sure scientific support. This did not reduce the political importance of the recommendations, but it did alter their position with regard to scientific fundamentals, and it made them more vulnerable to political objection. Research could sharply criticise the traditional educational system and put forward general perspectives for change. But in the following period, educational planning was concerned with the development of detailed models and the development of new scientific issues, one example being the increasingly problematic relationship between the education system and employment system.

Again, what is needed, in my opinion, in the present situation is more basic research, although publicly-expressed needs are mainly directed at practical advice. The mediatory role between science and practice is more difficult in this area but nonetheless necessary. Bodies, such as the Scientific Council and the Education Council, which provided advice to policy-makers, still are indispensable, particularly because this mediation between science and practice can never take the form of direct transfer. It is perhaps occasionally politically opportune for a **Land** or political party to do away with advisory bodies. The necessity, however, remains unchanged for the tasks of the advisory bodies to be undertaken again and again. The translation of research into policy-making advice must be assured in the future too.

What shape does the relationship between scientific consideration and political action take for the individual scientist, for the individual politician? In Israel I came across a strange phenomenon. Fallen politicians and especially retired generals often go back to the university either in Israel or America, do a doctorate, and make use of the academic title to gain access to new positions, or in some instances to obtain posts as lecturers in universities. This can of course occur the other way round. At the moment one of the leading Arabic scholars and Islamic experts in the Hebrew University in Jerusalem is the Civilian Governor of the West Bank, i.e. of the occupied Arab territories. I cannot pass any judgement on his policies. I merely wish to observe that politicians regard with misgivings a scientist who has previously published far-sighted papers on the relationship between Arabs and Jews. At the same time, the scientific community feels itself almost to have been betrayed by a man who daily, in his problematic position as an occupier of Palestinian territory, sees himself as being forced to take decisions which contradict, to say the least, basic liberal convictions. There is therefore a danger that a scientist, in the political application of science, becomes unfaithful, or at least is regarded as a traitor in the eyes of his colleagues. A scientist dirties his hands when he enters the world of politics. A science which regards itself as positivist is quick to consider even the giving of advice on policies, as breaking the laws on scientific thinking. An additional factor is that all advisory bodies are nearly always confronted with issues which cannot, even by prolonged scientific investigation, be definitively clarified. Thus, they make recommendations on the basis of hypotheses which, in turn, are based on scientific considerations, but which cannot be proved conclusively through scientific evidence. This is true not only for energy issues or nuclear strategy, but also for every aspect of finance or school policies. Thus, a development whereby universities once again draw back from the border areas to subject-restricted research, and take refuge within the so-called safe laws of science, i.e. within a mainly positivist-conception of science, is all the more dangerous.

Then politics, in particular the provision of advice by scientists to policy-makers, increasingly looks like an injustice to science. There is a danger that the level of enlightenment in politics may fall, a trend which can be observed today throughout the world. The great hopes for scientific and rational decision-making have been followed by a growing tendency towards irrational and prejudiced politics. The policy-makers are probably less to blame for this than the scientists themselves who, for fear of damaging their scientific integrity, are increasingly retreating into an ivory tower of irresponsibility *vis-á-vis* actual events. In this respect they overlook the facts that science can only maintain its position, if it constantly seeks to break through its own boundaries, to move beyond the bounds of individual disciplines.

Science as a life style can assume many different shapes today. It ranges from strict individual research endeavours of the traditional kind to bold cooperation with direct consequences for the fields of action. It is becoming increasingly difficult to withstand the tension between scientific considerations and political action and to remain a scientist in spite of this. However, our future depends on whether or not an increasing number of people would be prepared to live with these tensions.

At the same time a policy based on an ideology and an administration suffocated by bureaucracy must be judged in terms of whether they slowly become able to absorb the spectrum of scientific reasoning and to use this as a basis for their own actions. The contradiction between science and bureaucracy which is so often felt today is false. Both stem from enlightenment and were originally elements which belonged together. If it were possible to rediscover this feeling of solidarity, then there is a chance that a lively, rational adminis-tration could develop from a bureaucracy which blocks action. Gershom Scholem has said that we are living in an un-messianic age. Science cannot free politics from its responsibilities, nor can politics free science from its moral obligation to clarify the field of action as far as it can. Bureaucracy and administration are not relieved of their responsibility by politics or science, but they can only assume this responsibility if they absorb the power of the knowledge of science and the dynamics of politics into the administration.

It remains to be seen whether the individual can achieve this through an exchange of roles or a combination of roles. No thinking or acting individual can for one minute forget the mutual dependency of science, politics and administration. If he does, then he himself could be responsible for provoking catastrophes in science, bureaucracy and politics. What people lack at the moment is the political imagination to create the institutional preconditions for linking science, politics and administration in such a way that threatening catastrophes can be avoided. It depends on each one of us whether we succeed in creating them in the years to come.

References

AEBLI, H,: Die geistige Entwicklung als Funktion von Anlage, Reifung. Umwelt- und Erziehungsbedingungen. In: ROTH, H. (Hrsg.): Begabung und Lernen. (Deutscher Bildungsrat. Gutachten und Studien der Bildungskommission, Bd. 4.) Stuttgart 1968, S. 151–191.

ALBERS, W., OBERHAUSER, A., MICHALSKI, W., THIEL, E., SCHMITZ, E.: Sozialprodukt, öffentliche Haushalte und Bildungsausgaben in der BRD. (Deutscher Bildungsrat. Gutachen und Studien der Bildungskommission, Bd. 5.) Stuttgart 1969.

BECKER, H.: Welche Antwort fand die Arbeit des Bildungsrates bei den zuständigen Politikern? In: Neue Sammlung 5/1975, Göttingen.

BECKER, H.: Beitrag und Einfluß der Bildungsforschung auf die Arbeit des "Deutshen Bildungsrats". In: Zeitschrift für Pädagogik, 21. Jg. 1975, Nr. 2. Weinheim.

BECKER, H.: Auf dem Weg zur lernenden Gesellschaft. Klett-Cotta, Stuttgart 1980.

DEUTSCHER BILDUNGSRAT: Einrichtung von Schulversuchen mit Gesamtschulen. Stuttgart 1969 (a).

DEUTSCHER BILDUNGSRAT: Zur Verbesserung der Lehrlingsausbildung. Stuttgart 1969 (b).

DEUTSCHER BILDUNGSRAT: Empfehlungen der Bildungskommission: Strukturplan für das Bildungswesen. Stuttgart 1970.

DEUTSCHER BILDUNGSRAT: Zur Förderung praxisnaher Curriculum-Entwicklung. Stuttgart 1973 (a).

DEUTSCHER BILDUNGSRAT: Zur Reform von Organisation und Verwaltung im Bildungswesen. Teil I: Verstärkte Selbständigkeit der Schule und Partizipation der Lehrer, Schüler und Eltern. Stuttgart 1973 (b).

DEUTSCHER BILDUNGSRAT: Aspekte für die Planung der Bildungsforschung. Stuttgart 1974.

DEUTSCHER BILDUNGSRAT: Bildungsforschung. Probleme – Perspektiven – Prioritäten. Hrsg. von HEINRICH ROTH und DAGMAR FRIEDRICH. (Gutachten und Studien der Bildungskommission, Bde. 50/51.) Stuttgart 1975.

FLECHSIG, K.-H., HALLER; H.-D.: Entscheidungsprozesse in der Curriculumentwicklung. (Deutscher Bildungsrat. Gutachten und Studien der Bildungskommission, Bd. 24.) Stuttgart 1973.

HARNISCHFEGER, H., HEIMANN, G., SIEWERT, P.: Rechtsfragen der Gesamtschule. Lehrer- und Raumbedarf in Gesamtschulen. (Deutscher Bildungsrat. Gutachten und Studien der Bildungskommission, Bd. 13.) Stuttgart 1970.

HECKHAUSEN, H.: Förderung der Lernmotivierung und der intellektuellen Tüchtigkeiten. In: ROTH, H. (Hrsg.): Begabung und Lernen. (Deutscher Bildungsrat. Gutachten und Studien der Bildungskommission. Bd. 4.) Stuttgart 1968, S. 193–228.

LEMPERT, W., EBEL, H.: Lehrzeitdauer, Ausbildungssystem und Ausbildungserfolg. Grundlagen für die Bemessung des Zeitraums der Ausbildung bis zum Facharbeiterniveau. Freiburg i. Br. 1965.

LUTZ, B., WINTERHAGER, W. D.: Zur Situation der Lehrlingsausbildung: (Deutscher Bildungsrat. Gutachten und Studien der Bildungskommission. Bd. 11.) Stuttgart 1970.

MEYER-ABICH, K. M.: Physik, Philosophie und Politik. Festschrift für Carl Freidrich von Weizsäcker. Carl Hanser Verlag, München 1982.

OEVERMANN, U.: Schichtenspezifische Formen des Sprachverhaltens und ihr Einfluß auf die kognitiven Prozesse. In.: ROTH, H. (Hrsg.): Begabung und Lernen. (Deutscher Bildungsrat. Gutachten und Studien der Bildungskommission. Bd. 4.) Stuttgart 1968, S. 297–355.

RECUM, H. VON: Der Finanzbedarf eines expandierenden Vorschulsystems. (Deutscher Bildungsrat. Gutachen und Studien der Bildungskommission. Bd. 18.) Stuttgart 1971.

ROBINSOHN, S. B.: Bildungsreform als Revision des Curriculum. Neuwied Berlin 1967 (a).

ROBINSOHN, S. B. (zusammen mit J. C. KUHLMANN): Two Decades of Non-Reform in West German Education. (Zuerst 1967, wiederabgedruckt) In: DERS.: Erziehung als Wissenschaft. Hrsg. v. F: BRAUN u. a. Stuttgart 1973, S. 363–386. (1967b).

ROBINSOHN, S. B., THOMAS, H.: Differenzierung im Sekundarschulwesen. (Deutscher Bildungsrat. Gutachten und Studien der Bildungskommission. Bd. 3.) Stuttgart 1968.

ROTH, H.: Begabung und Lernen. (Deutscher Bildungsrat. Gutachten und Studien der Bildungskommission. Bd. 4.) Stuttgart 1968.

SCHEUERL, H.: Die Gliederung des deutschen Schulwesens. (Deutscher Bildungsrat. Gutachten und Studien der Bildungskommission. Bd. 2.) Stuttgart 1968.

SCHMITZ, E.: Die öffentlichen Ausgaben für Schulen in der BRD. (Deutscher Bildungsrat. Gutachten und Studien der Bildungskommission. Bd. 1.) Stuttgart 1967.

The Case of France: Higher Education

BY ALAIN BIENAYMÉ

> "Au fond des victoires d'Alexandre
> on trouve toujours Aristote".
>
> Charles de Gaulle[1]

This paper confines itself to higher education, mainly because of the limitations of the author's own experiences. He has collected testimonies through interviews and by correspondence with former ministers[2] and researchers who have spent time and led teams on this topic.[3]

Three main points emerge from this enquiry:

1. The *direct* influence of scientific research has been and will probably remain weak.

2. The *indirect* influence is a little more substantial but hard to assess.

3. The *potential* influence might be improved.

*   *   *

I. The direct influence

Almost no administrative and political decision could be credited unquestionably as a precise and unique result of a piece of scientific research. This is rather obvious but some comment is due here, in order to obtain a better understanding of what follows as regards indirect and potential influences.

1.1 General reasons can first be mentioned. Science and policy belong to widely different spheres

The scientist's ethos contains several features which are not shared by the policy-maker: the scientist is committed to truth and clarification; his way of

---

[1] "Deep at the heart of Alexander's victories you always find Aristotle."

[2] Mr. Edgar FAURE (Minister of Education 1968–1969), Mr. J.P. SOISSON (Secretary of State to Universities 1974–1981), Mrs. A. SAUNIER-SEITE (Minister of Universities 1976–1981).

[3] MM. P. BOURRICAUD, L. SCHWARTZ, PP. VALLI, J. VINCENS have answered our questions.

thinking, even if he uses systemic analysis, is reductive; unexpected results from experiments are thrilling.[4] The policy-maker is, or becomes of necessity, a politician. Even if he is himself a scientist, and a committed researcher, as a policy-maker in the government he deals with politics. Truth, clarification, reductionism, unexpected results from experiments and discussion must give way to other specific features. A policy-maker has necessarily to deal with broader aspects of reality, and with conflicting interests: his responsibility is to find compromises for helping people to get along. His action is purposeful and he will try to deny the unintended results which prove harmful to society.

The political situation often makes it very difficult to call on scientific advice: in normal cases, in quiet periods of history, the policy-maker's requirements are of an incremental type.[5] They have to be met, from the policy-maker's view point, with a step-by-step analysis; the commissioned research is meant to take for granted that all other conditions remain equal. When the political scenery is upset (see France in 1968, 1981) and prerequisites for an overall reform seem to be met, the whole system can be modified provided an emergency proposal can be designed.

Both contexts are unfit for political decision based on solid scientific results. In the first case, the scientist wishes to reformulate the problem submitted and refuses to rely only on data and assumptions given by the political establishment. In the second case, he is unable as a researcher to give advice on vast topics which require emergency answers and instant value judgements. He remains himself committed to exhaustivity and wariness. Exhaustivity means that the relevant analysis of a social situation (surplus of medical students, faculty staff's careers etc.) has to be placed in its adequate context; a minister of higher education who wonders how graduates in social sciences coming from universities get jobs cannot discard the problems arising from their competition with graduates from *Grandes Ecoles* coming under other ministries: Health, Defence, Agriculture . . .

As one of my correspondents puts it, policy-makers as well as every other human being, have their "sacred cows". In France many topics in higher education remain uninvestigated, such as the level of satisfaction and motivation of students, the level and quality of commitment of academic staff, the comparative costs and efficiency of institutions, the innovation processes.

The conclusions one is allowed to derive from a scientific study are often ambiguous, and raise new problems. Besides the fact that the researcher is not quite free from his own prejudices or value judgment, his work does not necessarily lead to clearcut policy recommendations. Correlations remain blind

---

[4]Max WEBER, "Politik als Beruf. Wissenschaft als Beruf" 1919 and R. ARON's introduction to the French edition, "Le savant et le politique", Plon, 1959.
[5]Centre d'Etudes et de Recherches sur les qualifications (CEREQ): "La recherche en sciences sociales comme aide à la décision", January, 1982. This research centre was created by the Ministry of Education in 1970.

to causalities; they may be biased by wrong specifications of concepts and data; they may be unstable. Multivariate analyses lead to proliferating typologies, but the results are by no means clear and helpful especially if the classes are composed of changing elements through time.

Finally, the direct influence of a specific research, R, on a specific policy decision, D, is and will remain weak, because the field of investigation – the French Higher Education system – has become a highly political arena in recent decades. With roughly 50,000 teachers, the academic community has inevitably become a political problem in itself. Independently from his own political opinions, the researcher is viewed from outside as a member of a tribe which must have concealed vested interests. This may open a new field of investigation in political science; but it does not entitle the researchers as such to determine through specific research the solutions to a political issue. In a democratic country the political decision is the final and visible outcome of a long underground process; trade unions, students' associations, employers, various other lobbies and authorities each play a role of their own, besides the Parliament and governmental policy-makers, which prevent the scientific community as such from dictating any solution, however unanimous this community may be.

1.2 More specific reasons reduce the chances that political decisions regarding higher education could be directly influenced by a scientific investigation

The political context in France makes it always a very difficult task for a minister. Education as a whole and universities in particular are very controversial areas. Teachers' unions have very powerful strongholds. Neither the student turmoil of 1968 nor the victory of the leftist political parties make it an easier task for the Minister in charge of higher education.

A highly prestigious authority such as L. Schwartz whose political opinions are well known has recently published a somewhat blunt diagnosis on higher education from which he derives recommendations which are not in accordance with the stereotypes of the Left; in spite of the soundness of many of his suggestions it will take a long time to get the trade unions to accept them.[6]

The main policy-maker, the Minister, has his own idiosyncrasies. His intellectual and professional background has some influence on his links with the research community. Two of the ministers interviewed had personal previous experience on academic faculties. Two of them had at the time of their appointment very strong political commitments. Only one of them had previous experience as a Minister, even as a Prime Minister, and was known as an outstanding historian. Their propensity to give weight to sound scientific achievements was not on par.

---

[6]Rapport sur l'enseignement supérieur, Documentation française, 1982.

The scientific community as such is not deeply committed to research in its own field of action. One of the ministers interviewed told us that research on pedagogy was useless in higher education, much as it might be useful at secondary and primary levels. The eye is not able to observe the eye. But we must add that if the urge for research is not very commanding, the need for investigations through *ad hoc* committees is more strongly felt by the academic community.

This is one of the main ways through which researchers may exert indirect influences on the political decision process.

II. The indirect influence

It may well be that questions such as: How do researchers and policy-makers relate? How difficult is it for them to communicate? are more provocative than relevant. It is inherent in political decision-making to require time. Time is needed to mature, to draft legislation, to implement decisions. This requirement results from the fact that in essence a political decision has to be accepted by those who are involved in its coming into force. Time is then at the core of an interaction process in which scientific achievements may contribute through many channels of influence to the political outcome.

1. The Minister himself obviously derives advantages from his own knowledge and experience. His most important decision is to choose his advisers. The number of knowledgeable experts and scientists who are on the Minister's staff and the expertise represented by officials makes it almost certain that important and reliable information and new data and ideas are conveyed, tested, screened and politically assessed. But these scientific materials are bound to compete with opinions, arguments, judgements and votes expressed in many different consultative bodies (National councils, University Presidents' conferences, Parliament).

2. On specific occasions the ministers benefited from and found counsel in commissioned research (B. Schwartz was consulted for example in 1974 on the problem of youth transition into professional life, J. L. Quermonne and others on the faculty staffs' careers and so on), or from permanent research centres, one of them having been created by the Minister in 1970.

Such was the case with research in the reforms introduced for the first time in 1975 in the fund-allocating process between universities, for the creation of new vocationally oriented curricula and degrees (*Naîtrise de Sciences et Techniques, Diplôme d'Etudes Supérieures Spécialisées*) at the graduating level and for post graduate studies. It was also the case for the promotion of research within universities and for other curricula, for example, in I.U.T., first cycle degrees or in secondary education.

The opinions of the ministers and of the researchers are worth quoting because they reveal some contrasts.

In the first case, the Minister who had launched the commissioned research reached the end of his term of office a few weeks after the report was submitted to him.[7] His successor did not actually implement the two-stage program of reforms suggested, but preferred to rely on the recommendations of an internal body of his own administration who had in some underground way carefully drafted its own proposal. This team had been heard by the official committee a few months before but the results had then been presented as purely descriptive and analytical and not at all as prescriptive.

In the second case, three main sources of information have been consulted by the policy-maker: the conclusions of sectorial groups including faculty staff, experts and representatives from fourteen broad groups of professions, the annual reports written by the *Grandes Ecoles*, and the C.E.R.E.Q. The latter is a research centre under the aegis of the Ministry of Education and universities. These three sources express their views and convey information on careers, future prospects in professions, appropriateness of curricula and so on. The C.E.R.E.Q. has built a permanent observatory (E.V.A.: entrées dans la vie active), gathering information on the individual careers of the French school-leavers: a large sample of them is subjected to a survey one year after they have left school and to a new survey 5 years after. A growing mass of first hand and precise information is then reaped and helps to understand how young people get along with their careers when they enter "active" life. But, in spite of this, the researchers feel that these surveys have made a poor contribution to the design of effective new policies in higher education. Their contribution was more obvious in the design of new technological curricula at the secondary level. One of the reasons for this lies in the fact that the degree of precision of information required by the Minister of universities was higher than the data could yield. Another reason stems from the fact that the research centre was not directly requested by the highest level of policy decision to conduct its research, but by intermediate administrative levels. This kind of situation is frustrating.

The third case is perhaps more paradoxical. The French *Conseil Economique et Social* is a semi-political body of 200 part-time members representing business executive associations, trade unions, agrobusiness and farm activities, craftsmanship, and including qualified experts in economics. It was asked by the Prime Minister to advise on how to organise and develop research activities within the walls of the higher education system.[8] In spite of the fact that only very few advisers are academics or scientists, this consultation can be considered from a political point of view as a genuine part of a rationalised

---

[7]"Le financement des Universités", La documentation française, 1975. The same misfortune hit the official Report on University autonomy (La documentation française, 1981).
[8]Conseil Economique et Social, "L'organisation et le développement de la recherche dans les établissements de l'enseignement supérieur", Journal Officiel du 4 avril, 1978.

process of decision. The Government after having consulted the *Conseil Economique et Social* is able to take its own decision: either to enact a decree or to bring in a bill. The paradox one may notice is that in spite of the fact that the report and the advice given were very well accepted and called upon by the Minister for justification of the reforms, these reforms only dealt with a minor point touched on by the report. The report was meant to focus on universities and *Grandes Ecoles* as such, not on the *Centre National de la Recherche Scientifique* which lies besides the higher education system and not within it. The political situation in 1978 was not felt by supreme authorities favourable enough for thorough reforms of institutions of higher education.

3. One of the ministers interviewed told us that the influence of scientific research was of a negative kind. Calling upon Karl Popper's authority, he argued that in the scientific process the tests to which the hypotheses are submitted can never tell what is the positive truth, but can sometimes at least rule out the wrong hypotheses. In the same way, he added that scientific advice may be useful to discard wrong or false ideas but is not a sufficient condition to give way to right ideas. He believed furthermore that on some rare occasions opinion polls which give more than a two thirds majority to a definite position may be worthy of consideration. But on the whole to a policy-maker science can only make a modest contribution, or help to formulate problems the solution of which cannot escape political responsibilities. The same Popperian philosophy could finally inspire new kinds of experimental policies which could be launched on a limited basis, assessed and then, if necessary and possible, extended to the whole society.[9] So it is in his view, the very process of science which prevents science from establishing a direct influence on policy-making.

Thus the influence of science can only remain indirect because scientific discoveries and results have to be assimilated through a wide body composed of non specialists or non scientists in order to be able to lead, at least partly, to policy applications. This irreducible gap does not mean that there is no prospect of improved communications between these two spheres of activity.

III. The potential influence

It might certainly be improved. Pragmatic measures could be taken in order to facilitate the communication of information between science and policy-making.

1. The scientific reports are very often unreadable. Efforts should be made to diversify the presentation of research in order to adapt its outcome to the requirements and reading capacity of the different audiences which might show interest. The draft frame law in 1982 discussed in the French Parliament on

---

[9]Edgar FAURE, "La philosophie de Karl Popper et la Société politique d'ouverture", Bulletin du Nouveau Contrat Social, février, 1982.

Research and Technology development stresses the obligation for every institute to attend to the diffusion of its results. This obligation is extended to each individual researcher as well.

2. One of the ministers interviewed emphasised the inadequacy of most statistical data produced by the relevant administration both under the ministry of education and the ministry of universities. He argues that statistical data may be both meaningful from a statistical or a financial view point, and meaningless from his point of view as an actor dealing with sociological realities in higher education. For instance, the number of grant-holders has to be compared with the number of students having part-time jobs, otherwise many comments may be irrelevant. Students' classifications remain very poor. There is no reliable figure on the repetition rates in the first 2 years of studies. The real curricula followed by foreign students were for a long time not satisfactorily assessed. In a general way, the policy-makers feel that the relevant figures which could give a rough estimate on pending political issues are not available. But an independent researcher retorts that decision-makers rarely address the relevant questions to the data already collected. This dialogue of the deaf could be somewhat improved if the minister felt committed to getting more directly in touch with a large part of the scientific community, especially those who are involved in studying higher education organisations.

3. Another minister, who stayed in office for only eleven months and eleven days, intended to create a long-range planning committee which would help him to identify the problems some 10 or 15 years ahead in order to frame broad guide-lines for education policy. This was also intended to free the minister from the influence exerted by his own administration departments. However, this idea did not germinate. Such a stillborn idea points out one of the shortcomings of a system which has to cope with heavy consultation processes through innumerable "bargaining" committees where compromises have to be found between conflicting vested interests.

One may presently have deep concerns about the massive consultation launched by the Ministry of Education in order to reframe the 1968 Orientation law. A questionnaire of 117 items has been sent to every university, which tries to reconcile an obvious concern for democracy with apparently scientific methods. But the questions are often formulated in a way which suggests ready-made answers, emotional reactions or value judgements. Furthermore the document conceals totally the actual weight which will be given to the information collected and fosters the idea that scientific qualifications and democracy can be harmoniously related. One may nevertheless reply that it is a good thing for the researchers to get out of their ivory tower, and to explain from a scientific standpoint why such and such proposals cannot work.

4. Assent could easily be found between our interlocutors from both sides on the idea that independent research centres and teams should blossom out in social science besides the administrations's own research teams. But some

ministers are less convinced of the validity and opportunity of developing specific research on higher education activity itself. In our view, however, many issues could deserve a good deal of investigation and enquiry: for instance, the differentiation of universities through autonomy raises problems of comparisons and calls for a more careful methodology than the "hit parade" classification made by newspapers.

5. The real challenge with which mass universities are confronted is the circulation of information on scientific research, its outcomes and its consequences on curriculae and organisation. One minister thought it of utmost importance to help autonomous universities to relate to a network similar to the network organised in the U.S. since 1973, or the German network of information in more limited fields of knowledge such as chemistry, medicine etc. The idea is to improve the government and management of each university by means of a more systematic information process. A special department has been recently created in the French ministry of universities in order to deal with this task.

6. The inducement and selection of research activities through the appropriation of public funds allocations is an attempt to meet objections at least from the research community. The heavy part of overhead wage costs limits the actual flexibility of the research resources. Furthermore the timeliness of a topic suggested for investigation on the one hand and the appropriateness of the teams selected on the other, should be assessed independently.

In order to improve the communication between both parties, the policy-maker should not expect too much from the data and findings provided by researchers; the researchers should devote more consideration to the political and sociological feasibility of their own proposals.

*   *   *

Are we then prepared to admit, like one of the researchers interviewed, that "policy decisions have never resulted from any serious research"? No. We are on the contrary struck by the fact that many ministers felt the need to consult reliable data, to resort to thorough research findings and commissioned research on several important occasions during the last 15 years. The researchers deny it, or underestimate their contribution for two reasons: a lack of information about the follow-up of their own ideas; a lack of understanding of the real nature of the policy-decision process. Research and reality are not interrelated in the same way as in Mathematics or in the Social Sciences.

Should we then agree with another comment of the same interlocutor according to whom: "In spite of existing (serious) research, it has never been of any serious help in the political decision process?". This seems to be an over-statement and conceals an overestimation of the potential uses of scientific research.

Finally, should we believe that with Left wing governments in France more obviously linked with the intelligentsia, things will be improved? This is pure politics, not science.

Almost everything being considered, General de Gaulle was right to detect Aristotle in Alexander's feats. But we would be wrong in ignoring Hector and Achilles' part as well. Courage remains a major component of political decision. Research, as such, may sometimes need courage too, but on its own account. Scientism, by which some pretend to provide permanent guidelines for policy decisions, is a plague. Science and policy-making follow different paths. They can ocasionally meet, as in a fugue, but cannot escape the risk of dissonance.

Issues in the Institutionalisation of Social Policy

BY JAMES S. COLEMAN

To discuss research and educational policy at a conference intended to honour Torsten Husén is a modern-day equivalent to the traditional English expression of carrying coals to Newcastle. For Torsten Husén has participated in research relevant to educational policy, and has been intimately involved with nearly every facet of this relationship, to an extent that would leave most of us breathless. We should be sitting at *his* feet, learning from *his* rich experience, rather than informing him of our own far sketchier experience.

But perhaps the topic of this conference is merely another example of his acumen – for I am sure he had some voice in selection of the topic. Not long ago Torsten carried out some research *on* educational research, questioning by mail a number of persons who had been involved in some capacity in research that served educational policy. I suspect him of taking the present occasion as the second stage of that research, bringing together a captive audience he could question at length, to extend his own experience by adding to it what he could find of use in ours. If my suspicion is correct, then I must say more power to him – though I hope that one way or another we will induce him to impart some of his experience on these matters.

*   *   *

Although most of my own experience in "policy research" concerns educational policy, I want to address issues that are slightly broader, what could be called *social* policy research. That is, I want to include in my remarks social welfare policies generally, and research related to these policies. The questions I want to raise are probably natural for a sociologist: They concern the *institutionalisation* of social policy research.

Social policy research is a relatively new activity in society, expanding enormously in the 1960s and 1970s from a very small base before that time. As with newly emergent phenomena generally, there has not immediately developed an institutional and normative framework within which it is carried out and used. Perhaps this is good, for we can see better now than we could in the 1960s some of the consequences of its taking one rather than another, or of following one set of norms rather than another.

First I will list a set of points which constitute problems in the relation between social policy research and social policy. All are drawn from American experience, but some may have their parallels in other countries. Then I will discuss what kinds of institutions might address these problems. Finally, I will reopen a question to which an answer has been assumed in the earlier parts of the paper: just how open should social policy research be?

Problems Relevant to the Institutionalisation of Social Policy Research as an Element in Societal Decision-Making

A common complaint of those who carry out social policy research is that it is not used by those in positions of policy, but left to gather dust on a shelf. At the same time, a common complaint of those in positions of policy is that social research designed to address questions of policy – whether it is research which evaluates a programme, social experimentation, or another kind of social policy research – is that the research as carried out is irrelevant to policy decisions. Thus both sides agree that social policy research is not used, though each places the blame on the other party.

At the same time, some social policy research does come to be widely used in ways that were not intended. In particular, it comes to be used in conditions where there is extensive conflict over policy and in which the debate over policy goes beyond the bounds of normal bureaucratic decision-making. For example, the report, "Equality of Educational Opportunity" prepared by the U.S. Office of Education under the Civil Rights Act, was never used by Federal agencies in formulating civil rights policy in education, but was widely used in the local conflicts over school desegregation, both in the courts and in the school boards. It appears from these and other cases that social policy research is most widely used where there is extensive conflict over policy, and is most used by those without direct control over policy, who challenge the policies of those in positions of authority.

In the United States, most social policy research is initiated by requests for proposals (RFP) from Federal agencies. When the research is evaluation of a social programme that is the responsibility of the agency, the research is – in partial contradiction to the complaint about irrelevancy above – sometimes used by the agency to support its request for budget allocation before Congress. However, three serious questions arise in this pattern of initiation and use: (a) Does the RFP ask for research that will provide information relevant to *all* interests surrounding the given policy, even including that opposed to the agency's interest? (b) Is the contractor sufficiently independent to design and carry out research that – even assuming an RFP attentive to a broad range of interest – could provide information inimical to the agency's interests? (c) If the results of the research do not support the agency's interests (e.g. interests in budget expansion), will the agency use and make known these results as widely as it would if the results supported the agency's position? The answer to all these questions is sometimes toward narrowly-defined RFP's, contracted for by captive or subservient research organisations which design, execute, and analyse their research in ways that will be most flattering to their clients, and resulting in reports that are buried if they would harm the agency's interests and used only if they aid that interest.

In the United States there have been other ways of initiating social policy research, most prominently one: The researcher submits an unsolicited proposal for research in an area which that research believes to be important. Most such proposals are submitted to agencies with a research responsibility but no responsibility for action programmes. The deficiencies inherent in this mode of initiation become apparent when one recognises that the principal motivation of many of the academic social scientists who submit these proposals is an interest in publication in academic journals.

The principal mode of initiation of social policy research is by the RFP prepared by an official of the agency. There appears to be no institutionalised separation between the bureaucratic interests of continuing or expanding a programme and the interests in finding out about its functioning or effects. Thus in a rather haphazard way conflict of interest may or may not be built into the design of the FRP.

In the United States, members of Congress are often suspicious of the result of evaluations of social programmes initiated by the agency of the Executive Branch which has responsibility for the programme, despite the fact that the evaluation has been mandated in the act of Congress which authorised the programme. This suspicion appears to arise principally from the potential conflicts of interests discussed in points 3 and 5 above, which in turn result from the failure to have institutional separation between responsibility for implementing a programme and responsibility for obtaining information about the functioning of the programme.

Some research which evaluates social programmes is done for the purpose of providing ongoing feedback to those with direct responsibility for the programme; some is done to provide those higher in the organisational structures of a government agency with information relevant to major modifications in the programme or its very continuation; and some is done to provide information relevant to the broadest social decision about the fate of the programme, which is made in the open, outside a bureaucracy, often in Congress with extensive public input. In these three different kinds of evaluation, research interests are aligned in different ways; yet the finding of research of all three sorts is often done from a single point within the agency, which is not insulated from the bureaucratic interests in maintaining or expanding the programme.

If results of social policy research favour one side in a policy dispute, there is ordinarily no means by which the other side can challenge the research results before they become fully public and are announced in the mass media. When these challenges come after that time, the result is a public squabble exploited and expanded by the mass media to extend its news value, but with the result of destroying the credibility of social research for the public, as well as neutralising any impact that social policy research might have in this policy area. An example is a report for the National Center for Educational Statistics (NCES) which I prepared with two co-authors, comparing public and private schools in the United States.[1] The report was released at a large conference (of about 300–400 persons) convened in Washington in April, 1981 by the National Center for Education Statistics.

At the same time, there was in Congress legislation pending for tuition tax credits for parents of children attending private school. Some social scientists were apparently concerned that the report's release would aid that legislation (since the results were generally favourable to private schools), and one organised a set of reviews of the report, some of which were critical, which he circulated in the hallway before, during, and after the conference. Although the report had been reviewed beginning in September, 1980, by persons inside NCES, by reviewers at the University of Chicago (where the research was done), and by outside reviews commissioned by NCES, the report went through no institutionalised process which was publicised and thus would have given all those with some expertise the chance to challenge the report before its release to the general public through the mass media. It is not clear what the appropriate institutional process would be, but in its absence the outcome is unsatisfactory.

A "science court" has sometimes been proposed for resolving issues in dispute which have relevance for policy, not only in social science, but in natural science as well. Although such a science court has not been implemented or even fully designed, its design would constitute some mixture of the scientific tenet of objectivity and the legal tenet of interest representation. This involves both the recognition that the methods of science are designed to insure objectivity and replicability, and the recognition that research outcomes have different consequences for different parties according to their interests. Thus each party with legitimate interests should have the opportunity to use the methods of science to challenge and probe the results which go against those interests.

The simultaneous initiation of more than one research project on the same policy-relevant issue has been suggested by some to help insure the correctness of results before they generally enter the public debate. But again, as with the idea of a science court, no fully developed institutional design (for example, for resolution of differences between two research projects on the same policy related issue) exist.

---

[1] James S. Coleman, Thomas Hoffer, and Sally Kilgore, Public and Private Schools, report prepared for National Center for Education Statistics, April, 1981.

The separation of social policy research into several stages, with different organisational structure for each stage, may be a useful way to introduce pluralism into social policy research without the duplication that would make such work prohibitively expensive. In the design of the research, and in the data analysis, it is valuable to have a range of interests represented, while for the data-collection itself (given design of instruments), standard field methods ordinarily make such insurance unnecessary. The Freedom of Information Act in the United States which makes publicly-collected data publicly available, is a step toward pluralism at the analysis stage but attention to enforcement and utilisation of that act is necessary if its value is to be realised.

These eleven points show the absence of any well-considered institutional structure for the initiation and use of social policy research and show also some of the ill consequences of this absence for social decision-making. In what follows, I will attempt some analysis of the problems and some suggestions of how – in the United States context – institutions might be developed to address the problems.

The Separation of Policy-Making from Policy Research

Social policy research that is currently carried out for the U.S. government is initiated through RFPs from agencies that have policy responsibility, and paid for with funds from the budget of those same agencies. Separation of the social policy research that is carried out to aid Congressional decision-making from the policy-making function of the agencies is necessary if the latter interests are not to contaminate the research, nor keep it hidden when it serves those interests to do so. The institutional focus for such research obviously should be an arm of Congress rather than within the agency. Two such arms already exist, the General Accounting Office and the Congressional Budget Office, and both have taken some steps in the direction of such research – although neither has the budget nor the responsibility to contract for such research from outside contractors. With institutional structures in which social policy research was carried out by one of these arms of Congress or a new arm created for the purpose, the use of social policy research by the policy-making agency itself to guide *its* decisions would still, of course, be necessary. This could generate in many cases two research projects designed to evaluate the same programme, an example of the two-project device mentioned above.

The Institutionalisation of Interested-Party Scientific Review Prior to Release of Research Results

Regulatory agencies in the United States have developed a practice of publishing proposed regulations some period of time in advance of the actual decision to impose the regulation. Hearings are scheduled in which interested parties are given a chance to present evidence relevant to the proposed regulation. This device has an obvious flaw, in that the regulatory agency is in the position of both judge and advocate (since the agency's own research is often challenged by the research results presented by the interested parties). However, apart from this flaw, the practice does provide an opportunity for challenge of research results by parties with diverse interests and other sources of data before any policy is established. An analogous procedure for social policy research that is merely being published or released is very likely a more complex procedure than is warranted by the potential impact of the research. However, some forum at which there was an opportunity for scientific re-examination of the issue before the research result entered into public debate through the mass media would seem to be useful. If this is done it is obviously necessary for the forum to be designed with full impartiality, and with rules which prevent its being "packed" by one set of interests. I have participated in at least seven such forums, which have seemed to vary greatly in their success.[2]

The general problem of institutionalising some form of scientific review which makes use of the special perspectives of interested parties prior to release of social policy research results that touch on sensitive issues remains an unsolved one. In most cases, research results will not engage the attention of the mass media until some time after results are released, and in such instances there will have been a period of time for review, reanalysis, and reassessment before the attention of mass media is engaged. But it is difficult to know in advance when a complex pre-release procedure is necessary, and when on the other hand it would be superfluous. The volume of social policy research is sufficiently great that review procedures that go beyond the kind of review process for academic publication could never be institutionalised for all but a

---

[2] Three of these concerned my research on so-called "white flight" from school districts that were undergoing rapid school desegregation, and four concerned my research on public and private schools. The first meeting on the school desegregation research, convened by the Urban Institute and held in the Summer of 1975, was held in private with research scholars and legal advocates in attendance, was probably the most successful. The second was held shortly thereafter at Brookings Institution, and was public to reporters. It was not designed to arrive at a scientifically correct conclusion, but to dull the impact of the (previously-released) set of findings. The third, held later at the Department of Health, Education and Welfare, consisted primarily of two conflicting presentations, but the presentation conflicting with mine was not made by an active investigator, and thus did not join the issue. The fourth was on April 7th, 1981, at the release of the public-private school report, and the fifth was a week later at the meetings of the American Educational Research Association. In neither of these had the reviewers of the report been able to carry out independent analyses of the data on which the report was based, so that their reviews lacked the full force that they might have had if alternative analyses of the same data had been carried out. The sixth and seventh, carried out on the public-private school report in the summer of 1981 by the National Institute of Education and the National Research Council, seemed to me distinctly more successful than earlier ones. These were closed meetings, consisting of small numbers of professionals (less than twenty in each case), each of whom had had the opportunity to study the report, and some of whom had carried out analyses of the data. These latter two meetings, however, were designed not as interested-party reviews, but as reviews by disinterested professionals.

very few research projects. Yet it is hard to predict just what those will be. For example, if the reports on public-private schools had been released in the Fall, 1980, attention from the mass media would have been unlikely and review procedures beyond those carried out by NORC and NCES would have been superfluous.

Perhaps a more important aspect of the prior review question concerns the danger of suppression of research results under a cloak of scientific criticism. I know of no general answer to this problem, nor even of a good set of principles that can guide specific cases. Yet any institutionalisation of review processes must be attentive to this problem.

*   *   *

In all that I have said so far, it is assumed that social policy research will be carried out on certain topics, and the central question has been the one of how to insure that the research results (a) get into the public debate and are not suppressed; (b) address questions of interest to all parties affected by the issue; and (c) enter the debate in a fashion that they elevate the level of public debate rather than misinform it or confuse it. Now I want to relax the assumption that policy research should be publicly available, and raise the question whether it should be privately held by the sponsoring government agency, or openly published.

I will begin with an example that illustrates this issue especially well. The example is that of negative income tax (NIT) experiments carried out at various locations in the United States. The first experiment was carried out in New Jersey and analysed by economists at the University of Wisconsin. The analysis focused principally on the question of labour supply: would the negative income tax (which provided a guaranteed annual income) reduce the amount which people worked, and thus greatly increase the extent of economic dependency in the U.S.? The result was that there was such an effect, but that it was quite small. Those results were openly announced, disseminated, and later when the Carter Administration was attempting to pass a NIT bill, the Department of Health, Education and Welfare called research analysts to testify before Congress, thus allaying fears of some Congressmen that there would be a drastic effect in reducing the willingness of people in the lower echelons of the labour force to work.

Another experiment was carried out in Seattle and Denver, and analysed at the Stanford Research Institute (SRI). Sociologists at SRI found a surprising result: the negative income tax sharply increased divorce rates and reduced remarriage rates. These results were treated very differently by HEW. The reports were subjected to extensive challenge, reports were buried rather than disseminated, and HEW did not call the researchers to testify before Congress. The results gained wide attention only after some members of Congress learned of the results and independently called for testimony on the results.

The reasons for the differential treatment of these two research results are several. One is institutional: the Institute for Research on Poverty (IRP) at the University of Wisconsin and the Assistant Secretary for Planning and Evaluation (ASPE) at the Department of HEW had very close ties, with some circulating membership; this was not true for the relation between ASPE and the SRI researchers. Thus there was a high level of trust and similarity of view point at IRP and ASPE. A second reason was disciplinary; ASPE and IRP were staffed largely by economists, and the labour supply results were obtained by IRP economists. The SRI researchers were sociologists, and were using mathematical methods of analysis that the IRP and ASPE economists only slowly came to understand and accept.

A third reason, however, and I suspect the most important, had to do with HEW's governmental policy role: it was the designer and promulgator of the Administrations's negative income tax bill. Thus it was interested principally in those research results which showed the benefits of NIT, or allayed fears about its harm. It was not interested in disseminating research results which would help defeat the bill (as in fact the divorce results, once disseminated, did). Thus HEW had a strong interest in preventing open dissemination of certain research results. In short, HEW was interested in the use of research results not primarily to frame policy, but primarily to help sell a policy already designed. Consequently, it was willing to suppress those results which were not helpful toward this goal.

This case of social policy research, and social policy research more generally, can be regarded as information feedback to guide social policy. The central question then becomes, who should it be fed back to? Who should have access to this information? Who should see the government-financed report on negative income tax and divorce? Who should see the government-financed report on public and private schools? Who should have access to the data on which these reports are based?

There are two models for feedback processes in a large society which give diametrically opposed answers to this question. One is the model of society as a cybernetic control system, with government officials as the decision-making agent, and social policy researchers engaged in contract research as the feedback instrument. In this model, the decision-making agent, i.e. the government agency within which direct responsiblity for the policy lies, frames the research questions necessary to inform policy, and the social policy researchers carry out the research and report the results back to that government agency. In this conception, it is entirely appropriate that the research reports on the negative income tax experiment go directly to HEW and become the private property of that agency, to use as it sees fit. It is not appropriate for the public to hear the results of government-funded research on private and public schools, nor for the researcher to discuss those results outside government.

This cybernetic conception of society, with social policy research as the feedback link in a sequence of action has been held up as a spectre of the future by the sociologist Jurgen Habermas. He envisions as a pre-eminent danger of a future society with a feedback process from policy effects back to policy-makers, bypassing the political process and emasculating the class interests generated by the institutional structure of society. The vision is of societies in which there is "the end of ideology", to use Daniel Bell's imagery, governed by non-political technocrats informed by sophisticated feedback mechanisms.

And the feedback mechanism, of course, is this recent arrival on the political scene of social policy research. Thus in this vision of the future, social policy research undermines the normal political processes by giving the technocratic policy-makers that most important weapon: information.

This suggests that social policy research aids the centralisation of power, helping to create a monolithic authority system. There is, however, a second model for feedback processes in a large society. This is a model of society not as one single rational actor, but as many actors. Societal decisions in this conception are not the product of a single decision-making agent, a government agency responsible for a certain area of policy. Rather, they are the outcome of a political process in which a great many actors, the whole spectrum of interested parties, press their interests via the existing political institutions. Some of these interested actors are in government, but most are outside. The policy is an emergent outcome of this political process in which the interests of many actors in society play a part.

In this model, the character of social policy research as a feedback instrument becomes very different from that I described in the other model. The research questions are *not* framed by a government agency; the principal feedback is *not* to a government agency. Rather, the research questions must be those of interest to the variety of parties affected by the policy, the interested parties, being mostly outside government. The feedback must be to that whole set of interested parties, who need that information to press their interests rationally. In this model, the feedback information must be a public good, with the full property of nonexcludability. For if the information can be withheld from any actor in the social system, that actor's interests are not informed. And as an increasing number of social policies come to be made at the national level, and as those policies come to be increasingly complex, rational response increasingly requires systematic feedback from social policy research. Thus interests which are excluded, in either the process of framing the policy research questions or in receiving research results, are increasingly emasculated.

The first of these two models, that of society as a single rational actor and social policy research results as private goods directly fed back to the government policy-making agency, may be termed a cybernetic model of societal decision-making. The second, that of society as a multitude of rational actors, with social policy research results disseminated openly to all as public goods, may be termed a pluralistic model of societal decision-making.

Often the question is seen as one of openness of inquiry, a question of the rights of the researcher compared to the rights of the policy-maker. But I believe the question properly put has nothing to do with the rights of the researcher. It has, rather, to do with the rights of those in direct control of social policy, that is, government agencies, vs. the rights of those who have interests in the effects of social policy, that is, those affected by the policy. What Habermas calls the cybernetic model places all information-rights in the hands of the former, the *controlling* parties, and the pluralistic model places all information-rights in the hands of the latter, the *interested* parties.

Some argue that the "cybernetic" model is wholly incompatible with a democratic society, where information-rights must lie in the hands of the interested parties with social policy research results as a public good. But if that is the stance one takes, there are several points which should be noted. First, social policy research has characteristically not been carried out according to the model of pluralistic policy research. In particular, economists' conception of the role of economic inputs into the policy process is characteristically that of adviser to the prince, implicitly using the cybernetic model of a single decision-maker. Nor are sociologists characteristically much closer to the pluralistic model in their policy research, for they ordinarily accept the policy research problem as framed by a government agency; and if they have less often acted in the role of adviser to the prince, it is because the prince has less often found the information they come up with useful.

More generally, if one accepts the model of pluralistic policy research (and I think there are some appropriate caveats to such total acceptance), then it is necessary to recognise that nothing less is being discussed than an augmentation of political rights for the population as a whole, to cope with a social structure that was not originally envisioned by the architects of democratic political theory. While these theorists created constitutions which insured freedom of expression and political representation of interests in government decision-making, they did not foresee the information-asymmetry and information-scarcity which could exist in a complex and massive society. Consequently, they neglected to insure representation of interests in the acquisition and dissemination of information relevant to policy. Subsequent institutions have developed to help rectify this omission. In the United States, these are principally the institution of public hearings on proposed legislation by Congressional committees, and public hearings by government policy-making agencies, such as the regulatory agencies. Lobbyists are the principal sources of such information. But with the explosive growth of social policy and the concomitant growth of social policy research, complementary institutions are necessary to insure that the variety of parties affected by a policy not only have an arena for input to policy, but also a means for becoming informed about the potential effects of that policy on them.

It is, I suggest, a task of social science, probably consisting of a mixture of social policy researchers and political theorists, to design such institutions. I can only point out that our current conceptions are simplistic and naive. We need to begin from a conception of the political process in which the feedback of systematically-gathered information plays a part, and in which information rights are dealt with as explicitly as are voting rights.

It is clear, that the task of devising appropriate institutions for protecting citizens' information rights cannot be left to government agencies. To do so would be to give the fox the key to the henhouse. For policy-making agencies in government have an interest in releasing or withholding policy-relevant information to fit their policy goals, that is, in policy-relevant information as a private good. Rather, this is a broader task, one which touches the discipline of social science in two ways: as the technical experts who gather such information and as theorists who conceive of appropriate institutions to insure that information rights are as broadly distributed as voting rights.

Contextual Problems of Educational Reforms: A Swedish Perspective

BY URBAN DAHLLÖF

Introductory remarks

Our Symposium is designed to contribute to a comparative project including the United States, West Germany, England and Sweden. This immediately raises the problem of comparability, especially with regard to the conditions under which political and administrative decisions are taken in the different national settings. In addition, we are faced with the "regular" problems of direct and indirect influences, short-term or long term effects, cumulative evidence vs. one-shot reports, variations between different types of issues, including the differences between reform decisions and continuous renewal.

I shall avoid discussing the case of Sweden only in terms of the comprehensive school reform and confine myself to personal experiences and points of view which hopefully will contribute to a problematisation of some issues.

Sociological and educational perspectives

First of all, a special word about the Swedish reform. No doubt, most educational reforms in Sweden have had broad social goals and should be seen as broad policy attempts directed towards the promotion of social equality. Indeed, this is one of the most thoroughly investigated areas by empirical studies related to school reforms in their planning phase. Most of these studies have been conducted by researchers with a background in differential psychology who at the same time hold chairs in Education. Above all, Torsten Husén and Kjell Härnqvist should be mentioned, not only for their pioneer work in this field but also for their sustained interest over a long period, ending up in several longitudinal follow-up studies over decades by themselves or by collaborators. (For summaries and further references see Husén & Boalt, 1968; Husén et al., 1969; Husén, 1972, 1973, 1975, 1981; Dahllöf, 1973; Härnqvist, 1966, 1968, 1973; Härnqvist & Svensson, 1980). With regard to the sometimes complex relationship between educational and sociological perspectives on education in the international research field, this means that in Sweden educational researchers have been more open to sociological perspectives and variables than many colleagues abroad. Sociologists and statisticians often tend to consider educational variables in terms of programme structure, curriculum content, option systems or performance levels among subgroups of students.

Yet, all reform efforts have taken place within a frame of reference which also takes into account the need and demand for different kinds of specialised education in Swedish society at large. Even though the time for differentiation has been postponed in order to counteract the influence of social background factors, this does not mean that problems of curriculum contents and competence can be dispensed with. Nor can one ignore the influence of the financial study support system or the rules for access to various specialised secondary or post-secondary programmes, the contents and merit value of which strongly influence their attraction. Thus, sociological and statistical studies which do not take such educational characteristics into account – and particularly the political decision-makers' view on them – are likely to become somewhat misleading.

Consequently, there are two types of risks involved in an analysis of social goals and sociological variables in education. The one is the superstitious belief in reforms in terms of organisational changes of the educational system as the main instrument of bringing about social change, irrespective of the problems and processes on the labour market or income and taxation policy. The other risk may be labelled "oversociologisation" of the whole debate, in which problems of merit value, formal and actual competence and curriculum contents are more or less disregarded. Researchers who disregard those aspects are not fair to the political decision-makers. There are, however, other participants in the debate who would gladly attribute the school reform to pure social goals, sometimes far more radical than the ones intended by the decision-makers themselves. No wonder, then, that such writers so often complain about the complete failure of the Swedish school reform. Sometimes one may suspect that it is in their own interest to arrive at an entirely negative conclusion, since their general political ideology makes them suspicious of any kind of reformism. In such a case, selective perception makes it easy to register failures. This is particularly understandable, since the common statistical indicators, which are commonly used as criteria for reform evaluation, are quite crude. It is somewhat of a paradox that Sweden with its elaborate social welfare policy offers indicators which do not even allow the positive outcomes, if any, to come through. Instead, the official national statistics almost invite the readers to draw negative conclusions about the social outcomes of the educational reforms. A person who wants to follow up the reforms in the way I find necessary has to dig into sophisticated special reports often available only in Swedish. Thus, the lack of adequate indicators does in fact provide overcritical radicals with quite a good excuse for their negative conclusions.

What has been said so far does not, however, imply that I am prepared to defend the position that the Swedish school reforms have proved a great success in relation to stated social goals. It is not my specific field of competence nor my duty to go into all the details necessary to support a balanced view of the successes and failures of the Swedish reforms. Nevertheless, there are in my opinion enough indications of at least a limited and moderate success in relation to the goals agreed upon by the majority of the political decision-makers, given the general situation which provided the starting point for the reform cycle. It is definitely a myth that the Swedish educational reforms have ended in nothing but a complete failure. It is also a myth that researchers in the social sciences have done nothing else than provide the political establishment with a legitimisation of their preconceived opinions, or political decisions already taken before a Royal Commission work starts.

On the other hand, we have found more problems than anticipated at least by the most optimistic reform spokesmen. I find myself in the rather peculiar situation of feeling a need to defend the social and educational aims of the Swedish reforms of schools and universities, as well as the main characteristics of the reform strategy, and at the same time to draw attention to several types of difficulties both of a general nature and in the interaction between researchers, politicians and administrators. Moreover, some of these difficulties have not been discussed at any length before. The mere fact that additional difficulties are added to an already complicated picture, will probably increase the frustration among those who want clear-cut answers to simple questions. If social scientists have any role to play as a partner in the political life, it is almost by definition that of detecting and analysing problems. In this particular case, some of the main problems seem to take the shape of seven crucial Cs.

Seven Crucial Cs: Criticism, Contextual Conditions, Comparability, Constructive Contributions and Cooperation.

Everybody familiar with the modern epistemological debate about the role of the social sciences recognises that the seven Cs mentioned above could lead straight into a long intellectual journey, if not over the seven seas but into a number of complicated theoretical problems for which there is no room here. Let me therefore be very pragmatic and at the same time take the risk both of being quite personal and of sticking my neck out in making some quite sweeping statements about the crucial issues mentioned above. The statements are made within a frame of reference where education is viewed as a social science. This includes a macro-micro dimension. Educational research is regarded neither as an application of psychology in any reductionistic way, nor as any kind of applied sociology (see Dahllöf, 1974, 1979).

Criticism

Without discussing the Frankfurter school or any other headquarters of a critical social science, I would like to make a distinction between *societal criticism* at large and *systems criticism* on the political premises of the existing society. In the former case the scientific efforts are concentrated on the economic, social and cultural fundamentals of different types of societies. Of course, educational research can make contributions to such critical studies, but it seems difficult to defend a position that this should be the main arena for education in relation to macro-sociology, social anthropology, general economics and political science. Consequently, it seems more appropriate for educational researchers to concentrate on the more limited area of the society's – formal and informal – educational institutions or systems. The term institution is here used with its sociological meaning. Then, it becomes an important part of the scientific procedure to pay due attention to the premises on which the educational system is resting in terms of ideology and goals, social structure and available resources. As regards the relationship between reform intentions, implementation and long-term outcomes it becomes a difficult, but important, task to describe the actors' general view of the actual field situation and their specific reform intentions. This holds true for various actors in the political parties, in the administrative bodies as well as among those social scientists who were consulted or who took part in the debate. Of course, both explicit and implicit motives and functions are of interest in an appraisal of the planning process and its later outcomes. Other problems include the successive change of relevant parts of the environment in which the educational system operates and the consequences of such changes for a specific reform. As a typical example can here be taken the recent Swedish governmental committee on the secondary school and the very restrictive budget restrictions issued by government just before the committee completed its work (SOU, 1981, 96).

Another specific problem should also be touched upon in this connection. The problem concerns concepts and connotations used by different reform evaluators and the role of the evaluator in relation to the objects of his study and the participants involved. I clearly recognise the difficulties connected with a congenial interpretation of motives and proposals according to the actors' own frames of reference, and I don't by any means deny the evaluator the right to look at the evaluation object from another perspective or from theoretical points of view not held by or perhaps not even known to the parties involved. At least from a scientific point of view I think, however, that it is more interesting if the evaluator demonstrates willingness and ability to describe and interpret the phenomena under study in terms of the frames of reference held by the actors of the times, which does not at all exclude conflicting views or other types of tensions. This seems to be so in line with the general and original meaning of hermeneutics, long practised by historians and linguists, that it may appear superfluous even to mention it here. Nor does such a subordination by the evaluator to the frame of reference held by the actors preclude other approaches, especially not if the new frame of reference is openly discussed and systematically related to the original one.

Now, what I am concerned about is the ambiguity which sometimes arises when the concepts and connotations of grand theories of societal criticism are used in evaluation studies – or even in actual planning processes – of the system's type when all main actors are working within another frame of reference. A typical example is different varieties of more or less orthodox Marxism applied to reform cases in which the representatives of the labour parties or trade unions involved did not use any such type of Marxist theory as a basis. I admit that even an orthodox Marxist analysis may be elucidating. But when it is applied to a specific reform case it is not particularly interesting from the point of view of scientific social or educational evaluation, unless it is open to modification regarding the empirical findings.

What I think particularly difficult are people who write about or even participate in an actual planning process, in which the political participants work within a frame of reference of the second type, while our expert uses the terminology of the first type, without making clear what connotations and interpretations this will mean, or in what way and how far the expert's hidden value premises will influence his or her recommendations. In a committee or local planning team there are often members representing the labour party, or central and local trade unions. Inasmuch as they base their standpoints on a way of thinking which – at least up to a certain limit – accepts industrial rationalisation as a legitimate goal, or as part of their basis for a "salary policy of solidarity", it is not very convincing to describe them as traitors to the true interests of the working class, nor to regard all kinds of state or municipal authorities, including planning committees within a labour dominated government, as nothing but an oppressive instrument of the ruling class.

Thus, the big difference resides within the political left. Tensions may arise in the planning and evaluation processes when there is ambiguity about the premises for the work in terms of societal or systems criticism. In the long run such ambiguity may affect the credibility of the social sciences as partners in planning and evaluation processes. Nor is it particularly healthy from the point of view of theory building: evaluation studies in field settings are, after all, one of the cornerstones of a better understanding of educational phenomena at least at the macro-level. An ambiguity of the type described above can at least for young researchers – deliberately or unintentionally – be used as a tactical means of being accepted by both sides. A not very pleasant second or third cousin are those "mature" researchers who have used up lots of research grants from state authorities, and who think they sharpen their progressive profile or gain credibility as radicals by making statements about the need for revolutionary pedagogics in a country like Sweden; or who complain about their feelings of being prostituted, as if the democratic planning and evaluation processes had not given them enough room to get involved in a critical discussion on the premises offered by the present societal order.

Once again, and in order to prevent misunderstanding, societal criticism and research based on such theories are relevant and justified. From the point of view of educational planning and evaluation based on other premises, it should, however, be a first consideration to investigate such problems on the selfsame premises as the decision-makers, before one resorts to quite other types of explanations of less successful efforts.

Contextual conditions

Contextual conditions are important in at least three ways. Instead of trying to cover the whole field of determinants I think we should concentrate on a limited number of typical circumstances which should be regarded as examples.

1. The overall economic order, degree and kind of social stratification as well as cultural traditions are of great importance both for the meaningfulness of priorities of educational reforms and for the likelihood for them succeeding. I do not think I need to elaborate this theme in relation to the differences between the so-called developing and developed nations, nor between socialist and non-socialist societies. But I want to emphasise that contextual conditions vary considerably also *within* the western sphere. I am here thinking about the differences among the regions of the western civilisation and in particular in small, relatively homogeneous nations, like the Nordic countries and New Zealand on the one hand, and countries like France, Great Britain and West Germany on the other.

The distinctive characteristics between these two groups of nations are, among other things, the degree of social stratification in combination with a cultural heritage which to a large extent relates to quite distinct social and economic patterns. Taken together, these background factors with their strong historical roots provide a quite different and much less fertile ground for educational reforms in France, Great Britain and West Germany.

Historians may find larger differences also between different members within the two main groups of nations which we have juxtaposed here. But for the purpose of this paper our division is sufficient, as it also points out some common factors which may be of relevance for a comparative study of reform strategies. If from the very beginning one starts with the assumption that all nations should be treated as unique cases, then comparative education is doomed beforehand in relation to its possibilities of generating fruitful conclusions about common trends which cut across contexts. Since we do not know the limits for meaningful generalisations – and since these limits in addition may vary with topic and times – I think we had better keep the door open for the comparability of contexts, provided that careful case studies form the basis for the conclusions. The fact that educational phenomena at least to some extent are context-bound does not mean that all ambitions about generalisations have to be eliminated. Even though it means a warning against regarding education entirely as a behavioural science of high generalisability, it makes it in my opinion much more interesting as a social science. It emphasises the role of partial theories with a moderate coverage, for which economic, social, cultural, and other contextual frame factors may play a decisive role. These general considerations on the macro level of the territory of education as a social science seem to be supported by a research group of mine concerned with sub-systems within a nation (Dahllöf, 1967, 1969, 1971a–c, 1974; Dahllöf, Lundgren & Sjöö, 1971; Lundgren, 1972) which later was developed further by Lundgren (1977, 1979) and his collaborators in the relation between context, curriculum and teaching (see also Gustafsson, 1977; Lundgren & Pettersson, 1979).

In any case, the observation about the two main groups of nations mentioned above does not only lead to the conclusion that the conditions for educational reforms may be better in countries like Sweden than in England, France and West Germany. The distinction will also draw attention to the fact that most grand theories of societal criticism emanate from philosophers and researchers in the latter group of social and cultural contexts. This could, of course, lead to a long discussion of the difference between the big, relatively strongly capitalist western economies on the one hand, and the small mixed economies and welfare societies like Sweden on the other. For obvious reasons grand theories of societal criticism have been little concerned with the tiny western fringe areas. Nevertheless, they might constitute a much more interesting case for societal analysis than is generally recognised both by continental writers and their protagonists here, who not only do their best to introduce them to us, but also to convince us about their general validity. It may even be true that – from certain points of view – there is no fundamental qualitative difference between the big capitalistic states and the small welfare societies, but even differences of degree in some combination of crucial background factors may lead to far-reaching consequences for cultural and political policy.

2. Other contextual conditions are found at the level of political and administrative processes and their ideological and cultural background both in general and with education in particular. Here it may suffice to point to the federal character of the United States and West Germany, to the strong traditions of local freedom at the municipal level in the United States and England as opposed to the high degree of centralisation in France and to a moderate "Länder-Centralisation" in West Germany. A classification of the Nordic countries among those having a highly-centralised system might be formally correct, but it should be borne in mind that as entities they are small, and on the level of a single American or Central European metropolitan area.

Moreover, there are differences between nations both with respect to the ways in which different parts – primary, secondary, tertiary – of the educational systems are monitored by their respective top authorities and regarding areas which are kept under more systematic control by national or federal authorities. In a systematic treatment of educational reform strategies these areas represent a key to understanding what room there has been for a national or federal planning process, and also for interaction between professional planners and social scientists. In a national and federal setting, where the main monitoring of the educational system takes place entirely in terms of budget allocation or state grants, there is only room for interaction with economists. A quite different situation exists, when the Parliament takes the decision about the allocation of teaching time to subject areas or even main curriculum units. In discussions of reform strategies and their interaction with educational research, both areas of decision-making should thus be recognised.

I take it for granted that conditions like the preceding ones will be treated in a much more detailed way in the comparative project to which this paper is intended as a contribution. What has been said so far is, however, only a prerequisite for another preliminary conclusion concerning the applicability of various theories or models about strategies for educational innovation or reform. Irrespective of how we define the concepts of change, development, innovation, and reform in relation to each other, most of the international literature on the subject has its origin in the United States and England and is derived from economic, cultural and administrative settings which are profoundly different from those in the North European scene. And inasmuch as they have had any concern for experiences from this part of the world, the descriptive tools available have probably not been of the best.

3. Finally, there are also some other factors worth mentioning which influence the opportunities for interaction between policy-makers and different types of social scientists. Let us disregard local innovation within the existing school structure and concentrate on structural changes at a state or national level.

In Sweden, the main units of study then become governmental committees. A single issue can, however, have a long preparation time. Sometimes a problem area is investigated by, and a bill built upon the work of, one single committee. Sometimes several committees have been involved before a decision is taken. In the latter case, even the same groupings of people may be found behind different committee labels, although in slightly different formal roles. This is part of the explanation why earlier in this paper I warned against identifying Sweden with the comprehensive school reform even over such a long period as 1946–1969, during which at least five planning commissions were at work. It goes without saying that any valid conclusion – even for a relatively specific national context – has to rest on more than one or two single cases, if the study is to live up to conclusions beyond the roles played by individual actors.

Another challenge has now to be introduced: the number of educational researchers available. Interaction implies participation of several researchers. Common sense makes it also reasonable to assume that there must be at least a number of candidates for society to choose from as interaction partners. The first professor who comes to hand is not necessarily well-suited for a specific type of consultation or commissioned research. It is necessary for the researchers to be familiar with the general role and specific importance the research area has for the reform issue, in relation to time limits and other working conditions.

In Sweden, the behavioural sciences, Psychology and Education, were for a long time joined in one chair in Education, of which there were only three, until the middle of the 1930s when the University of Stockholm also got one. The first Education professor was appointed in Uppsala in 1910, the second in Lund in 1912, and the third in Göteborg in 1919. The first division into separate chairs of psychology and education took place also in Uppsala in 1948, and it was not until 1956 that this process was completed. At about the same time a new School of Education was established in Stockholm under the National Board of Education. It was later followed by others, and in 1977 these schools were integrated into the new system of universities and colleges. The first education professor to occupy a chair was – after invitation – Torsten Husén (1956), who in 1952 had become Professor of Education at the University of Stockholm and who in 1971 returned there on a chair to which the Institute of International Education was attached.

"The new era" started with the 1940 governmental school commission and its invitation to the four professors of education to give their views on a great number of educational issues (Anderberg *et al.*, 1943). The basis for commissioned empirical research was restricted to these four men and the small number of assistant professors or doctoral students around them. All in all, the number of young, active researchers who were advanced enough to be trusted with independent research responsibility was limited to less than ten in the whole country. From what we now know about developments during the 1950s, the first and most important acquisition was made by the military authorities, when they enrolled Torsten Husén on to their staff for the development of their new personnel assessment system. It should be noted that some of his research findings (Husén, 1947, 1948) as well as the dissertation by Gunnar Boalt (1947), who later was to become the second Swedish professor of sociology, were quoted on a strategic point in the governmental bill (Prop 1950) on the comprehensive school. That bill was based on the report by the 1946 School Commission (SOU, 1948, 27), which was the first educational planning committee to commission empirical educational research. They asked one of the four professors, John Elmgren in Göteborg, to investigate the relation between theoretical and practical intelligence with regard to the differentiation problem (Elmgren, 1952).

In any case, at the starting point of the major reform cycle there were very few behavioural science researchers available for any type of investigations requested by the authorities; nor was there any established research tradition within the field of education.

Urban Dahllöf

Conclusions about contextual conditions

What is the outcome of these general considerations about the contextual conditions? As far as I can see, they lend themselves to the following, tentative conclusions.

* There are contextual conditions on different societal levels which may all exert an influence on the role of school reforms for social and educational changes, as well as for the chances of successful reform.
* Fundamental economic and social structural conditions determine to a large extent the degree to which an educational reform is meaningful in relation to other strategies for change, as well as the probability of reform ideas being accepted and implemented without the support of other, concomitant, changes in society.
* The degree of centralisation and the key factors under federal or national control determine to a large extent which type of planning process will take place and what type of experts among the administrators or researchers will play a role.
* These two main factors are given only as examples. They can at the same time be regarded as covering the demand side for educational reform planning processes.
* With regard to social and educational research, the availability of a sufficient number of suitable candidates as leaders of commissioned research may also be taken as a restrictive contextual condition on the supply side.

If this minimum set-up of conditions are combined and applied to the five countries mentioned above, representing at least three main clusters, the outcome of the analysis may take the form of a matrix shown in Table 1.

TABLE 1.
Hypotheses about Some Crucial Contextual Conditions Concerning Reform Demands and Probabilities in Some Selected Countries

| Country | Fundamental conditions of society at large | | Educational system | | Research community in social and educational sciences Supply |
	Social change demand	Room and probabilities for educational reforms	Reform demand	Reform probability	
France	High	Low	High	High	Moderate
W. Germany	,,	,,	,,	Moderate	,,
England	,,	,,	,,	Low	High
USA	High*/Low	Low	Low	Low	High
Sweden about 1950	Moderate	High	High	High	Low

*For certain specific strata, otherwise low.

The main message of Table 1 is the following: In the central European group of countries the social and economic stratification is so deep that educational reforms as a social change strategy have low probability, even though the educational systems as such could be ascribed a high reform priority. Within the group there is considerable variation both with regard to educational administration and its potential for reform implementation and with respect to the supply of researchers.

When the U.S. and Sweden are added to the picture some paradoxes are even more evident. One of them is that the supply of researchers seems to be highest in national and federal settings where the educational systems do not readily lend themselves to reform, and where the room and probability for reforms also, for more general reasons, seem low. The other paradox seems to be Sweden where the supply of researchers was low about 1950, but the specific educational reform demand high, as well as the degree of freedom for it with regard to general economic and social structure.

Comparability

It goes without saying that the preceding discussion about contextual conditions has far-reaching consequences for international comparisons of reform strategies and the role of research in them. Contextual factors like those exemplified above are considered to form an important part of the theoretical framework for an interpretation of available descriptive data. There is also the risk of applying models and theories stemming from a more limited context than the authors are always themselves aware of, to other national conditions for which their validity can be questioned.

But the influence of contextual conditions may also have a positive side for comparative research. In principle this has at least to some extent been recognised in standard texts on comparative education, but the focus on a specific problem like reform strategies, and the role of behavioural research, highlights the problem. One positive aspect is, as already indicated above, the potential theoretical power with respect to the interpretation of cases from different contextual settings. Another possibility lies in concentrated efforts to find and study several cases which have some overall characteristics in common, but within which there may be differences in the political or educational situation which might further a better understanding of necessary and sufficient conditions for reform strategies.

As an illustration, I can point to the problem of models for distance education in tertiary education (Dahllöf 1977, Willén 1981) or the development of professorships and equivalent types of permanent positions (Dahllöf 1980, 1982). In both cases the Nordic countries have several prerequisites in common as to population size and density, and it is also convenient to include countries like New Zealand, the Australian states and the Canadian provinces in the analysis, especially in the case of distance education.

Constructive contributions

First, the term "constructive" does not imply anything else than a reminder of an ideal that research contributions should have a constructive relationship to the reform issue. This does, however, *not* imply that every research should end in practical recommendations. What we wish to emphasise is, however, that a critical analysis of dysfunctions, tensions or unsuccessful educational efforts may also contain a constructive element, at least with regard to explanations helpful for model- and theory building.

Second, we should recognise the need to distinguish between direct and indirect contributions. The *indirect* contributions of research can often be expected to have the character of cumulative evidence over longer periods, either in terms of a pattern of research findings or in terms of statistical trends of a descriptive kind. In its most diluted form, an indirect research contribution is offered by data presented as an immediate outcome of an administrative process, e.g. by the National Bureau of Statistics, behind which, in turn, is hidden a former research contribution in terms of the measurement of a new set-up of variables, methods of analysis or problems of definition. The distinctive character of *direct* contributions will then mean either new variables, or more reliable and/or valid information about an earlier investigated problem, possibly also with a new pattern of outcomes or new combinations or interpretations of relations between factors.

So far we have dealt with contributions from the research community at large. If we turn our attention to the mechanisms behind the contributions from the individual actors, we may also talk about a direct or indirect researcher influence. On the one extreme of the continuum, we have the university professor who after a period of "pure" or "commissioned" research produces research findings of immediate importance for decisions on a specific policy issue. Somewhere in the middle, we have the former graduate who now works as a civil servant dealing with relatively advanced problems of planning or development, who reads the professional journals in the field and now and then takes up a problem in his or her former speciality, participates in professional conferences etc. At the other extreme, we find the former university student who does not take any deliberate steps to consult the active researchers but who nevertheless has got a basic frame of reference for his assessment of the problem area, and for his ways of handling problems.

Influences of the last mentioned type are never credited to the research community, or very seldom if they are due to the middle man. Yet, it belongs at least to the rhetoric of public speeches at academic ceremonies to emphasise the importance of academic training to the shaping of sensitivity, creativity and ways of thinking which enable the former student to adapt professionally to new circumstances in his field of competence.

What about educational reforms in this perspective of direct and indirect influences against the background of the preceding discussion about contextual conditions?

If we accept a major structural change as the distinctive part of the definition of an educational reform, this leaves out both a mere quantitative expansion of the number of schools and curricula, and teaching innovations which are kept within the boundaries and timetables of the existing subject matter. Even so, what is reform in one country might not be a reform in another, depending upon differences with regard to the degree of central control and the means and content of that control.

There is, of course, a point where it is no longer meaningful to talk about "major structural change". If the educational system is built in such a way that it is very sensitive to consecutive changes in demands – from students, society or both – and if it is possible to keep a proper balance between various pressures without jeopardising the basic educational ideas guiding the school system, then (and only then) there seems to be no need or even room for reform in terms of major structural change.

These considerations might lead to the conclusion that reforms and reform-makers should do their best to make themselves superfluous. The challenge for the educational and social researchers would then be to assist in designing the system with regard to decision-making, type of monitoring and kinds of regulators, so that it is capable of renewing itself without big and difficult structural changes. Then, the more a direct, dramatic influence, often associated with a piece of reform, could be converted into an indirect, continuous influence in terms of a flexible and sound national educational administration exerted by intelligent and sensible civil servants, the more successful would that particular country be – or would it? To paraphrase Ben Bloom's (1971) statement about mastery learning: Reform-busy professors – a vanishing species?

This may seem seductive, but it nevertheless appears too optimistic to expect a perfect self-regulating educational system without running the risk of being too market-adapted or too much in the hands of short-term interests and/or of strong social and economic pressure groups. Another risk is that the system becomes too expensive or too varied with regard to standards and competence. A third – and greater – risk is that the political decision-makers may lose control of the system to the bureaucracy. It may also become more difficult to assess long-term trends and their cumulative effects. As can be demonstrated, the Swedish development is already suffering from a lack of information about long-term trends in the allocation of teaching time to different subject areas. We should also be aware of the fact – as Richardson (1978) has shown for the 1940s – that to a great extent educational planning is often some kind of adaptation to changing societal conditions, rather than a strong future-oriented, ideological task. But that does not make any profound difference in this particular case.

Thus, the main difference may, ultimately, lie in the amount of control and the amount of structural changes necessary at any given time in relation to the extent to which innovation and quality can be promoted without any structural changes.

Cooperation

We shall now tackle problems involved in the cooperation between researchers and policy-makers taking place within a governmental planning committee or in a permanent National Board which may also have responsibilities for evaluation and planning.

A number of environmental frame factors (Dahllöf, 1969, 1971a–c; Lundgren, 1972) influence "the operational field" and its degrees of freedom in terms of total time at disposal, size of staff, available resources for operating costs, and the consequences of these factors for the choice of overall design and methods of research projects. This is the positivistic side of the interaction. We suppose that some type of original research contribution in terms of new empirical data is needed, which has so often been the case in the Swedish reform setting. But we should not disregard the problems connected with the time available for interaction between the political decision-makers and the researchers – and the actual use of that time – in the early planning period before specific investigations are launched; and after the research findings are reported, when the specific outcomes have to be interpreted and discussed in relation to additional information about practical solutions, or alternative strategies for structural changes.

In the case of Sweden we should pay special attention to the fact that two main avenues of reform bills have opened up during the post-war period. The principal one has been the *ad-hoc* committee, appointed by the Ministry of Education, who reports back to the ministry in the form of a printed book in the series of *Statens Offentliga Utredningar* (SOU). The committee may in its turn use fairly readily available resources for commissioned research of different types. It may of course also rely upon every other type of information available, including research reports which have been conducted as commissioned research requested by the National Boards involved. In a governmental committee these National Boards have most often been represented by some of its top officers.

The other principal alternative is when the reform proposal is prepared by the National Board itself, as part of its general responsibility for the development of the educational system under its supervision. Deliberate steps were taken in the 1960s to give the National Board of Education such a responsibility for the school system and the adult education sector, as part of what has been called a strategy of "rolling reform". A corresponding change was made somewhat later as regards higher education and the duties for the National

Board of Colleges and Universities. However, it should first of all be noted that up to now we have had very few "clean" cases of planning of the second type.

In this particular connection we should only take up those differences between the two main strategies which affect the conditions for cooperation between researchers and decision-makers. In the case of an *ad-hoc* committee, the following characteristics are combined:

- Among its members are often a number of top politicians representing the different political parliamentary parties.
- A special secretariat is set up.
- The whole organisation will, for a limited number of years, concentrate solely on the specific planning task.

In the case of a national board as the planning agent:

- The members of the proposal-making body are not in the same way representatives of the political parties. That order has however been practised in the National Board of Education since 1981.
- Both the board and its staff have to divide themselves between the specific planning task and a great number of day-to-day administrative matters requiring decision.
- The specific planning task is therefore often delegated to an *ad hoc* group within the national board who are put in charge of all the preparatory work. That sub-group then becomes the real discussion-partner for the researchers and other experts involved.

The conditions for cooperation between researchers and policy-makers are somewhat different in the two cases discussed above. However, in both cases there are quite restrictive conditions, primarily with regard to time limits and the opportunities to take up alternatives for discussions about the general planning strategy, about the specific research, about the interpretation of result patterns and about proposal packages.

Last but not least: The cooperation issue raises problems of time perspective and follow-up. When considering the conditions for cooperation in the two Swedish-type situations described above, we did not follow up longer than the time when a structural change is proposed. So far, there have been some quite substantial differences between them. But after that point there is an important common phase: evaluation in terms of a follow-up of the implementation programme and its outcomes. A reform evaluation in its turn lays the foundations for new structural changes and therefore becomes part of the next planning phase.

Sometimes treatises and textbooks on evaluation do not pay sufficient attention to the different cases or contexts of evaluation; sometimes they mix both phases and levels of analysis. An evaluation of a structural change as conceived here puts certain specific demands on the project concerning the level of analysis and its reference points. This implies a good deal of theoretical analysis before embarking on empirical work. Such an analysis contains at least three phases: 1. An analysis of the components of the reform goals, the intentions and their interrelationships, if that was not done before the reform package was presented. 2. An analysis of the recommended implementation programme and its relation to the reform goals as the decision-making bodies have perceived them. 3. Theoretical considerations about the consequences of 1. and 2. for the design of an empirical evaluation programme in terms of levels of analysis, selection of variables and assessment procedures.

Thus, reform evaluation as a special case has a certain duty to concentrate on the goals decision-makers have set up for the reform and on their conception of the relationship between ends and means. The former phase may be a question of a congenial interpretation of intentions, but it may also reveal inconsistencies and tensions which the researcher may identify thanks to his general knowledge of the field and of the relationships between different types of goals. Such types of conflicts, e.g. between equality and quality in school education, should not be confused with grand social conflict theories, since the conflicts discussed here are not specifically bound to certain social strata, but are a question of the function of an educational system which often has several types of goals, even for the same students. However, we should not overlook the possibility that the relation between two or several goals – e.g. knowledge acquisition and education for cooperation, to take but one classical example – can be dependent upon a third group of variables concerning basic patterns of teaching or methods of instruction and learning. So, the evaluator may have good use for any educational theory that takes these types of relationships into account.

This means that neither reform decisions nor reform evaluation programmes are entirely political matters. Since all political decisions about goals and changes of goals also include recommendations of means intended to promote the ends, and since the decision-makers may vary both in their ways of perceiving such relationships and with regard to the realism on which they build their proposals, reform evaluation by necessity includes important empirical elements.

This is the main reason why there is a need for politicians and administrators to have access to expertise which has been trained in the analysis of educational phenomena and interrelationships not only at the traditional classroom level but also at a macro-level of school types and educational systems. As an expert the educationalist should not, of course, try to take over the goal-stating role from the politician. Nevertheless, he has an important role to play both before reform proposals are decided upon and as an evaluator of the programme in bringing his research and analytical insights to bear on the relationship between ends and means. However, both the duty to analyse and detect new problems in time and the task of designing an evaluation programme put quite heavy demands not only on the individual researcher but also on the whole field of education as a social science. It is necessary to have a sufficient theoretical foundation both for the societal context in which it is intended the reform should take place and to the *intra*-educational relationships between the systems analysis at a macro-level, and intermediate curricula and organisational levels down to the classroom situation, and the interactions which should take place there. This also means that educational reforms, both in their planning and evaluation stages, call for a theoretical foundation adapted to the specific contextual conditions at hand.

We can draw only tentative conclusions about the issue under discussion here. The reason is simple: In spite of the theoretical development described and the recommendations for reform evaluation procedures referred to, we have not in Sweden yet experienced any completed reform cycle which lives up to the demands put forward here. Thus, the overall conclusion is that the most promising outcome of a study of the relationship between reform and research would perhaps be consideration of the conditions for rational decision-making about the educational system in a specific type of cultural and social context.

Some Specific Illustrations and Observations from Swedish Reform Research

In this section we will, finally, give some illustrative examples from each of the three levels of education.

Comprehensive school problems

The differentiation problem is now so much discussed – and still partly mis-understood – that I do not want to go into details about it. Let me just try to summarise my own interpretation:

• There existed definite social goals for which the responsible politicians were prepared to pay a price in terms of less emphasis on the academic areas in the curriculum of the new comprehensive school. They also criticised the old junior secondary school for "its medieval roots", and its too narrow intellectual orientation.

• At the same time one of the main reasons for the prolongation of the 7 year compulsory elementary school to a 9 year comprehensive school was the higher demands placed on the individual by the modern complex society, together with a quite deliberate wish to promote democracy and to increase the individual's capacity to participate in modern democratic decision-making. Thus, special emphasis was put on skills in Swedish and social studies.

• Comprehensive classes were regarded as an important means of bringing about the combined changes mentioned above by means of individualised instruction within intellectually and socially heterogeneous groups.

• Even though some general social statistics indicators do not seem too encouraging, there are, so far, signs of at least some positive social long-term effects of the comprehensive school

  – a much less stressful climate was created during grades 3–5 due to the abolition of an early transfer to junior secondary schools,

  – a considerably more relaxed situation was created for most teenagers in the grades 6–9 thanks to the option system and the opportunities for studies at the senior secondary level which were opened up by the new adult education system,

  – an equalisation has taken place in the transition of students to theoretical study lines in the senior secondary school among students of high academic ability. Thus, Härnqvist & Svensson (1980) have recently shown a very high transition rate among all categories of students who belong to the top 10–20 per cent in scholastic achievement, including those with a working class background. It should, however, be noted that there still exists a difference between the social groups, especially among the girls. I think that the reform-makers' intentions have been met, so far, since they regarded the theoretical study lines as a programme intended for academically-talented students. These intentions have, however, been counteracted by another tendency for quite mediocre or even relatively weak students from higher social strata to enter these theoretical lines. Thus, successes at the upper end are balanced by the losses at the lower end.

• The Svensson (1962) study was interpreted to show that ability grouping did not make any difference to the scholastic achievement of students with equal initial performance level and social status. My re-analysis (Dahllöf, 1967, 1971a, 1974) did show that such a conclusion was too far-reaching, since the content validity of the tests was generally low and particularly so for the positively selected classes. Considering the expectations held by the politicians, these outcomes were too good to be true. Proponents of undifferentiated schools were prepared to pay a price in terms of achievement for preferred social values. According to my re-analysis, there was such a price, at least as long as the traditional method of classroom instruction had not been replaced by an individualisation that worked. The price was paid both in terms of teaching time for achieving the same performance level in elementary units of mathematics and basic skills in Swedish (Dahllöf, 1970), and in terms of the number of more advanced curriculum units covered in the different systems. In principle, it seems to be quite in order to pay at least some price of that nature, provided that the cost is not too high and that there at least are some gains of the type pointed out above.

• Following on the introduction of the new comprehensive school reform there have been a series of changes in the timetables and, thus, in the balance between major subject areas. It is difficult to judge to what extent those changes represent a deliberate adaptation to changing general societal demands, and to what extent they are adaptations in order to keep a reasonable standard in some subjects, where there are clear indicators and strong pressure groups (as in Mathematics). But when a comparison is made for groups of students who before the reform went to the 7 year elementary school, it has been shown (Dahllöf, 1981) that the total time for the teaching of Swedish after a period of increase now is back again at the level it held in the 7 year elementary school. The same tendency holds for the whole block of social studies. In view of the professed goals for the comprehensive school reform this is indeed paradoxical.

When study lines preparatory for senior secondary schools are compared over time, a big loss is found not only for foreign languages, which apparently has been a quite deliberate price for the comprehensiveness, but also for humanities and civics.

It would be inappropriate here to specify what has been expanded, but we now have a series of practical and aesthetic subjects which are compulsory parts of the curriculum. This can be seen as a consequence both of the compelling needs of urbanisation and broadened educational goals. But I am still not quite sure that the responsible planners were quite aware of the effect of cumulative long-term reductions of such central subjects as Swedish and social studies when they took their decisions.

Some secondary school issues

Let me now point out some strategic research contributions to the 1960 *gymnasium* committee. One of them concerns the problem of the "two cultures" as discussed by C. P. Snow (1961). Here a juxtaposition of findings by Härnqvist & Grahm (1963) and myself (1963) revealed a bias towards too little science orientation in the old system, which later was counteracted in terms of an integrated science course for those students. Another small study concerned a comparison of study demands by the universities in Latin with the actual teaching content in the senior secondary school, which later ended in a much less extensive translation course than before (see Dahllöf, 1966).

The final example from this time is of specific interest, since it is about a "non-decision" by the committee. A proposal was made within the 1960 committee that separate 4 year study lines should be created for "late maturing students" parallel to the proposed 3 year lines. A theoretical analysis was made of the meaning and possible consequences of such a proposal. And at short notice Ahnmé (1963) carried out a quite strategic empirical study of the reasons for study difficulties on the 3 year lines of the old system, which finally led to a quite different device for handling difficulties of that kind.

A final word

In the preceding section I have chosen some remaining problems rather than successful contributions, although there are examples of that type as well. This has deliberately been done in order to underline two things which I think researchers and politicians have in common when the conditions are not too pressing: A wish and a need to understand how things in the field of education are interrelated, and open minds with which to discuss alternatives before proposals are made and decisions taken. A specific problem for both researchers and politicians remain the cumulative long-term effects. In my experience, top politicians who become representatives of the various parties in the standing committees in Parliament have given me a firm impression of seriousness of intent and an open mind to facts and explanations. This attitude is combined with a wish to guard their respective goals but to avoid unnecessary conflicts in matters of detail. The same cannot always be said about semi-politicians among administrators and *ombudsmen.* The conditions for the political process and educational planning are, however, not always the best, nor have the educational researchers always been the best possible counterpart for a constructive dialogue. So far as I can see, there is nothing that compels us to give up the basic model of interaction between policy-making and research that has now over a period of some decades been practised in Sweden.

References

Ahnmé, B. (1963) Underprestation i gymnasiet. In *SOU,* 41, ch. 3.

Anderberg, R. *et al.* (1943) Den psykologiska forskningens nuvarande ståndpunkt ifråga om den psykiska utvecklingen hos barn och ungdom m.m. In *SOU,* 19.

Attman, A. *et al.* (Eds.) (1973) *Social science research in Sweden.* The Swedish Social Science Research Council, Stockholm.

Bellack, A. A. & Kliebard, H. M. (Eds.) (1977) *Curriculum and teaching.* Readings in Educational Research 7, McCutchan, Berkeley, Calif.

Bloom, B. (Winter 1971) Individual differences in school achievement: A vanishing point? *Education at Chicago,* 4–14.

Boalt, G. (1947) *Skolutbildning och skolresultat för barn ur olika samhällsgrupper.* Norstedts, Stockholm.

Dahllöf, U. (1963) *Kraven på gymnasiet. SOU,* 22, Ecklesiastikdepartementet, Stockholm.

Dahllöf, U. (1966) Recent reforms of secondary education in Sweden. *Comparative Education,* 2, 71–92.

Dahllöf, U. (1967) *Skoldifferentiering och undervisningsförlopp.* Göteborg Studies in Educational Sciences 2. Almqvist & Wiksell, Stockholm.

Dahllöf, U. (1969) The need for models in curriculum planning. *Western European Education,* 1, 12–19.

Dahllöf, U. (1970) Elevgruppering och undervisning i svenska. *Rapporter från Pedagogiska institutionen, Göteborgs universitet,* 44.

Dahllöf, U. (1971a) *Ability grouping, content validity and curriculum process analysis.* Teachers College Press, New York.

Dahllöf, U. (1971b) Relevance and fitness analysis in comparative education. *Scandinavian Journal of Educational Research,* 15, 101–121.

Dahllöf, U. (1970, 1971c) Curriculum process analysis and comparative evaluation of school systems. *Paedagogica Europea,* 21–36.

Dahllöf, U. (1973) Aspects of school research. In *Attman,* 250–263.

Dahllöf, U. (1974) Trends in process related research on curriculum and teaching at different problem levels in educational sciences. *Scandinavian Journal of Educational Research,* 19, 55–77. Also in *Bellack & Kliebard,* 1977.

Dahllöf, U. (1977) *Reforming higher education and external studies in Sweden and Australia.*

Uppsala Studies in Education 3. Acta Universitatis Upsaliensis/Almqvist & Wiksell International, Uppsala.

Dahllöf, U. (1979) Evaluating recurrent education reform or reforming recurrent evaluation in higher education? In *Dahllöf, Löfgren & Willén,* 1–20.

Dahllöf, U. (1981) Timplaneförändringar på grundskolestadiet i ett långtidsperspektiv. *Arbetsrapporter från Pedagogiska institutionen, Uppsala universitet,* 43.

Dahllöf, U. (1982) *Faculty profiles in a long-term and comparative perspective.* Paper presented to the Fourth European AIR Forum in Uppsala, August 25–27, 1982. Uppsala: Department of Education, Uppsala university (Mimeo).

Dahllöf, U., Lundgren, U. & Siöö, M. (1971) Reform implementation studies as a basis for curriculum theory: Three Swedish approaches. *Curriculum Theory Network,* 7, 99–117.

Dahllöf, U., Löfgren, J. & Willén, B. (1979) Evaluation, recurrent education and higher education reform in Sweden. Three papers to the 1978 Lancaster conference on higher education. *Uppsala Reports on Education,* 6.

Elmgren, J. (1952) *School and psychology.* Ministry of Education and Ecklesiastical Affairs, Stockholm.

Gustafsson, C. (1977) *Classroom interaction.* Stockholm Institute of Education, Department of Educational Research, Stockholm.

Husén, T. (1947) Begåvningsurvalet och de högre skolorna. *Folkskolan,* 1, 124–137.

Husén, T. (1948) *Begåvning och miljö.* Gebers, Stockholm.

Husén, T. (1972) *Social background and educational career.* OECD/CERI, Paris.

Husén, T. (1973) Two decades of educational research. In *Attman,* 225–239.

Husén, T. (1975) *Social influences on educational attainment.* OECD/CERI, Paris.

Husén, T. (1981) *Torsten Husén. Tryckta skrifter 1940–1980.* Almqvist & Wiksell, Uppsala.

Husén, T. *et al.* (1969) *Talent, opportunity and career.* Almqvist & Wiksell, Stockholm.

Husén, T. & Boalt, G. (1968) *Educational research and educational change. The case of Sweden.* Almqvist & Wiksell, Stockholm.

Härnqvist, K. (1966) Social factors and educational choice. *International Journal of Educational Sciences,* 1, 87–102.

Härnqvist, K. (1968) Relative changes in intelligence from 13 to 18. *Scandinavian Journal of Psychology,* 9, 50–82.

Härnqvist, K. (1973) Educational measurement. In *Attman,* 264–270.

Härnqvist, K. & Grahm, Å. (1963) *Vägen genom gymnasiet. SOU,* 15, Ecklesiastikdepartementet, Stockholm.

Härnqvist, K. & Svensson, A. (1980) *Den sociala selektionen till gymnasiestadiet.* SOU 1980, 30. Utbildningsdepartementet, Stockholm.

Lundgren, U. P. (1972) *Frame factors and the teaching process.* Göteborg Studies in Educational Sciences 8, Almqvist & Wiksell, Stockholm.

Lundgren, U. P. (1977) *Model analysis and pedagogical processes.* Stockholm Institute of Education, Department of Educational Research, Stockholm.

Lundgren, U. P. (1979) *Att organisera omvärlden.* Liber/Publica, Stockholm.

Lundgren, U. P. & Pettersson, S. (Ed.) (1979) *Code, context and curriculum processes.* Seven papers presented at the annual meeting of the American Educational Research Association 1979. Stockholm Institute of Education, Department of Educational Research, Stockholm.

Prop. (1950) 70 angående riktlinjer för det svenska skolväsendets utveckling. Riksdagen, Stockholm.

Richardson, G. (1978) *Svensk skolpolitik 1940–45.* Liber, Stockholm.

Snow, C. P. (1961) *De två kulturerna.* Verdandi-debatt, Malmö/Lund.

SOU (1943) 19: *1940 års skolutrednings betänkande och utredningar.* Bilaga II. Ecklesiastikdepartementet, Stockholm.

SOU (1948) 27: *1946 års skolkommissions betänkande med förslag till riktlinjer för det svenska skolväsendets utveckling.* Ecklesiastikdepartementet, Stockholm.

SOU (1963) 41: *Specialutredningar om gymnasiet.* Ecklesiastikdepartementet, Stockholm.

SOU (1981) 96: *En reformerad gymnasieskola.* Utbildningsdepartementet, Stockholm.

Svensson, N.-E. (1962) *Ability grouping and scholastic achievement.* Stockholm Studies in Educational Psychology 5. Almqvist & Wiksell, Stockholm.

Willén, B. (1981) *Distance education at Swedish universities.* Uppsala Studies in Education 16. Acta Universitatis Upsaliensis/Almqvist & Wiksell International, Uppsala.

Researchers and Policy-makers in Education: The World Bank as Middleman in the Developing Countries

BY MATS HULTIN

Urge to Transfer Knowledge

"Manpower estimates and rate of return calculations are useful in education planning, but should be applied without overbelief in their accuracy."

"Achievement studies of the IEA-ECIEL type may help to find remedies for the high attrition rates."

"A diversification of curricula might narrow a gap between school and community and increase the relevance of education, but there is no guarantee that it would solve a vocational education problem, and workshops are costly to equip and run."

"An extension of teacher-training may not improve school instruction; teacher quality may rather be more closely correlated to entrance criteria of teacher colleges and to teacher salaries."

"An increase in school class sizes could reduce recurrent costs considerably and might be done without a reduction in pupil performance."

The above truths (or untruths) reflect discussions between World Bank staff and policy-makers of the Third World during work of World Bank education loans. Bank staff is required to appraise education project proposals, and to know the state of the art and the appropriate technologies in education. The Bank is supposed to provide developing countries with knowledge as well as capital. This is a responsible and far-reaching task as the Bank is the largest aid agency with education loans in most developing countries. It is a risky and difficult task for all who work in education in the Third World. To do it properly, Bank staff have to stay abreast with educational research. They must understand what findings would be relevant to a specific country situation. Bank operators may talk about "academic research", with a slightly negative connotation, but, nevertheless, use research findings in their work. The Bank serves as a catalyst and as a middleman between researchers and policy-makers in the developing countries. It is urged to transfer "know-how".

165

This paper describes linkages between research and the Bank's policy in education and the application of that policy in Bank-financed education projects. The first section will discuss the Bank's education financing procedures and programmes in general. The second section will describe the role of educational research in the Bank's policy development and research as a component in educational projects. The third will review project items particularly depending on research and discuss project cases. A final section will discuss education issues in the 1980s and urgent research needs. The paper intends to show how the World Bank transfers existing knowledge in human resources development to developing countries. The Bank's education policies will not be discussed, although the making of those policies will.[1]

World Bank Education Financing

The support of education has become an important part of the World Bank's work for economic development. It is justified by research evidence. The non-oil exporting nations whose economy grew the fastest during the 1960s and 1970s had literacy rates which were higher than those of the countries with a slower economic growth in the same income per capita brackets. Although it cannot be strictly proven, circumstantial evidence shows that the cause-effect relationship was in the direction *from* literacy *to* growth. The social rates of return on investments in education appear to be high compared with many investments in physical assets in developing societies. Research indicates, furthermore, that educated workers, including farmers, produce more than the uneducated, other factors being equal. Life expectancy is an important economic and social indicator and the correlation between life expectancy and literacy is positive and high. It is higher than the correlation between life expectancy and any other of nine important basic needs indicators (including caloric intake, access to clean water and health care). Thus, there is ample research evidence to show the importance of education and its impact on development. Good educational systems, formal and nonformal, are necessary although not sufficient for economic growth. For these reasons, the World

---

[1] In lending for education, the Bank seeks to promote educational development on the basis of the following five broad principles: (a) Basic education should be provided for all children and adults as soon as the available resources and conditions permit. In the long term, a comprehensive system of formal and nonformal education should be developed at all levels. (b) To increase productivity and promote social equity, efforts should be made to provide educational opportunities, without distinction of sex, ethnic background, or social and economic status. (c) Education systems should try to achieve maximum internal efficiency through the management, allocation, and use of resources available for increasing the quantity and improving the quality of education. (d) Education should be related to work and environment in order to improve, quantitatively and qualitatively, the knowledge and skills necessary for performing economic, social, and other development functions. (e) To satisfy these objectives, developing countries will need to build and maintain their institutional capacities to design, analyse, manage, and evaluate programmes for education and training.

Bank assists, on request, its member countries with education, including training.

Nevertheless, at the start of the Bank's financing of education 20 years ago, in 1962, the Bank's justification for lending was rather unsophisticated and the approach narrow. The lending was primarily justified on manpower grounds. Programmes and projects in agriculture, transportation, etc. in developing countries could sometimes not be implemented as well and as efficiently as planned because of shortages of skilled manpower at different levels. Consequently, the Bank financed the establishment of agricultural and industrial schools, vocational training centres, university departments of engineering and agronomy. It supported also a "prevocationalisation" of general secondary schools through curriculum diversification, in an expectation that this would increase the supply of middle-level technicians.

In the early 1970s, the Bank began to see education in a wider development perspective. The policy became more comprehensive. Macro-economic reasons for a general support of human resources development began to be accepted. The reduction of poverty and promotion of equity also became important concerns in educational financing. At the operational level, such factors as unequal access to schools and low education quality in addition to manpower shortages became important reasons for lending. In this way, the Bank's lending expanded during the 1970s in scope and volume. It came to cover, and still covers, many types of formal and nonformal education and training. It came to reach and still reaches from simple classroom constructions to the construction of advanced administrative buildings, from primary school textbook production to the provision of research equipment in university laboratories, from the training of special teachers to studies to trace school-leavers. The comprehensive policy and the expansion of the education financing reflect a Bank reaction to borrowers and UNESCO's requests for a wider Bank view of education but reflect even more a Bank reaction to educational research over the last decades. They show the Bank's perception of the state of the art and should convey a message to the borrowers about the importance of education for development. Already the application of certain research-based lending policies in education has made the Bank a middleman between researchers and the policy-makers of the Third World.

Its current education lending is substantial and diverse. The World Bank approved education and training loans for an amount of US$1.1 billion in fiscal year 1981. The distribution in education lending proper is shown in Table 1.

During the 1970s, the percentage of lending to primary and nonformal (adult) education increased. The increase reflected the role of basic education for development. The low percentage going to agricultural education reflects, in some part, a Bank perception of the lack of an appropriate model for agricultural education in the developing world, rather than low manpower

TABLE 1.
World Bank Education Lending in 1981

Level	%	Curriculum	%	Outlay	%
Primary	23	General	29	Construction	23
Secondary	15	Technical	45	Equipment	57
Tertiary	42	Agricultural	9	Technical Assistance	20
Nonformal	20	Teacher Training	10		
		Management Training	5		
		Health Training	2		
	100%		100%		100%

needs – it is an area where research has not been able to help the decision-makers much, so far. The Bank's role as an explicit or implicit intermediary has been most significant in the financing of the development of curricula, learning materials and media and of education planning and management, which amounted to 21% of its lending in 1981.

Despite its current comprehensiveness, the Bank's education lending has not become unconditional. Each project is preceded by studies of the borrowing country's education sector (preferably conducted by the borrower). Needs and priorities are identified often in cooperation with UNESCO. Possible solutions to educational problems are suggested and discussed by the borrower and the Bank. Project preparation and appraisal are followed by negotiation, in which agreements on project objective, scope and size are reached and reflected in formal loan agreements. The agreements may contain conditions as to specific education needs, priorities and problems. Procedural suggestions and conditions might be specific and detailed, and Bank staff may refer to evaluations, pre-investment studies, economic or sector work or basic research. A condition for lending implying a change in a country's education policies would not make sense if it did not reflect an attempt towards education improvement, based on the current body of knowledge. In this way, Bank (and UNESCO) staff act as brokers of education research findings at the operational level during the entire project cycle, with a culmination at the loan arrangements.

Project approval is followed by project execution. The Bank's middleman role in project implementation is more limited. The small number of Bank education staff (120 educators, economists and architects) in relation to the number and size of projects prevents a role in project implementation similar to that during project generation and preparation. The intensive activity during the first phases of the project cycle reflects the desire to ascertain sound investments. The less glamorous project execution is often seen to need performance monitoring only. Nevertheless, the need for continued work to improve policies and programmes is also realised. As a consequence, the percentage of Bank education lending going to technical assistance has increased from 3% in the 1960s to 20% in 1981. This increase is contrary to the expectations 10 years ago. However, the type of technical assistance needed has changed. High-level experts on short visits, training seminars and study fellowships at advanced institutions at home or abroad are increasingly funded. Technical assistance components would, in this way, serve as a major vehicle for the transfer of know-how and the execution of policies and programmes agreed upon between the borrower and the Bank.

Project evaluation is the last stage of the project sequence. Research competence is particularly important in this work. Evaluation of completed projects did not become a serious concern until in the early 1970s. It was originally seen as a concern among the Bank management and staff and its Board of Executive Directors, and the first evaluation report dealt primarily with project execution problems as seen from the Bank's perspective. A change gradually took place. It was realised that evaluation must go beyond financial audits, reviews of the school buildings constructed, and student counts. There must be a performance audit and the evaluation must assess project impact. It should be more thorough, quantitative, scientific and less impressionistic. It should be formative as well as summative. In addition to *ex post* evaluations, the Bank increasingly requires the building in of monitoring and evaluation systems in projects. It has eventually been accepted that a proper evaluation requires baseline data, must be institutionalised at the time of the project conception and be a major responsibility for borrower institutions–universities, institutes of education or research arms of ministries of education.

The discussion between the Bank and the borrower and among Bank staff of appropriate evaluation of educational projects has been intensive during the last few years and is probably a beginning of the most comprehensive transfer so far of know-how between researchers and policy and decision-makers in Bank-financed education projects. The strategy has been to see evaluation not primarily as an assessment of past activities, but rather as a management tool and a means to identify new priorities. By doing so, the threatening and historical aspects of evaluation would be downplayed and the experiences and lessons learned used in the identification and preparation of future projects in a continued Bank–borrower cooperation. Student achievement measurements, school resource surveys and tracer studies would be conducted and seen as future-oriented operations. The word "research" should, in fact, be avoided in the context. The evaluation requires a considerable input of researchers and a close cooperation between them and the educational administrators. The Bank hopes that the evaluation programme which currently includes 125 studies will create a bridge between researchers and policy-decision-makers in education and also assist in the development of an indigenous education evaluation capability in developing countries.

Educational Research

This section will deal with the role of educational research in policy development and as a component in educational projects.

The World Bank's Education Policies have been presented in "sector policy papers", produced approximately every 5 years. As has been the case of the Bank's lending, the policy papers have become increasingly comprehensive. The first paper was simple and a few pages long, and based on a report by a consultant. The last paper, which was finished late 1979, ("Education Sector Policy Paper", World Bank, April, 1980) was preceded by a considerable review of educational research by Bank staff and consultants and an extensive cooperation with UNESCO's Statistical Bureau. The recent developments of education in the Third World were, of course, of particular relevance for the paper, but education in the OECD countries was also studied.

The paper was carefully reviewed prior to its completion. In addition to discussions of the draft paper among Bank staff, some twenty internationally-known researchers were asked for comments. Their assessments were followed by ten seminars with 200 government administrators and educators in Central and Latin America, Asia and Africa. The paper, which has a large bibliography, came in this way to serve as a bridge between researchers and policy-makers even during its preparation.

Much attention has been paid to the dissemination of the Bank's Education Policy Papers.

The 1980 Paper has been printed in English, French, Spanish, Arabic and Japanese, and the Chinese Government has translated it into Chinese for distribution among Chinese educators. In total, some 40,000 copies have been printed and distributed worldwide to developing as well as developed countries. The Paper has been used as a textbook at universities, including the British Open University, and additional seminars have been organised with the Bank's borrowers. The paper appears to have met a need both among policy-makers and scholars.

The 1980 Policy Paper also discusses educational research needs. In addition to educational policy and programme reviews and recommendations, the Paper explores the situation of educational research in the developing world. It states:

> Most of the research in the developing countries is restricted in scope and unrelated to policy largely because the institutional capacity is still inadequate in many countries . . . Research is hampered by the lack of qualified personnel and the failure to accept it is an integral part of the policy-making process. Further research activities are inadequately financed because they are not considered expensive. This could be true in the short run, but in the long run they may lead to substantial improvement in the efficiency of the education system.

The Bank could hardly have made a stronger statement as a middleman between researchers and policy-makers to endorse the role of education research in policy development.

The Bank in the 1980 Paper goes far in its support of research. It makes a plea for the improvement of the research capacity in education of the developing countries and suggests expanded programmes, staff training, etc. It claims that the research should be pursued in two broad categories: (a) education as a social force that interacts with the economy and society during the development process, and (b) education as an individual learning process-determinants of learning, acquisition and retention of skills, etc. The Paper, finally, makes explicit reference to the value for the developing countries in active participation in international research networks, such as the International Association for the Evaluation of Educational Achievement (IEA). As a consequence of its endorsement of research, the Bank is financing research out of its own administrative budget and a large number of studies through its loans. It directs, in this way, the attention of the education policy-makers of the developing world to research.

The Bank is conducting its own educational research primarily as part of its policy development. It became evident during the 1970s that it could not rely solely on the educational research produced by universities and other institutions for its policy development and broker role. A major reason for this conclusion was the meagreness of educational research in the developing world. A Bank programme which covered both meta-analysis and basic research developed, consequently. The annual allocation of educational research funds has averaged US$800.00 during the last few years.

A list of research published by Bank staff and consultants includes about 100 papers during 1974–1981. Forty-two studies financed by the Bank's Research Committee cover:

Internal Efficiency	17
External Efficiency	16
Cost and Financing	3
National Capacity Building	4
Access and Equity	2

Of the 42 studies, 36 deal with efficiency and cost problems. The emphasis on efficiency and costs reflects what ought to be the Bank's primary concern in educational financing and the areas in which the Bank should have a comparative advantage and be able to talk with education and financing authorities of the developing world with some authority. There are a few research areas where the Bank has possibly played a major role: the power of education and literacy in determining productivity and the influence of school quality on achievement in low-income countries. Bank research has also led to the questioning of a few sacred dogmas about the determinants of school achievement in low-income countries and about representation in higher education. The findings of the Bank's research is discussed in Bank seminars, and the papers are distributed to a large number of institutions (including ministries of education) and individuals in developing countries and elsewhere. The research findings will hopefully find their way to policy-makers in addition to helping Bank staff in policy development.

The Bank's role, as a research broker, is also reflected in its financing of research in the developing countries as a part of lending in education. A 1981 review listed 69 ongoing research studies at an estimated cost of US$20 million in Bank-financed education projects; 15 covered efficiency, 20 education and work, 7 costs and finance, 11 capacity building and 16 access and equity. A 1982 review showed, furthermore, 75 tracer studies and another 125 sector or subsector studies. The quality and impact on the policy-makers of these studies which are primarily undertaken by local institutions with some foreign assistance will vary, but their execution is monitored by Bank staff as a part of their project responsibility. As was the case in evaluation, the findings are being used in discussions with government officials, particularly in connection with new loans.

Education Projects

The Bank's role as a middleman between researchers and policy-makers has been particularly significant in the financing of development of curricula, learning materials, media and other "softwares".

The Bank's early educational financing was "hardware"-oriented. It was felt that other agencies should take care of the "software" components. It proved, however, difficult to coordinate efficiently the work among the agencies along those lines. Assistance policies varied, furthermore. Hence, the Bank has increasingly been financing total packages, including occasionally "hardware" and "software" with co-financing of the total project package. The software financing includes support of policy changes, modes of delivery, training seminars, etc. Changes in policies and modes of delivery are of specific interest. Table 2 shows the number and type of policy changes supported in Bank-financed projects and reported in the project appraisal reports.

TABLE 2
Projects with Policy Changes

Policy Change	FY 1981	Total FY 1963–81
Diversification of Curricula	3	97
Reform of Curricula	8	108
Change of School Structure	3	54
Class Size	4	20
Double Shifting	5	61
Multi-grade Teaching	3	9
Language of Instruction	1	10
Teachers Qualification	11	74

Table 2 is retrieved from a computerised recording of the content of Bank education project appraisal reports. Changes not specifically mentioned in the reports are, therefore, not listed and the extent of policy changes may vary considerably among projects.

Table 2 shows that the Bank staff has discussed advantages and disadvantages of diversified curricula in at least 97 cases, the problems of teacher training in

74 cases and appropriate class sizes in 20. The proposal to initiate policy changes through a Bank-financed project may come from the borrower, but the inclusion in a project can only be done after a discussion between the borrower and the Bank, a discussion that requires an understanding of the state of the art by both participants.

The introductions of new modes of delivery have also been frequent. This is shown in Table 3.

TABLE 3.
Projects with various Modes of Delivery

Modes of Delivery	FY 1981	Total FY 1963–81
Textbook Production	7	29
A-V Materials Production	4	55
Educational Radio	–	28
Educational TV	–	18
Mobile Training Units	1	25

The Bank financing of new modes of delivery includes generally programme preparation, programme testing, equipment, staff training and delivery of the services. Again, a discussion of these project items must be based on a knowledge about the state of the art and recent research. Costs and cost-effectiveness have been as important as learning impact in these discussions. Some textbook projects are large (perhaps 100 million textbooks), and it would have been irresponsible for the Bank to enter upon such financing without a good perception of the role of textbooks in learning and of the costs. In some cases, such as in educational TV and satellite transmission, the Bank's role might be to dampen the enthusiasm of the education authorities for the innovation. Some of these authorities have occasionally been overly thrilled by technical innovations and underestimated costs and logistical problems, and the Bank has had to refer to research findings from other countries to show their limitations.

Three current projects will now be used to illustrate the Bank's middleman role. The first project is a basic education project in Colombia, the second is a combined primary and secondary education project in Tanzania and the third is a major sector loan in the Philippines to improve primary education.

The *Colombia* project supports basic education in rural areas. Education in those areas is characterised by low achievement, difficult access, high attrition, incomplete programmes, and few and unqualified teachers. The project report analysis of the system draws upon the IEA-type survey which has been conducted in Colombia by ECIEL (Programa Conjunto de Estudios de Integracion Economica en America Latina) and also of other studies on returns to investments in primary education, on curricula, school participation rates, etc. The use of these studies has facilitated the formulation of concrete proposals to remedy the situation. The proposals cover curriculum content, instructional methods, teacher recruitment, testing and promotion policies, use of multigrade schools, and flexibility in student intake and output. As in many other countries, cooperation between the research community and the governments has not been close. In Latin America the relationship is, in fact, often tense. As a result, some of the Colombian research data used for the project were not known to government officials until Bank staff brought them to their attention. Then, the data were jointly analysed and used by the Government and the Bank in the loan formulation. New education policies have been adopted by the Government and there is a reasonable expectation that they will lead to an improvement of rural education in Colombia. The project is a good example of how the Bank served as a middleman.

The *Tanzania* project is designed to improve primary education by means of teaching materials and better teachers and by providing poor rural districts with greater access to primary schools; it will also improve the quality and increase enrolment in secondary schools, particularly in science education. The findings of research and studies play an important role in the project. The rapid expansion of formal education in Tanzania during the last decade has led to a public concern about a possible deterioration in school achievements. As a consequence, systematic performance evaluation is being introduced and the Ministry of Education is organising itself to promote the use of research, evaluation and monitoring. The project includes, therefore, several studies on (a) the project's contribution to the quality of primary education in rural areas; (b) factors in secondary education which particularly promote learning in sciences, mathematics and practical subjects; (c) effects of differential primary educational attainment on the efficiency of farmer households; and (d) necessary teacher and physical resource profiles and organisation for small primary schools in low density population areas. The National Examination Council will also be strengthened through the project. It includes, furthermore, "schoolmapping" using techniques developed by the International Institute for Educational Planning (IIEP) in Paris. The inclusion of the above and five other studies reflects intensive discussions between Bank staff and the Government of knowledge gaps in Tanzania's education and constitutes a condition for the project, although the studies would tap only a few per cent of the project funds.

Another condition for the Tanzania project is an increase in class sizes in secondary schools where the current small size is pedagogically unjustifed and uneconomic.

A comprehensive US$400 million programme for the development of primary education in the *Philippines* comprises the third case selected among recent Bank loans. The Bank is financing the development of curricula and instructional materials, equipment and education management. The cooperation between Bank staff and Philippines policy and decision-makers in the development of this loan, even more than the two previous cases, reflects the reliance on research. Student admission, student progression and teacher utilisation were discussed in a policy statement for elementary education submitted by the Government to the Bank in connection with the loan and the Government agreed to consult with the Bank in the event that major changes in those policies would be contemplated. The Bank–Government discussions covered student achievements and interregional differences, entrance ages, grade repetition policies, teacher–student ratios, class structure, class contact hours, languages of instruction, and impact of textbooks on learning. Frequent references were made to findings from Philippine and international research, including that of IEA, during these discussions. The Government of the Philippines had previously showed interest in the use of educational research in the formulation and execution of its education policies, particularly in connection with a large Bank-financed textbook project. The primary education programme meant a further development of the link between research and policy.

The three projects illustrate efforts to link research findings to project content in the Bank's education financing. The most important goals of those projects – increased access, improved learning and useful employment of school graduates will more probably be reached – thanks to this linkage. The responsibility of the middleman to interpret the research findings correctly and work with the policy and decision-makers to formulate appropriate programmes is evident. There is also a risk that Bank staff eager to produce projects and the borrower eager to borrow will agree on educational policy changes which may have proven beneficial in other contexts, but might be less suitable in this specific case and even socially or culturally unacceptable. The Bank with its emphasis on economy and cost-effectiveness may also tend to believe that economic rationality alone governs decisions and actions – this is, of course, far from true.

Research Needs in the 1980s

The quantitative development of education in the Third World countries has been very impressive during the last two decades. However, there are indications that the qualitative development has been less impressive, perhaps not because of the rapid quantitative development but primarily because of the serious deterioration of Third World economies accelerated by the worldwide recession.

Data on school performance in developing countries are scarce. Despite the studies of IEA, ECIEL and others, little is known about student achievements. The World Bank has the world's largest bank of data from achievement studies, but only fifteen Third World countries are represented. However, the data which do exist indicate that the performance in science and reading comprehension is very low among students in developing countries. There is a gap between developed and developing societies in average student performance which might even have increased during recent years.

It would by no means be surprising if a performance gap exists and is widening. The resources allocated to education in developing countries are stagnating or diminishing, as measured in constant dollars per student. The World Bank has grouped countries by income per capita level in five major categories – four with an income per capita under US$2,500 and one category on par with OECD countries. Using this grouping, the allocation of education funds per student has been calculated. Figure 1 shows how the gap between the

PUBLIC EXPENDITURE IN EDUCATION
Per Year/Per Student 1960–78
(Current Prices)

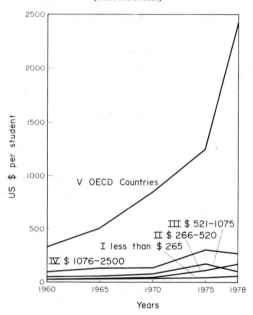

Figure 1.

richest and the poorest countries has increased. A ratio of about 16:1 has grown to 50:1 between 1960 and 1978. The OECD countries have been able to compensate for inflation, while the very poorest countries representing 60% of the population of the other four groups have had to reduce their allocation per student to half or less in real terms. High education funding does, of course, not guarantee high education performance. But the low allocation in the poorest countries reduces teacher salaries in real terms to such a low level that it becomes difficult to attract people to the teaching profession and forces teachers to take one or more extra jobs which lowers the quality of their teaching seriously. Furthermore, salary costs occupy often 90% or more of a recurrent cost budget. As a consequence, very little is being left for maintenance, materials and textbooks.

Despite meagre funding, education absorbs an increasing proportion of the government's budget in many developing countries. In a Bank paper written seven years ago, it was predicted that the poorest countries (particularly in Africa) would have to allocate over 50% of their government's budget to education in the mid-1980s if they wanted to have universal primary education and a reasonable quality secondary and tertiary education system without introducing measures – sometimes drastic – to rationalise their systems. They seldom have rationalised and a country like the Ivory Coast is, in fact, approaching the 50% figure and faces a serious financial situation. The Ivory Coast might be an extreme case, but the average poor developing country is now devoting as much of its national budget to education as measured in per cent as the rich developed countries did just before the oil crisis. Despite such financial efforts, many poor countries still have a good way to go to achieve education targets set in the 1960s and 1970s.

The unfortunate economic and financial development with its impact on the performance of the education system calls for a systematic research effort in education in the developing countries. It is necessary to find ways to make their educational systems more cost-effective, as soon as possible. The poor countries need more and better managed learning at lower costs to prevent development gaps relative to the rich world from increasing. In an effort to remedy the situation, Bank education staff has conducted discussions during the last year about the establishment of a consortium of donor agencies to support and develop educational research in the Third World, with an emphasis on ways to increase achievement within the existing economic framework. Use of the IEA network has been suggested. The outcome of those discussions is still uncertain. What is certain is the need for research funds and increased educational research in the developing world.

The World Bank is assisting educational research, as far as it goes, through its project loans and its own research programme. The Bank is serving as a middleman between researchers and policy-makers. It expects to continue these activities in the 1980s.

Effects of Educational Research on Educational Policy-making: The Case of Sweden

1. What is Educational Policy?

The relationships between researchers and policy-makers in education are usually illustrated from the standpoint of the researcher. They are less often seen from that of the policy-maker. The researcher judges how far the policy-maker assists or hinders him, and how the policy-maker uses or ignores his results. The researcher takes a different view of his role if he is conducting research commissioned by policy-makers, if he is concerned with so-called "free research".

To the distinction between free and commissioned research, we can add another, namely that between basic and applied research. Commissioned research can, as we know, just as well be basic as applied. In addition, researchers themselves often distinguish between discipline-oriented and decision-oriented research.

Research can thus be described in several dimensions. Educational policy, on the other hand, is seen as an integral unit. But this policy, too, can be of various kinds. And, of course, the interplay between researchers and policy-makers will therefore be further structured. It will differ both according to the nature of policy, and the nature of research.

Educational policy is part of a wider social policy with education as one of its instruments. Educational policy is the expression of numerous forces, some of them clearly defined, others only "experienced" in a general manner. It reflects people's hopes, needs, and judgements of what should happen. It is an expression of their efforts, both conscious and unconscious, to achieve by education certain social and cultural objectives.

II. Two Levels of Educational Policy

If educational policy in this vague and general form exists over a broad field, it is still only a few individuals who give it verbal expression. These include members of Government, and politicians in Parliament. They are the policy-makers and constitute a group *per se*.

Their policy-making, however, has to be implemented, and translated into specific organisational measures and programmes of action. Those responsible for this constitute a second category of policy-makers. They are the administrators and executors of educational policy. Let us here distinguish them from the former group and call them the policy-executors.

A national board of education, a board of higher education, or a local school board, have to operationalise and make concrete a general educational policy, expressing it in organisational and functional terms. What the policy-makers, as we have defined them above in our first group, say and decide in general on such matters as the democratisation of education, equality of educational opportunities, or the relationships between the schools and society, is derived from the larger framework of educational policy which has to be filled with tangibles. The administrative and executive apparatus of educational policy is usually required to do at least the following three things:

1. Interpret the goals of educational policy. The goals set up by policy-makers in Parliament and Government allow for different interpretations and different practical arrangements. The education-policy arm is often perfectly aware of this, and thus leaves the detailed interpretation to executive agencies at the central and local levels.
2. Take a position when goals conflict. Educational policy decisions can be mutually incompatible, or at least be perceived as such. It is the task of the executive apparatus to clarify the situation, to resolve conflicting aims and to arrive at a mutually compatible interpretation.
3. Set priorities between different goals. Often, it will be impossible fully to implement decisions on educational policy with the monetary funds or other resources appropriated. Here, the educational policy-executing arm is required to set priorities, and to set up the timetables and resource schedules that the first category of policy-makers have refrained from providing (Marklund, 1980). Educational policy can be described also in other dimensions. One such relates to whether its purpose is to alter the formal system of education, or simply to implement an already accepted policy. To this dimension can be added yet another, namely policy at different governmental levels: central, regional or local policy-making. I shall leave out these policy dimensions in my present analysis, and confine myself only to the distinction made above between policy-making and policy-execution.

3. The Interrelations between Educational Research and Educational Policy

In Figure 1 I am trying to illustrate the relationships between the representatives of research and of educational policy, and thereby also the conditions and constraints under which the latter utilise the results of research.

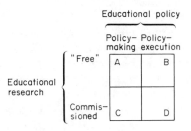

Figure 1.

The cells A, B, C and D provide four different types of relationships. The aim of commissioned research is not to provide "solutions" to educational problems, but to increase our knowledge of these, and of the conditions governing the implementation of proposals and decisions in educational policy. At the policy level, represented by the cells A and C, there is a certain amount of research in Sweden. I can mention here the studies on differentiation made by Elmgren (1952), Härnqvist (1960) and Svensson (1962), and the studies on curricula conducted by Dahllöf (1960 and 1964). These studies are, by the way, clearly "basic" research, in spite of the fact that they were commissioned. Studies of type C are usually initiated in Sweden by *ad hoc* central Government commissions.

Representatives of educational policy at this level normally content themselves with expressing general goals and recommendations. An example of this is the Swedish governmental report on educational research and development (*Skolforskning,* 1980), in which the following needs and priorities were mentioned as guidelines for the R & D programme in coming years:
– the obligations of educational R & D should be based not only on issues concerned with changes within the educational system but also on external educational conditions,
– it is important for educational R & D to find instruments to realise the aims and objectives of politically-stated curricular guidelines,
– educational R & D should be carried out in close contact with everyday school situations and be directed to the problems experienced in them,
– long-range projects should be promoted, but the focus of interest should be on problem-oriented R & D related to actual school questions,
– it is important that R & D be done in close collaboration with the schools,
– it is important that there be project planning, so that some projects are conducted every year and give place for new ones.

Research initiated by state committees, that is to say research of type C, even more than other types, has as its point of departure the intention of policymakers to *alter* the structure and function of the educational system. It is concerned with educational reforms, and the conditions under which these can be carried out.

Research of type D relates more to the *implementation* of existing decisions of educational policy. However, the boundary between C and D is fluid. It has sometimes been suggested, above all by researchers, that the policy-makers and "executors" here "commission" certain specific results, and that they know in advance how the problem to which the study relates is to be solved. I am not familiar with any case of this kind. That the policy-maker should know the goal he wishes to reach is not the same as knowing the solutions required to achieve that goal. The researcher and the policy-maker differ only to a negligible extent in their satisfaction or disappointment over the research results produced by a project.

In Sweden, in recent years, the liveliest contacts have been those of type D, that is to say contacts between academics conducting commissioned research and policy-executors. The great bulk of educational research is also to be found in cell D. The main policy-executor in Sweden is the National Board of Education (NBE), an independent central authority, the closest counterpart to which in other countries is the administrative branch of the Ministry of Education. The NBE is responsible not only for the central administration of schools and adult education, but also for R & D in these fields. Since 1962, the NBE has had its own appropriation for this purpose. There is a corresponding authority for higher education, the National Board of Colleges and Universities (UHÄ), which since 1969 has received a corresponding, although considerably smaller, grant for research on higher education.

These grants are known in Sweden as "sectorial" grants. By a decision of the Swedish Parliament in 1979, various sectors of public administration receive such grants for research in their respective administrative fields. Health and medical services, social care, energy and water supplies, defence, traffic and communications, agriculture, forestry etc., all have special grants for research in their particular sectors. In the majority of cases, these grants are handled not by the Government, but by central administrative authorities. By the same parliamentary decision, the research for which these funds are earmarked are to be conducted primarily by university research departments. No independent research institutes should thus be established for this purpose. (A limited number of such institutions already exist, although none for education.)

For the research not tied to sectors, there exist, in addition to the permanent research positions at the universities, certain resources for basic, "free research", which are administered by the four state research councils.

In discussing the relationships between researchers and policy-makers, I shall restrict myself to educational research, in particular relating to the schools. It follows from the sectoral principle that contacts will be of type D. The NBE has a bureau for research and administration, but no research units of its own. As regards the content of specific research efforts, the Swedish NBE has over a number of years stressed the following priorities for new projects:

1975/76.   Relationships between the schools and society, and their cooperation with particular emphasis on adult education and equality through education,

1976/77.   Factors creating "inequality" in school education; the connection between preschool and primary school; and curriculum work, with the emphasis on the subject of Swedish,

1977/78.   Education of immigrants; questions relating to sex roles,

1978/79.   Decentralisation of decision-making in education; instruments for local planning and evaluation,

1979/80.   Basic skills; recurrent education; the educational environment in the upper secondary school; reading and writing difficulties of adults,

1980/81.   Adult vocational education; the integration of handicapped students into the regular educational system.

A list of this kind may suggest that priorities vary from year to year. Since, however, individual projects last for several years, there is also a substantial continuity.

4. Effects on Policy-making

There is no simple way of describing how the policy-makers and executors "use" research results in their decision-making. Nor, probably, would many be prepared to admit that they "use" research, although they will cheerfully say they are influenced by it. It is therefore more correct to speak of the "effects" or impact of research, rather than the "use" of research.

The effects are of various kinds. They are often more indirect than direct, more long-term than immediate, and more concealed than visible and apparent. The results of research normally produce no effects *per se*, but only in combination with the policy in whose context they are presented.
Research produces effects when it,

1. Arouses interest and debate among the policy-makers and executors,
2. Influences their perceptions and attitudes,
3. Gives rise to suggestions for new organisational structures in education,
4. Influences the formulation of curricula or curricular guidelines,
5. Contributes to the introduction of new teaching and learning methods,
6. Produces new teaching aids (Marklund, 1981).

The effects, as is clear from the above, can be both general and specific. Their actual impact on educational policy is not connected with this in any obvious manner. A study performed by the above-mentioned Educational Research Committee shows, for example, that basic research appears to have had quite tangible effects on educational policy, greater perhaps than the effects of what has been regarded as applied research.

The effects can be negative, as well as positive. In educational policy, where different value judgements are opposed, the results of research can increase polarisation. One example of this is research into the integration of handicapped children with the regular educational system. Of importance in this context are the circumstances which – regardless of the actual results of research – contribute to effects arising, or alternatively perhaps tend to prevent such effects from arising. In its analysis of this subject, the Educational Research Committee distinguished between effects and "effect correlatives". These include:

1. Degree of clarity in the research "message",
2. Channels by which information is disseminated,
3. Existence of channels of information, and liaison persons, between research and policy-making,
4. The receivers' readiness to receive the research message (knowledge, needs and interest),
5. The amount of new knowledge contributed, and the degree of practical as well as theoretical assistance offered.

One of the NBE's experiences concerning the effects of research is that the dissemination and use of a project's results are matters which should be incorporated in planning at an early stage. It is also of importance that the reporting of results, and their dissemination, be adapted to the knowledge and requirements of the primary target group. The manner in which researchers write, and deploy their conceptual apparatus and terminology, has sometimes been thought to hinder communication with the policy-makers and executors. Experience suggests, however, that this problem is exaggerated. Behind the supposedly technical difficulties presented by the researchers' reports lie equally often – unfortunately – what is quite simply a vague conceptual apparatus and poor writing on the part of the researchers.

5. Freedom and Constraint in Educational Research

The "freedom" of research presents a large and complicated question. In this context, I will simply offer a couple of remarks concerning the effects of the policy-makers and executors being in a position, by their grants, to give priority to a particular type of research. My remarks are based on experience as a policy-executor of the collaboration between researchers and the NBE. One important question is how research is initiated.

In the years 1971–1980 the NBE received 831 proposals from the research institutes for research projects. The majority of these came from institutes of educational studies at the universities and teacher training colleges. Of these 831 proposals, 304 – or 37% – were accepted. Of the proposals accepted, the great majority were initiated by the researchers themselves. A small number, perhaps 20–30, had been initiated by the NBE, which had contacted the researchers and invited them to produce proposals for projects on high-priority problems.

The projects accepted did not always acquire the scale and content first proposed by the researchers. In the course of subsequent, regular contacts, the original proposals were reduced in scale (mainly for economic reasons), and their contents changed. The latter type of modification, to which the researchers themselves were as a rule positive, was an effect of the priorities established by the NBE on the basis of its research policy.

Contacts between the research institutions and the NBE have consistently been lively. Since 1977 they have assumed the form of frequent consultative meetings, sometimes on subsidiary questions within the NBE's research programme in established consultative groups, sometimes on acute problems. Numerous proposals for projects have emerged from this consultative process, the initiative for which it would be difficult to assign specifically to the researchers or the policy-makers. The previous system of applications and detailed project plans has in recent years been more or less abandoned. Research institutes have been asked by the NBE to describe the "profile" of their research. Depending on the questions arising in its planning, the NBE has then invited different institutes, depending on their fields of competency, to draft proposals.

This, naturally, is a kind of steering. With occasional exceptions, however, the researchers do not appear to have experienced this as a constraint upon their freedom. The majority appreciate this consultative process, and consider it enriching. An important condition for this form of commissioned research in consultation between the researchers and policy-makers is that the former should have an opportunity to seek grants for projects of the "free research" type, which they themselves initiate. As already mentioned, grants of this type can be obtained from the national research councils. The NBE and the research councils in fact have regular contacts for the purpose of establishing jointly what granting agency the researcher should most suitably work with. Not infrequently, researchers submit the same project proposals for both "free" research and commissioned research.

Each commissioned research project is managed by a professor, or by what we term in Sweden a "researcher of professorial competency". The bulk of research workers on these projects, however, are young graduate students. Most contacts between research policy now take place at this level. Such obstacles to "free" research as the researchers may experience will not stem exclusively from the representatives of educational policy. The research community itself sets certain limits for research. These include the qualifications and formal competence required to obtain research, and rules on merits and job descriptions formulated by the research community itself. The funds for "free" educational research – over and above those available to the holders of research positions – have not increased at the same rate as grants for commissioned research. The fact that the latter type of research is administrated by the policy-making arm, is only one form of constraint upon research. Other constraints upon the freedom of research are applied by the research community itself.

186 Sixten Marklund

References

Dahllöf, U. (1960) *Kursplaneundersökningar i matematik och modersmålet.* Empiriska studier över kursinnehållet i den grundläggande skolan. ("Studies on the curriculum for mathematics and the mother tongue in basic education".) SOU, 15, Ecklesiastikdepartementet, Stockholm.

Dahllöf, U. (1964) *Kraven på gymnasiet. Undersökningar vid universitet och högskolor, förvaltning och näringsliv.* ("The demands on upper secondary education by universities, colleges, administration and industry".) SOU, 1963, 22. Ecklesiastikdepartementet, Stockholm.

Educational Research and Development at the National Board of Education (1976) A summary compiled by Bo Estmer. The National Swedish Board of Education, Stockholm.

Härnqvist, K. (1960) *Individuella differenser och skoldifferentiering.* ("Individual differences and school differentiation".) SOU, 13, Ecklesiastikdepartementet, Stockholm.

Marklund, I. (1981) Educational Research in Sweden: Reform Strategies and Reform Policy. *International Review of Education,* **XXVII,** 109–119.

Marklund, S. (1980) *Educational Administration and Educational Development.* Studies in Comparative and International Education. No. 1. Institute of International Education, University of Stockholm.

Skolforskning och skolutveckling (1980) ("School Research and School Development".) SOU, 2. Utbildningsdepartementet, Stockholm.

Research and Policy-making in Higher Education: Six Observations by an Academic Bureaucrat

BY JAMES A. PERKINS

"Research" and "policy-making" appear to be clear and simple entities and the interplay between them also appears to be a clear and simple relationship – until you start to think. Then, as Torsten Husén's paper (see p. 1–36) records, each of these words and concepts is seen to cover a wide range of activities that almost defies description let alone precise analysis. Thus at the very outset we are faced with the classical dilemma: To think precisely we must distinguish and particularise but to think at all we must simplify and generalise.

Each contributor to this symposium will see this important complexity from the vantage point of his or her own experience. Mine is that of a former professor of social sciences, university administrator, foundation officer, and the manager of an international educational organisation. I have lived and now live in the territory between the researcher and the policy-maker while being involved with both, not really claimed by either.

Given the real complexities and my detached involvement, what can I contribute to a seminar made up of distinguished researchers and policy-makers? I can only plunge ahead and offer six observations arising out of my own experience.

I. Research on Higher Education is a Relatively New Enterprise

It is told that higher education is to the professor as water is to the goldfish – they live in it but never think to study it. This arresting comparison is, of course, not entirely true. There were important historical and philosophical books on higher education and the university long before World War II. One has only to mention Newman, Rashdall, Paulson, Flexner, Hutchins and Ortega y Gasset – and many others.

However, the explosive growth in the size and the importance of higher education in the last three decades has had three interrelated effects. Long-range policy-making, both in private and public sectors, became a social and political imperative. Research on higher education attracted serious scholars. And the proper and effective relation between research and policy-making became a matter of increasing concern.

187

But we must remember that the very newness of this development has put some necessary constraints on its early competence and effectiveness. As in all new fields of study, standards must be established, limits of effectiveness must be understood, policy-making and policy implementation must be distinguished and the connected but different purposes of enlightenment and policy analysis must be discovered. In short, it will take time for the parties to this relationship to become sensitive to their roles and mission and the necessary etiquette in their relations.

Perhaps the field of agriculture has evolved the most stable and harmonious relationship between research, policy and practice. In the United States, this process has been evolving for more than one hundred and fifty years. Can the far more complicated field of higher education be expected to do as well in one-sixth of the time?

II. Research on Higher Education Requires an Integrated Infrastructure

For the development of quality research in any field there must be a supporting institutional network of positions, publications, funds, and an interested audience. For the development of policy-making there must be a recognised need and a sense of priority among administrators, civil servants and politicians. Before 1950 these conditions hardly existed in America.

In that year there were in America only three professors whose titles had to do with higher education. Today there are hundreds. But even more importantly, first rank scholars from the social science and humanistic disciplines are now at work on problems of higher education. Professional opportunity has arrived and will probably grow. The same development has led to a plethora of journals, special newspapers, professional associations, publishing houses, and private (particularly in the U.S.) and public funding of research activity.

It is hardly surprising that these developments would lead to specialised activities, such as policy research and increased attention to the processes by which policy is designed and implemented, and this attention has involved the whole reciprocal process of research and policy-making into the cultural and political realities of the societies concerned. And this, in turn, has led politicians and government administrators to become increasingly concerned with the processes and arrangements for intra-government management and relations with the research/policy-making complex.

III. Research, Policy-making and Their Relationship Vary Markedly from Country to Country

Federal and unitary systems present distinct differences in the promotion of research, the process of policy-making and the relationship between them.

Even a casual look at the United States and Sweden immediately highlights the contrast between the two constitutional arrangements. The same might be said of Australia and Japan, Canada and England, Germany and France, not to mention Nigeria and Ghana.

Research and policy-making in federal systems turn on the distribution of responsibility and funding between the federal and state government and no two federal systems are alike. And these internal differences between countries must be taken into account. Centralised responsibility in Australia, for example, brings that country's practice close to Sweden's, but in decentralised Canada, practice is more like that in the United States.

It should be noted that once again there is a tendency towards the middle as well as a tendency for polarisation. Unitary states are experiencing the urge to decentralise through a variety of regional arrangements. As they do so, they will acquire both the flexible arrangements of federal systems and the attending complications of necessary national policy-making. In the last two decades federal systems have become more centralised with increasing responsibilities to the federal government as higher education is seen to serve national purposes. The differences are still there but they are, today, not so stark.

Another factor that affects the nature of this relationship is the presence or non-presence of a private sector, and more specifically the presence of private institutions. Policy-making (above the level of the institution itself) that embraces private institutions is a very difficult matter and, indeed, in many cases an impossible one. Harvard does its own research or makes use of research outside of Harvard, but it selects the results thereof and applies them through the arcane process of faculty debate, administrator impulse, and eventual decision-making. It is, of course, true that federal and state laws, like those having to do with the enforcement of equal rights for minorities and federal and state funding, both apply to private institutions and can affect a research/policy-making relationship. But these are peripheral matters, as important as they may be. The pluralistic system in the United States has federal, state and private authorities, each considerably independent of the other. Generally speaking, this means that research is prepared and presented for the enlightenment of those who feel the need for it while its use in policy-making depends almost entirely on the initiative of the government authority relevant to the problem and/or the academic institution that would wish to design and pursue a policy line.

A third distinction stems from different values, ideologies and intellectual styles. Socialist countries are likely to give more attention to utility to the socialist system and to show less interest in research for improved under-standing. Democratic-pluralistic systems are more likely to give increased weight to concern for individual or small group justice. The former will doubt-less emphasise the potential contribution to establish social goals while the latter may be more concerned with the enlightenment of an interested public.

In an interview with the Vice Minister of Education in Bucharest, who was telling me that the new law on foreign languages would stipulate that every third grade child would start one foreign language and every fifth grade child would start a second, he was certainly giving me an illustration of a centralised management system in its starkest outlines. While there are some attractive features to one who had been embroiled in the problems of getting a national language policy established in the face of anarchic pluralism, the jealousy was fleeting because Romania has obviously a cultural ethic which cannot be ignored as a factor in helping to shape this relationship.

Surely Islamic and Protestant Christian countries have considerably different attitudes towards empirical research and how it can be best applied in the shaping of public policy. There may be also a difference between Protestant Christianity, Catholic Christianity and Judaism on the same score. The Koran and Karl Marx are quite different sources of authority for the making of policy than a carefully considered collection of facts, even when they are collected' and presented under the impulse of an avowed social purpose. And those who like to argue from first principle to specific cases are likely to have different attitudes toward the research/policy-making relationship than the more typically Anglo-Saxon and Scandinavian notions of information and facts that clarify and help shape policies.

The question is how we can study comparatively the relationship between the research and the policy-making enterprise without reference to the cultural and constitutional backgrounds in which this process takes place.

IV. Academic Freedom, University Autonomy, Research and Policy-making

With respect to research and policy-making in higher education and the university, the fundamental ideas of academic freedom, faculty control of the academic programmes and the autonomy of institutions (particularly the university) represent constraints and conditions of primary importance.

Academic freedom and considerations of social responsibility have always maintained a precarious balance. And external authority that would raise social considerations as guides to professional instruction and behaviour is frequently viewed as the nose of the Philistine camel under the academic tent. Policy-making that takes into account social considerations, let alone political objectives, is viewed with attentive scepticism. The same view will obtain for policy-making by the university president, the college dean, the department chairman or even a majority vote of peers if it restricts his freedom of teaching or research. A professor of political science in a leading American university once said that any serious effort to establish a consensus in his department, let alone a formal agreement, on what should be taught and how it should be taught, would destroy the department. Perhaps this is the reason that the reports of the

Carnegie Commission, while attentively studied by government officers and community administrators, were so generally ignored by the professoriate.

Ergo – research to be digested and policy-making to be accepted requires the participation of the university community but particularly the faculty.

And what is true internally is true externally. The doctrine of university autonomy is a shield protecting the necessary freedom for teaching and research from outside interference. Swedish universities were not completely happy with the government's policies that evolved as a consequence of the U-68 report, and that concern led to important modifications in the implementing legislation. And perhaps these same concerns for university integrity explain the increasing influence of associations of university rectors, vice-chancellors and presidents who speak for these institutions. A comparative study of this phenomenon in England, France, Spain and others would be illuminating.

With this well-articulated set of resistance both in widely accepted doctrine and quite disparate ways of providing institutional support thereof, the business of research on higher education relating in any systematic way to policy-making is not without its complications. As has been mentioned, in more authoritative centralised systems, or even in those countries where ministers of education deal more or less directly with the professoriate on the one hand and the internal budget office on the other, they all do have in common to one degree or another the capacity to protect against the more obvious and direct ways of having the research/policy-making cycle implemented without their participation and, when necessary, their vigorous opposition. It is not to be wondered that the nature, direction and priorities of both research and policy-making must take into account the institutional and doctrinal environment in which the relationship must work. Academic freedom and institutional autonomy are two powerful ideas that make the educational enterprise different from other areas where research and policy-making proceed without this particular kind of resistance.

V. Initiative in the Research/Policy-making Cycle

Policy-making is an administrative, social and political exercise; research is an intellectual exercise. The two represent – as Torsten Husén indicates – two worlds imperfectly connected. It is my observation that research involved with policy-making is generally initiated as a response to social, economic and political initiatives. But research for the purpose of enlightenment can be and is initiated by scholars whose work may influence policy-makers even though that was not the initiating force.

It does seem to me important to note that a good many of the major innovations in higher education have not come as the result of research at all. Research, in any modern, empirical sense of the word, has not been part of the process of the policy design or even policy implementation. Frequently research is undertaken to support, attack or clarify policies already established. I subscribe to Husén's notion of the necessity of having a modest view of the role of research in educational innovation.

To support this general view, one has only to think of the role of Morrill and the Land Grant Act of the 1860s – one of the most important educational initiatives in the United States. There is no visible sign that research played any significant role in either the initiation or the implementation of this law. Rather, it would seem that individual states and their institutions developed according to their own environmental and internal dynamics and produced institutions as widely different as MIT in Boston, Michigan State University and that hybrid public-private institution known as Cornell University. President Elliott of Harvard introduced the notion of elective courses because of student resistance to a too tight prescription on classical studies. Aydelotte introduced the honours system to Swarthmore College because of his concern for the loss of high talent in the flood of students. Hutchins had an even more elitist notion of the role in the university and proceeded, as did Aydelotte, to implement his ideas because, like Elliott he could implement them as president of the university. James Conant, who became convinced of the need for schools and colleges to combine both vocational and academic subject matter, started his study on secondary education in order to prove a conclusion that preceded the inquiry. His high school studies started, as he flatly stated, to prove that comprehensive schools were both desirable and possible, and in order to demonstrate their possibility he said to John Gardner and me on one occasion that it was like proving that there could be a left-handed violinist. All you had to do was to find one. All he wanted to do was to find schools that were and had been able to combine academic and vocational tracks. Then he would develop his doctrine from that discovery.

The Carnegie Commission on Higher Education and the following Carnegie Council are another interesting case in point. The Commission was originally conceived by the Carnegie Corporation to study the financing of higher education at a time in the mid-1960s when problems of financial stability began to appear large on the academic stage. However, the Council had hardly been established before it was realised that finance was only one important part of a complex of interrelated problems of admission, management, faculty recruitment and institutional coordination. So the Commission early on decided to study all of higher education as a complex and interrelated system. The Carnegie Commission had an original and continuing interest in research, but the presence of academic and business administrators made it inevitable that a concern for policy would be kept alive.

The relevant point to make now is that because of its mission and composition the Council was contracting research studies and framing policy all at the same time, and not necessarily with any clear causal connection between them. Stated policies came from the experience of the Commission and Council. It would be fruitless to try to disentangle the effect of Carnegie deliberations and publications from the effect of the social impulses then at work. Most of us who were members are very much inclined to believe that the Carnegie enterprise rode the tide of an increasing public concern for social justice in higher education and a preoccupation with financial and social stability within its institutions. For these reasons federal policy was in the focus of interest, although state institutions, faculty and students also received direct attention. But it was in the federal government in both its legislature and its executive and, in several cases, in its judiciary that it would be fair to say lay the chief interest of the Carnegie enterprises.

And, of course, all this was swept away with the Reagan economic plan that involved severe cutbacks in federal appropriations for education. Hopes and even demands for increased federal funds which were at the centre of Carnegie preoccupation now seem naive and quaint, when in 1982 we are only hoping that projected cuts won't be too great. The moral in this particular case is that commissions like the Carnegie enterprises will long be remembered for their enlightenment rather than their long-run impact on policy implementation. Information, criticism and recommended policies will be referred to for years to come by those interested in higher education.

VI. Some Preliminary Conclusions

1. Research and policy-making are carried on through a complicated network of institutions concerned with thought and action. These institutions include universities, foundations, scholarly associations, and various public authorities.
2. As a relatively new activity, it has yet to establish adequate standards for research whether for enlightenment or policy-making. It will also take time to develop constructive working relations to protect both intellectual integrity and public responsibility.
3. The special nature of academic institutions that emphasise academic freedom and university autonomy requires the involvement of faculty and administration in support of both research and policy-making.
4. Different social values and systems of governance require that research and policy-making should be in tune with the style and philosphy concerned.

References

Conant, James B. (1959) *The American High School Today.* McGraw-Hill, New York.
Perkins, James A. *et al.* (1974) *Higher Education: Crisis and Support.* International Council for Educational Development, New York.
Priorities for Action: Final Report of the Carnegie Commission on Higher Education (1973) McGraw-Hill, New York.
Sponsored Research of the Carnegie Commission on Higher Education (1975) McGraw-Hill, New York.

Research and Policy-making in Education: Some Possible Links

BY T. NEVILLE POSTLETHWAITE

> "But I dare say sustained thinking
> is a minority occupation amongst
> Ministers, though I've always found
> it helpful".
> (Crosland in Kogan, 1981, p. 157)

Various experiences on the international scene in the last two decades have played a key role in forming my views on the relationship between researchers and policy-makers. I shall recount some experiential anecdotes and then extract some principles which I think important.

Some Experiences

First Experience: In 1960, I undertook a study which could loosely be described as social psychological in nature. The focus of the study was the working conditions and attitudes of "au-pair girls" in England. Whether or not au-pair girls were "exploited" was a frequently occurring theme in the newspapers at the time. The results of the research were discussed by a pressure-group, and were widely reported in the media. The results were used in preparing new legislation in Parliament.

Second Experience: In 1965, I had been invited to a celebratory retirement party for an eminent professor of education in a bilingual West European country. The Director General of Education for that country drove me back to the capital after the party. I had just completed an analysis examining sex differences in mathematics achievement according to whether the boys and girls were in separate schools, mixed schools but with boys and girls taught in separate classes, or mixed schools with mixed classes. The results indicated that the more the segregation the wider the difference in mean scores and the more mixed the closer the mean scores.

The country in which I was had many separate schools and provided one of the country's data sets which I had used in the analysis. I asked the Director-General, by way of making conversation, if there was any problem with having so many sex-segregated schools. His reply was that there was no problem whatsoever. However, I further elicited from him that he was not in favour of large sex differences in achievement. This was, for me, a puzzling situation. I continued to quiz the Director-General and by the time we reached the capital city it became clear to me that a "problem" only existed for my kind policy-making driver if it had been raised in the Parliament, or by a teachers' union, or in the media or by vocal parents' groups. I then told him the results of my analyses and we parted. I never heard from him.

Third Experience: In the early 1970s a friend of mine told me the following episode which he had experienced. He had been a member of a multi-national agency's team to review the French national system of education. At that time grade repetition was frequently practised in primary schools in France. Indeed, it was said that by the age of ten about seventy per cent of an age group had repeated at least one class. In reporting to the Minister of Education, the team had pointed out that grade repeating produced a larger spread of achievement than an age promotion system, and also cost more – if children had to stay in school to complete the minimum number of grades. The Minister replied "Messieurs, je vous le crois mais qu'est-ce que vous voulez que je fasse. Le redoublement, c'est une tradition de la France!"

I have pondered much on this reply. My interpretation is that education is a very national business in that the voters (and in many cases the decision makers, too) are victims of the education they themselves experienced and they often think that "their's" is the best educational system in the world because they are unaware of the alternatives which exist.

To change attitudes towards an educational system – such as towards automatic promotion instead of grade-repeating – requires a powerful propaganda campaign. And an effective propaganda campaign can often take a long time, a longer time than before the next election! In this case, the reviewers (some of whom were researchers) communicated well with the policy-makers, but the policy-makers saw difficulties in implementing a reform. I was also told that teacher trade unions were in favour of grade-repeating.

Fourth Experience: In 1973, the first sets of results of the IEA Six Subject Survey appeared. The Minister of Education in an East-European country held meetings with the researchers from the national institute participating in the IEA research. The minister first of all inspected the mean scores in his country compared to the mean scores of other countries. His country was well above the international mean in general but he was struck that in one subject area it was below the international mean. He quizzed his researchers and subject matter experts on the adequacy of the tests. Having been reassured that the tests were adequate he sent school inspectors into the schools. They reported that certain aspects of the curriculum in that subject matter were not being adequately covered in that there was insufficient time being allocated. Within a short space of time, legislation had been enacted to ensure more time coverage. In this case, there was a direct link between the researchers and the top policy-maker, and the policy-maker was in a position to take direct action.

Fifth Experience: After the IEA Six Subject Survey had been completed and two years had passed, I was constantly asked about the "effect" of the studies. Had they really improved educational practice in the participating countries? I talked with the heads of the IEA National Centres. Of the twenty-one countries, something in terms of impact on legislation, curricular guidelines or policy action had happened in fifteen of them and nothing had happened in the other six. My general assessment of the reasons for this dichotomy was that in the countries where nothing had happened the researchers had no links with policy-makers and had also made no attempt to forge such links. Again, my impression was that the researchers were either poor communicators with policy-makers (or were too junior to attempt to forge links) or were very good academic researchers and disdained the notion of communicating with mere "administrative" policy-makers. Sometimes, the enormous task of communicating with policy-makers, where each of the hundreds of school districts is autonomous, was a major deterrent. In these cases, the research publication ended up as the proverbial "yet another dusty report on a dusty shelf". In some instances, it might have been the case that the policy-makers just did not want to know the results or had not any established channel for receiving data which they, themselves, had not requested.

Of those who did "something" there were various types of "somethings" which they did and in some cases facilitating circumstances existed. Some researchers deliberately forged links with policy-makers from the beginning of the research project. A typical tactic was to include on a "national committee" for the research one or more key persons from the Ministry of Education and in one case the Director General of Education was on such a committee. Indeed, the Director General was impatient for the results and was forever phoning the data processors for them. The key persons on the national committee reviewed all instruments and often helped with the translation of items and questions, and wrote special national questions for extra information which they wanted from a national probability sample of children or schools.

Two recent innovations have come to my attention which might be of some use in dealing with the problems of policy-makers and researchers. The first is in West Africa where the Anglophone West African Regional Educational Research Consortium was formed in 1977. The aim of this is to have joint pre- and in-service training for researchers and administrators in education. The second is in an R & D institute in a Ministry of Education in South East Asia. Within the R & D institute plans are being made to create a unit whose task will be to identify the major problems in education in that country which are being raised (in Parliament, in the press, or by teacher or parent groups) *or are likely to be raised,* and to bring together research from within the country itself and foreign countries and summarise the research results succinctly for distribution to the heads of divisions in the Ministry and, in some cases, directly to the Minister himself.

From Personal Experiences to Promulgation of Practice

The experiences given above exemplify key points. They have covered two themes: the links or communication between researchers and policy-makers, and policy-makers' reactions or non-reactions.

Before drawing the points together it should be mentioned that all decisions for implementation are political in that not only should policy-makers take into account research findings but they must take into account the funds required and the attitudes/desires of the various pressure groups within and outside government in the country. However, in many cases it is clear that the political decisions are taken first and the policy-makers *post hoc* search for evidence to legitimise their decisions. The alternative logical approach is to identify the problem, collect *all* information available – including extant research results and commissioning new research – and then taking the policy decision(s).

In what I shall present below I shall make the optimistic assumption that it is the latter approach which is being taken.

1. *Facilitating circumstances.* Where the problem being researched is widely discussed in the media and is emphasised by pressure groups within the country, and where the various levels of policy-makers are motivated to have research results, then the probability is high of good links between researchers and policy-makers and of subsequent action being taken. But even under these circumstances it may be necessary for the researchers to make the effort to forge links with the policy-makers. So often one cannot take on board the ultimate objectives to the policy-makers because these are determined by values and ideologies which are unknown to the researchers or not shared by them.

2. *Which links with which level of policy-makers*? One proposition which I would like to make is "the more links the better". Where research is being undertaken at the state or national level and achievement in one or more subject areas is one of the variables being measured, it is, to my mind, usually desirable to involve the appropriate persons responsible for curriculum development in these subject areas. This is at a level where action is usually fairly quick. When objectives are poorly achieved curriculum developers usually examine the materials they are producing and make modifications. This is also a link which has been under-utilised.

Another major link was that between the researchers and the central unit responsible for curriculum development in the country. Since all six subject studies produced accurate estimates of the percentage of the target population children answering an item it was very important for the curriculum developers to know which objectives were being well or poorly achieved. This link was useful for the revision of curricular materials.

A third link was to the teacher unions. In some countries deliberate efforts were made to arrange lecture and discussion groups with the major teacher associations. In general, these were successful for spreading the results.

A fourth link which occurred was a direct link from the researchers to the teachers. Pamphlets were written about the results in language understandable to teachers and distributed to teachers in schools. In one country in which I visited schools, I was most impressed to discover that IEA was a household word among teachers.

The message of this experience for me was twofold: first of all it is very important that researchers forge or strengthen links with the policy-makers from the inception of a major national research project; the second was that there are different levels of policy-makers from the Minister through the Director General, the various divisions within a ministry, the curriculum developers, the teacher unions and associations, and the school principals and teachers. It is important to have links with all. In some countries this is becoming a necessity in that to undertake research in any school a series of prior permissions are required. In the country where I work, researchers must obtain permission from the state school authorities and then for each school from the school principal, teachers, parents and students. In effect, this means that the research team needs one more or less full-time person for "public relations". This person can also be responsible for feeding the results back to the various groups who have participated in the research.

Sixth Experience: In the mid-1970s I was working in a curriculum centre in an East African country. It became clear that the curriculum centre needed close links with the examinations centre to ensure that the new curriculum fed into the examinations being prepared for the end of the school year after the new curriculum had been introduced. At the same time, links were also needed to the teacher training colleges. Even though the Director General of Education understood the problem and its urgency very well, it still took 2 years to establish the links. It was the slowness of the bureaucracy and the power play within it which caused the delay.

A similar experience was in a small Asian country where I was also working in the curriculum centre. There was no link between the curriculum centre and the university department of education where all pre- and inservice training took place. The teacher trainers in the university had no motivation or intention of changing the content of their teaching despite the Ministry's desire to implement new curricula in the schools. The university and curriculum centre were both financed by the Ministry. The Minister, when asked to intervene, was unwilling to take any action because although the university was financed by the Ministry, the university was "constitutionally autonomous"! To what extent research results have affected educational practice through teacher training institutes is debatable.

Seventh Experience: In 1975, I was the chairman of a seminar consisting of senior educational planners from a West European country with some senior Ministry of Education officials from neighbouring countries. We were discussing research results pertaining to organisational factors of schools and their "effects" on achievement. Two points became clear to me: the first was that only a handful of the planners had any knowledge at all of how empirical research is undertaken, of the terminology of research (for example, the concept of a standard error was completely new to them) or of what criteria could be used to judge the quality of a research study put in front of them; the second was that, in general, they were blind to the alternatives which existed for a particular mode of organisation in their schools. They knew only what had been discussed and tried out in their own countries. They had very little idea of how other countries dealt with the same problem. This ignorance was in part due to language. Many major research findings are published in English and in certain countries senior administrators are reluctant to read in English. Of course, we also have the problem that many researchers write their reports in an excruciatingly complex way. In the country where I now work there is a saying "Warum soll man es einfach sagen, wenn es kompliziert gesagt werden kann"! Many academics – and researchers are usually academics – truly believe that complicated language is necessary in order to make a research report academically respectable!

A Comment

Although I was saddened by the ignorance of some policy-makers, I would defend them by pointing out two things: firstly, that many researchers are poor summarisers of their own research and, in particular, in pointing out the implications of their results for changes in practice; secondly, there are many research studies which appear that are either dealing with a trivial matter or poor in their conceptualisation or methodological execution. It becomes an onerous and difficult matter to read the mass of research reports and to sort out the trustworthy and important from the poor and/or trivial.

How can one deal with this problem? Firstly, the universities where future policy-makers and administrators are trained should include training on the general ideas and how research is undertaken, and the criteria by which to judge research and the applicability of research results. Secondly, the ministries themselves should organise more inservice training for their own personnel. Thirdly, the researchers should be clearer in their summary statements of results and the implications of results for practice. If I may digress for a moment, I find it particularly unfortunate that eminent researchers quibble in widely circulated documents. Quite often the quibbling is about a point of statistical analysis or about a conceptual point – defining a concept X in this way versus that way. It is not surprising, therefore, that some policy-makers view research as an academic points (for academic promotion) game rather than a serious endeavour to produce the best information possible as a basis for decision-making.

More recently there has been quibbling between two outwardly apparently conflicting groups – those promoting quantitative research and those promoting qualitative research. In my research experience, I have rarely come across a problem which has not required both quantitative and qualitative data. In the first place, any variable included in a research study needs to have been qualitatively (and historically?) isolated in the sense that one knows what the variable is, why it is thought to be important and how it interacts with other variables in a model. Secondly, in much of the research in which I am involved the statistical analysis can point to the fact that variable M is having a major effect on Y indirectly through variable (or latent variable) P. What the statistical analysis cannot tell us is what form or forms the interaction takes. Here we typically need the speculation of experienced practitioners (say inspectors or teachers if we are dealing with teaching behaviours in the classroom) and the collection of qualitative data to allow us to describe the interaction or at least give us insights into what it might be.

Where the "treatment" variables are of major interest for the improvement of educational practice (e.g. teacher, instructional, and management variables) it is usually relatively easy to involve the key people responsible for teacher training in the Ministry as well as key teacher trainers and teacher association members in the country.

Where structural and organisational variables are involved (e.g. research on comprehensive vs. selective systems, number of subject studied, grade repeating vs. automatic promotion, etc. as related to learning outcomes) it is, again, usually easy to involve the relevant key persons in the Ministry and other bodies. Indeed, if class size is involved the teacher unions are of course extremely interested.

It might be that I am taking too much for granted when advocating that close links are desirable. It can be argued that researchers should be independent, and be able to critique freely – even the policies of the decision-makers. Given close links, the researchers may come under funding threats and political pressures. Some would advocate that perhaps an arms length relationship is desirable (perhaps with an occasional hug!).

3. *What forms should the links take*? Ideally, the more the junior policy-makers can be involved in the practical work of the project the better. This can be in the form of curriculum content analysis, writing test items, deciding on indicators for variables, making *a priori* decisions on which variables form a latent variable, etc.

If this is not possible, every attempt should be made to involve the appropriate policy-makers in the organisational structure of a project; for example, on the overall steering committee or an instrument subcommittee. At worst, the researchers should attempt to have regular meetings with the appropriate policy-makers – say, every three months.

Once the results are known and an estimate has been made of how much credence one can have in the results, full discussions should be held on the practical consequences of the results.

4. *Forms of language to be used.* Too often researchers use jargon. I often admire the mathematical training of researchers but am uneasy about their training in the clear and parsimonious use of their mother tongue. Occasionally, some of them have an attitude of disdain towards those not versed in technical details. This is unfortunate. Often the people with whom one has to deal in life are technically ignorant but not stupid.

Researchers must learn to express their ideas in non-technical language and learn to use policy-makers where they can help. On the other hand, policy-makers not versed in research concepts and methods should attempt to learn some of the critical concepts.

The Dissemination of Results

It is rare for Ministers of Education to be interested in the detailed results of research studies or even in research itself, except where it has evaluated the relative efficacy of 2 or more ways of achieving a particular aim.

When discussing the use of research in decision-making (such as before deciding to encourage Local Education Authorities to implement comprehensive schools) Anthony Crosland who had been the Secretary of State (same as Minister) said some years later:

> . . . this argument (i.e. the use of research) had a natural attraction for an ex academic like myself. But as soon as I thought the thing through I could see it was wrong. It implied that research can tell you what your objectives ought to be. But it can't. Our belief in comprehensive reorganisation was a product of fundamental value – judgements about equity and equal opportunity and social division as well as about education. Research can help you to achieve your objectives . . . But research can't tell you whether you should go comprehensive or not – that's a basic value judgement. (Kogan, 1971)

Thus, when I talk about senior policy-makers, I do not mean the Minister or top permanent civil servant but rather the senior persons in each division within a Ministry.

One technique often employed is what I call the Churchillian technique – the important results and implications for practice are all written down on to one sheet of paper to be handed to the Director General or Minister. I find this an almost impossible task. As a rule caveats have to be entered into findings. A large study is virtually impossible to summarise on one sheet of paper. However, I do believe that most research studies can be summarised in some three to ten pages (depending on the richness of results and caveats to be made).

A technique sometimes used is that of discussions. It is usually possible to have a small group of top policy-makers meet for half a day or, in exceptional cases, for a whole day. The strategy I suggest here is that the researchers carefully summarise their findings together with their perceived implications for changes in practice. A discussion then ensues. It is my hope for the current

IEA research studies that small two-day regional meetings will be held for Directors General from three or four nations. It is my belief that if these discussions are well-planned and conducted they can be highly influential in improving the decision-makers' information bases.

The dissemination of results to curriculum developers is relatively easy, but the feedback should not overburden the developers with statistics and should not be seen as a chastisement of the developers. Ugly scenes have occurred when the feedback has not been handed with sensitivity!

Finally, the dissemination to teachers is very important. The " 'Set' research information to teachers'' mechanism used in New Zealand and Australia seems to me to be an excellent mode of dissemination. It does, however, require an editor who is skilful in transforming research reports into highly readable synopses for teachers. And, it requires a very good distribution system from the national educational research centre to schools. Apart from this direct form of dissemination, teacher newspapers and magazines can also be used.

The Beginnings of a Model

Research studies now exist in abundance and speculation based on experience can be tested empirically. Many (major) research studies provide data and the unit of analysis is a research study. It is the variance between studies which is analysed.

As with any model there is always one or more alternative models. The model presented below is to initiate the idea in the hope that it will induce others to produce better models. It is only a beginning and, for example, one can imagine different models according to whether the project is initiated by one interested group for their consumption only or whether the results are for general debate on public policy.

A Tentative Model

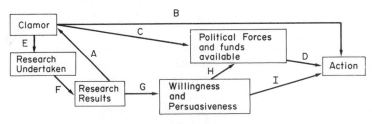

Figure 1.

In this model the unit of analysis is as mentioned above research projects. They can *either* be many different types of research projects in different countries or within a country *or* the same project (as in IEA) but in different countries. For example, the IEA Second Science project has some 40 countries participating in it and since it is just beginning, data about relationships could be collected in each country as the study proceeds.

Definition of Terms (constructs)

ACTION =	action occurs/does not occur; intensity of action; direction of action (e.g. perceived of a progressive or conservative). Each could in itself be taken as a separate dependent variable or a composite could be created.
CLAMOR =	Frequency and amount of noise from – parliament – teachers unions – pressure groups other than teachers union – media.
RESEARCH UNDERTAKEN =	Number and size of research studies initiated as a result of clamor. (The research could be undertaken anywhere within the nation)
RESEARCH RESULTS =	– existence/nonexistence of research results; – similarity/dissimilarity of findings; – strength of methodological criticisms from academic community. The research could come from anywhere in the nation.
WILLINGNESS AND PERSUASIVENESS = (within the major agency – typically the Ministry of Education)	– existence of permanent channel of communication of research results to policy-makers; – number of such channels; – existence of key persons in agency able to understand research reports; – research reports written in easily communicable language; – existence of mechanism for sifting good from bad research; – intensity of belief of agency's top personnel in utility of research; – to help policy-making; – the level of persuasiveness of key persons within the agency in their dealings with policy-makers and the treasury (Ministry of Finance).

POLITICAL FORCES AND — strength of acceptance or rejection of pro-
FUNDS AVAILABLE = posal for reform by key persons (or Parliament) in authority;
— strength of willingness to allocate (extra)
funds required.

Before proceeding to the links, two points should be mentioned:

(i) the variables making up the constructs should be thought of as manifest variables although their operationalisation may require indicators. In this case, the indicators would become the manifest variables and their compositing would mean that the variable would then be a latent variable.

(ii) the model should have a hierarchical structure. Thus, to take "Willingness and Persuasiveness", I suspect the model would be:

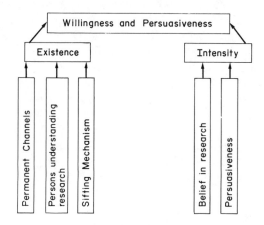

Figure 1a.

What Would the Links Be?

Clamor. If clamor arose, it could be because research results had become available which created the clamor (A). In this case, the link B could occur where the reform did not involve extra money (as, for example, in my au pair girl study or where the reform might involve changing the content inservice teacher training but not the number of days spent by teachers at inservice courses). Or the links C → D → Action could occur.

On the other hand, clamor could occur which would result in research being undertaken (E) and results being made available (F). At that point, A → B or A → C → D could occur. Or G → H → D, or in the case of no extra money being required, G → I.

Agency sponsored research. The agency (which is basically the "Willingness and Persuasiveness" box in the model) could itself initiate research culminating in research units (G, but this term in the reserve direction from the case mentioned under clamor which could then either feed back G → H → D or G → I. This would be what Coleman has called the "Prince" model. Or, it could go A → C → D or A → B, both of which, as I understand it, would be the Coleman "People" model.

How do the experiences mentioned earlier fit with the model?

Experience 1: A → B

Experience 2: The research results existed but link A did not occur and neither did G.

Experience 3: Link A did not occur. Link G occurred but there appeared to be an unwillingness to go either H or I. In fact, grade repeating is much less frequent in France now, so that in the period 1970 to 1980 something must have happened. It would be interesting to know whether H or I were used or whether there was another route – perhaps involving extra constructs.

Experience 4: G → H → D.

Experience 5: either G → H → D or nothing. In other words, the "Prince" model was tacitly assumed. Hence, some of my points in Part I refer to introducing or strengthening A.

Experience 6: In the both cases H and I never occurred.

Experience 7: The Willingness construct was weak and no links involving research were used.

Development of Model

It must be remembered that this model is concerned with situations where research occurs and where "policy making" does or does not occur. Of course, policy-making occurs without research at all but that is a different model.

It is also clear that the model probably needs more manifest variables and more constructs. By taking further examples, it should be possible to improve and extend the model. Or it could lead to the point where the model is abandoned and replaced by another. Finally, it is to be noted that it is a so-called "linear model" and it may be that another type of model (e.g. catastrophe theory model) may be more appropriate. What is clear is that complementing the existing qualitative data with quantitative data should help our understanding of the relationship(s) between researchers and policy-makers.

Reference

Kogan, Maurice (1971) The Politics of Education. Education Specials, Harmondsworth, Penguin, London.

Research and Policy-making in Swedish Higher Education

BY RUNE PREMFORS

Introduction

This paper examines the role of research in the development of Swedish higher education policy. To what extent and in what ways have various forms of research knowledge been utilised in policy-making? The concept of "research" used here is consciously broad, encompassing any piece of knowledge obtained through systematic conceptualisation, data collection and analysis. The concept spans from quite simple fact-gathering exercises to in-house policy analysis in government to elaborate research performed at university departments of social and behavioural sciences.

The analysis proceeds by three steps. First, I provide a general overview of research on higher education in Sweden, from the early efforts in the 1930s to the plethora of research undertakings occurring today. The second section of the paper starts from policy. To make this task manageable I have singled out five areas of higher education policy. These are: quantitative planning in higher education; social recruitment of students; localisation of institutions (regionalisation); governance; and, finally, teaching and learning. For each of these policy areas I seek the role of research in major policy decisions. While they do certainly not encompass all of Swedish higher education policy nor are they "representative" in any qualified sense of that term, these areas have all been among the most salient ones during the period of investigation. They all seem to belong to a limited set of recurring, basic problems of higher education policy, not only in Sweden but elsewhere as well.

Following the analysis of the five policy areas, a third section is devoted to a discussion of five general features of the policy area of higher education, features which are deemed to be of particular relevance to the problem of research utilisation.

The conclusions of this study should perhaps best be viewed as suggestive rather than conclusive; the empirical arguments are almost without exception open to refutation. However, in general I believe that the greatest burden of proof with respect to research utilisation in public policy-making lies with those who take an "optimistic" stance. Recent literature on knowledge utilisation has, in my view convincingly, shown the complexity of the relationships involved, and the problematic character of simple views which more or less take utilisation for granted (see e.g. Premfors, 1979, Weiss, 1980 and Wittrock, 1982). Social researchers and policy-makers alike have tended to be overly optimistic with respect to the rationality of policy-making processes and the importance of analysis and research in such processes. Using the terminology of Charles Lindblom and Aaron Wildavsky, there has been a strong tendency to underestimate the role of "social interaction" as problem-solving mechanisms, while giving too much weight to "analysis" (Lindblom) or "intellectual cogitation" (Wildavsky). In their view social interaction – having two major forms: politics and markets – is generally the basic determinant of outcomes in social problem-solving in general, as well as in that particular form, public policy-making (Lindblom 1977, Lindblom & Cohen 1979, and Wildavsky 1979). When analysis or intellectual cogitation enters policy-making it usually takes the form of "partisan analysis" (see also Lindblom, 1980) or "political ammunition" (see e.g. Bulmer, 1982 and Orlans, 1973). It is used to support policy positions already adopted.

While the prevailing attitude in the literature is one of "pessimism" with respect to research utilisation, this is usually not the whole story. The scepticism is most often confined to what is commonly termed the "engineering model" of the research-into-policy process. Briefly put, this implies the use of research knowledge as a direct input into specific instances of decision-making. This may not be its major role, however. Several theoretical formulations and many empirical studies have argued that the role of social research fits better into an "enlightenment model". To quote Carol Weiss:

> Evidence suggests that government officials use research less to arrive at solutions than to orient themselves to problems. They use research to help them think about issues and define the problematics of a situation, to gain new ideas and new perspectives. They use research to help *formulate* problems and to set the agenda for future policy actions. And much of this is not deliberate, direct, and targeted, but a result of long-term percolation of social science concepts, theories and findings into the climate of informed opinion (Weiss, 1976, p. 534; see also Premfors, 1979).

Another important insight from the research on knowledge utilisation argues that the extent and forms of use are largely determined by the character of policy-making processes (see e.g. Rich, 1981). In line with this argument we would expect considerable variation in research utilisation between policy sectors. Janet Weiss (1979) has identified important characteristics of policy sectors which seem important in explaining utilisation; in the third section below I will use her formulations in an analysis of the policy sector of higher education.

Research on Higher Education in Sweden: An Overview

It began in the 1930s. A government *ad hoc* commission was appointed in 1933 to investigate the supply and demand for university places and university graduates. The commission was set up against the backcloth of increasing student numbers and a fear of what had hitherto not been experienced in Swedish higher education: graduate unemployment. A statistician at the University of Lund, Sven Wicksell, and a civil servant, Tor Jerneman, were asked to perform the study. Data collection was not an easy task (despite the limited size of the Swedish higher education system: less than 2000 new students a year) since no aggregate statistics on students and their performance in the labour market was available on a nation-wide basis. The methodology and general framework of their study (published as SOU, 1935, 52) would, however, prove to be very influential on future efforts in the same vein. One of their substantive proposals was for a national system of higher education statistics. That proposal was adopted by the Swedish *Riksdag* and the new statistical system began operation in 1937. However, it turned out to be much less ambitious than originally conceived by the Wicksell-Jerneman Commission (see SOU, 1979, 47, pp. 16f).

The next major round of national policy-making came immediately after World War II. A University Commission was appointed in 1945. Its work was, however, focused on the creation of new teaching and research positions, and its deliberations contained little research apart from the simplest fact-gathering. More important from the point of view of higher education research was the work of another *ad hoc* commission. In 1946, the Minister of Education appointed a Student Aid Commission. Headed by Ragnar Edenman, himself a future Minister (and a political scientist by training), the Commission asked a professor of statistics at the University of Lund, Carl Erik Quensel, and his assistant, Sven Moberg, to conduct research on the social background and attainment of students. The Commission published its report in 1948 (SOU, 1948, 42). Drawing on the research of Quensel and Moberg, it argued that there existed among Swedish youth a substantial "reserve of ability" (the term itself is said to have been coined by Edenman) which, given the appropriate support, could manage to study at university level. Sven Moberg later continued the analysis of the data in his doctoral dissertation (Moberg, 1951).

In 1955, the time was ripe for another major *ad hoc* commission, the 1955 University Commission. Ragnar Edenman was again appointed chairman with Sven Moberg as head secretary. Compared to the 1945 University Commission its terms of reference were considerably broader. It was to inquire into all major aspects of university education in Sweden, including quantitative developments, teaching and learning, research, and governance. A number of ambitious analyses were initiated at an early stage. In particular, the research focused on the "reserve of ability" problem (Härnqvist, 1958) and the manpower needs of the Swedish economy. It also made forecasts of student demand. In the area of governance it asked for the assistance of *Statskontoret* (the Swedish Agency for Administrative Development) which produced a special report on the topic (SOU, 1963, 11; see below).

A decision by the Swedish *Riksdag* in 1956 meant that the National Bureau of Statistics, which in 1937 was given responsibility in this area, could start developing a more elaborate system of higher education statistics. In the late 1950s the 1955 University Commissions proposed that a separate institute be created for manpower forecasting. It argued that the institute should be an independent body possessing its own resources. While the Cabinet generally accepted the idea of a unit for manpower forecasts, it decided to make it part of the National Labour Market Board. A group had actually been active within that agency since 1956, and the decision by the Cabinet and the *Riksdag* only meant additional resources for an on-going activity. However, these allowed the Board to intensify its work relating to manpower forecasting. In particular, much energy was spent on methodological development in this field by economists and statisticians. The overall aim was, in line with recommendations of the 1955 University Commission, to develop a forecasting model covering the entire Swedish labour market.

The problem of student aid was addressed by a second commission appointed in 1959. It was chaired by Olof Palme, future Minister of Education and Prime Minister. It embarked upon a fairly ambitious programme of analysis with respect to the social recruitment and living conditions of students (SOU, 1963, 44, 53 and 74).

Barely were the forecasts and proposals concerning student numbers published by the 1955 University Commission before they were made obsolete by reality. The student explosion incited the creation within the Ministry of Education of a special forecasting group (known as the "P-Group"). It was headed by Sven Moberg who had now been appointed under-secretary in the Ministry. (Ragnar Edenman became Minister of Education in 1957; he was succeeded as chairman of the 1955 University Commission by Torgny Segerstedt, professor of sociology and *rector magnificus* of Uppsala University.) The pressure of numbers continued and in 1963 the Minister appointed an *ad hoc* commission to investigate alternative courses of action in coping with expansion. The Commission (known as "U63") was chaired by Sven Moberg. Its terms of reference were primarily concerned with quantitative aspects of policy, and the Commission was asked to make cost analyses of three alternatives for expansion. The analytic work of U63 mainly dealt with problems of costs, but much energy was also spent on the decision about where to locate the four new institutions it proposed. In addition, a study was commissioned on the impact of higher education institutions on the regional economy.

The work of the 1955 University Commission was the first sign that the pedagogical aspects of higher education were becoming an important concern for national policy-makers in Sweden. However, little research was involved in the Commission's deliberations. But in 1965 the reformed Chancellor's Office appointed a major commission of its own, with the explicit task of investigating the area of university pedagogics. Torgny Segerstedt became the chairman of the Commission (known as "UPU") and among its members were several well-known educational researchers. UPU was asked to address the whole range of issues associated with teaching and learning in higher education in view of improving the efficacy of instruction. The Commission on University Pedagogics worked for 5 years and produced an impressive number of reports. Many of these were directly based on pedagogical experiments and research projects which the Commission had initiated. The final report of UPU, published in 1970, was characterised by a firm belief in the possibilities of educational technology within a rationalistic framework of teaching and learning (see below).

Half-way through its work UPU proposed that a permanent institutional framework be created for pedagogical R & D activities in Swedish higher education. The proposal was favourably received, and from 1969 onwards R & D units began to be set up within the institutions. In 1970 the Chancellor's Office established its own R & D unit.

Meanwhile Sweden had in 1968 seen the appointment of another *ad hoc* commission for higher education, the well-known U68. Its terms of reference were very broad. Although largely confined to undergraduate education, it was asked to inquire into the status of all post-secondary education in Sweden. In particular it was to address issues of quantitative planning, the localisation of institutions and governance. With respect to the first two areas, the Commission soon launched an ambitious programme of research. A major topic was manpower planning. The Forecasting Institute – which had in 1964 been moved from the Labour Market Board to the National Bureau of Statistics – was asked to assist U68 in developing a "flow model" of the entire post-secondary sector. The Institute had in fact started that work already in 1967. U68 also commissioned research from economists concerning the feasibility of using cost-benefit analysis as a basis for quantitative planning in higher education. The social composition of the student body was another important topic in the research programme of U68. With reference to this problem we may note that the National Bureau of Statistics had already started to collect statistics on a regular basis in 1962. Every student who enrolled was asked to provide information on his or her social background. Now U68 asked a sociologist at the University of Lund to analyse this and other sets of data on social recruitment to higher education. Social recruitment was also a prominent feature of the research commissioned in the area of regionalisation. This research was performed by a team of geographers at the University of Umeå.

An important area which had largely been left outside the mandate of the U68 Commission was admission policy. The reason was not a lack of concern, but the fact that another *ad hoc* commission had been set up in 1965 to investigate this policy problem. That commission – the so-called *kompetens-utredningen* – launched an ambitious programme of analysis from 1966 onwards. The research mainly consisted of knowledge reviews relating to the predicative value of various admission criteria in higher education, including reviews of research and experiences of other countries. Several educational psychologists were brought in to assist the Commission in its work. The final report was published in 1970 (SOU, 1970, 21; research reports were also published in SOU, 1968, 25 and SOU, 1970, 20). In 1972, the Swedish *Riksdag* adopted a series of guidelines for important reforms of admission policy, but it also stated that further inquiry was needed. Another *ad hoc* commission – the *kompetenskommittén* – was set up for that purpose. Again, experts in educational psychology were brought in (mainly from the University of Umeå), this time to assist, in particular, in the development of an aptitude test to be used in a reformed admission system in higher education (see SOU, 1974, 41).

Following its creation in 1970, the R & D unit of the Chancellor's Office soon developed into the most important sponsor of Swedish higher education research. To begin with it inherited many of the projects initiated by UPU. This inevitably implied a focus on pedagogical research. Remarkably soon, however, a drift away from educational technology and didactic rationalisation began (Premfors & Wittrock, 1979; Johansson, 1982). The R & D programme was focused on three sub-programmes: research, local development projects, and pre- and in-service training of teachers. The subprogrammes were already from the start characterised by considerable autonomy and they developed in quite different directions.

The research programme was, as indicated, initially dominated by research on didactical problems. As many as 13 out of a total of 16 projects were performed at departments of pedagogy or psychology in 1971. In 1975, the number of academic disciplines involved were nine, including for example, history and political science. This marked development toward a multi-disciplinary approach was parallelled by a considerable broadening of the policy problems covered. In 1975, the proportion of research topics under the headings of "the internal work of higher education", "higher education in society", and "higher education as a system; structure and governance" were 35, 42 and 23 per cent respectively. This broadness in terms of both disciplinary perspectives and problems treated has continued to characterise the research subprogramme in the late 1970s and early 1980s. Important emphases during the last few years have included the study of knowledge traditions in higher education (both non-academic and academic) and, perhaps even more significantly, research on research organisation and policy.

The subprogramme concerned with pre- and in-service training of teachers was given high priority by policy-makers. The objective was clearly to use pre- and in-service training as an important mechanism for disseminating R & D knowledge. Soon, however, this straightforward approach would prove quite unrealistic. The subprogramme has successively been transformed into a general programme of staff development in Swedish higher education. Its current links with other R & D activities are not uniquely intimate compared with those of many other parts of the National Board.

Although disposing of much larger resources than the research subprogramme, the development subprogramme was initially a minor activity of the central R & D unit. It largely consisted of the central administration of R & D activities within institutions. In the mid-1970s this changed rather abruptly. As part of the 1975 *Riksdag* decision for a major reform of Swedish higher education, the R & D unit was given the responsibility for evaluating the implementation of the reform. A major follow-up programme was launched as part of the development subprogramme of the R & D unit. The specific design of these projects has varied greatly. Some were given an action-research format. while others implied a fairly traditional commissioning of research performed at university departments. Most projects have now been reported, and current discussions with respect to the future of the follow-up programme point toward a transformation of it into a routinised programme for evaluation and policy studies. Furthermore, the Cabinet appointed in 1979 an *ad hoc* commission consisting of MPs whose task was to review and draw politically relevant conclusions from the follow-up activities and other evidence of the implementation of the higher education reform. Due to political conflicts, the commission was dismantled before it could report in 1982.

Since the mid-1970s, the interest expressed by national policy-makers in the problems of research and research policy has increased considerably (see, for example, Premfors, 1979a). This has also been reflected in the growth of various kinds of research on research. A number of *ad hoc* commissions have worked in the area, many of them producing important new knowledge.

A similar trend towards a greater emphasis on the research function in higher education has characterised a set of activities not mentioned earlier in this account. This is the evaluation programme carried out by the *Riksrevisions-verket* (the National Audit Bureau). This central agency reviews all government agencies in the cause of promoting efficiency and effectiveness. Starting in about 1970, the NAB has carried out close on 50 projects related to higher education. While some have been very limited in time and scope, others have been quite ambitious evaluations of major functions in higher education. Here as well we can note an increasing interest in the research function of higher education.

Finally, another body supports research on higher education, particularly on the research function. This is the *Forskningsrådsnämnden* (the Council for the Coordination and Planning of Research). It is currently engaged in launching a set of projects under the heading of "the role of the university in the Swedish research system". It is also involved in a major evaluation project on the Swedish student aid system.

*   *   *

The growth of research on higher education in Sweden since the early efforts in the 1930s is by all counts impressive. In terms of quantity, the development outlined above has shown how isolated efforts associated with the work of *ad hoc* commissions in the 1930s and 1940s have developed into the plethora of projects in the 1970s and early 1980s. While the early efforts were primarily focused on the input (student recruitment) and output (number of graduates and their subsequent absorption in the labour market) aspects, research has successively come to include almost every conceivable aspect of the higher education system. Following a preoccupation with the educational process from the mid-1960s, the early 1970s saw a shift of emphasis toward other processes and structures in higher education, including, from the late 1970s, a growing interest in the research function of the system. The predominance of statistical and pedagogical approaches to the study of higher education has successively been replaced by the involvement of almost the whole range of social and behavioural sciences as well as some of the humanities.

This impressive growth of higher education research has been intimately linked with the development of government policy in the area. As was demonstrated, the early efforts virtually all occurred within the context of *ad hoc* commissions (see Husén, 1976). Two processes of institutionalisation have diminished this role of *ad hoc* commissions for the enterprise of higher education research. First, beginning already in the 1930s but gaining additional momentum from the late 1950s, an important institutional structure has been created for statistically oriented analysis. Second, about 1970 the build-up started of both a central R & D programme and local R & D units within the institutions. Despite fairly limited resources, in particular for the research sub-programme within the National Board of Universities and Colleges, the central R & D programme has succeeded in initiating and supporting a very substantial research effort, an effort which seems to have no or few equivalents in comparable countries.

Very little research on higher education has been initiated outside these three settings – the *ad hoc* commissions, the agencies responsible for statistical analysis of various kinds, and the R & D programme of the National Board – and consequently, few research efforts have been financed through the regular channels of research funding such as general university funds or the research councils. There may be an increasing tendency for other agencies than the National Board to become involved; apart from the examples cited above, there is, for instance a recently launched project on the work environment of academics financed by *Arbetarskyddsfonden*, a foundation for research and development activities in the field of working life and industrial democracy.

Upon reflection the predominance of a few public bodies should come as no surprise. Apart from pedagogy, higher education is no "natural" research area for any discipline. And pedagogical researchers have been heavily preoccupied with school reforms and other educational problems outside higher education. More than most policy sectors, higher education has, in other words, been dependent on earmarked resources for research and development in order to make use of the services of outside researchers.

Research-into Policy: Five Case Studies

Having outlined the development of Swedish research on higher education, we now address directly the problem of the use of research in policy-making. Each of the five policy dimensions mentioned above is analysed according to the following format. First, I outline briefly what I consider to be the main policy problems in the area. Second, Swedish policy developments are described. Finally, I examine the evidence to hand concerning the role of research in policy formulation.

Quantitative Planning

The basic policy problems here concern the determination of the overall student numbers in higher education as well as their distribution between different fields of study and institutions. Elsewhere I have argued that, put simply, the problems which governments face in quantitative planning can be expressed as a choice between two basic approaches (Premfors, 1980). On the one hand they may rely on the demand for places expressed by qualified individuals; this is what may be termed a *private demand* approach. On the other hand, governments may decide to provide places in higher education according to some definition of society's need for trained people; this is the *social demand* approach. The two approaches pose different analytical problems. The main task within the context of the private demand approach is, of course, to predict future levels of student demand and plan the allocation of resources accordingly. If a social demand approach is adhered to in quantitative planning, some conception – more or less explicit – of society's need for various types of graduates is needed. The latter type of analysis can of course be performed in a very crude and *ad hoc* fashion in response to perceived imbalances between supply and demand. However, there are also more elaborate analytical techniques available, such as manpower planning. In brief, this approach attempts to specify a desired future manpower structure in terms of the number of individuals needed with specific skills, and to translate that need into numbers and types of graduates. The major difficulty involved is to make sufficiently accurate and detailed forecasts of future manpower requirements. A partly competing analytical approach is more market-oriented and is commonly termed the rate-of-return-approach. In brief, it purports to determine the profitability for the economy of investments in educational programmes. An important assumption of this approach, and many would argue its chief weakness, is that individual earnings reflect the "social value" of various forms of training.

Traditionally, Swedish policy on student numbers relied on a combination of private and social demand. Private demand was allowed to determine numbers in the so-called free faculties of the universities, encompassing most programmes and courses in the humanities, law, and social and natural sciences. All applicants from upper-secondary schools possessing the appropriate certificate were allowed to enter such courses in higher education. However, many programmes also practised restricted admission. This was true for, for example, medicine, dentistry, and technology. No doubt the main reason for restricted entry was the obvious link of most of these programmes with the labour market. In addition, many of them were relatively expensive.

The 1955 University Commission did not question the inherited policy of combining open and restricted admission. In general, it strongly emphasised the value of overall higher education expansion. However, current trends pointed to a future substantial mismatch between supply and demand in the humanities. But the predicted surplus did not convince the Commission of the necessity to restrict student numbers in that area. Such a policy measure would be too detrimental to other values such as flexibility, individual freedom of choice and social justice (SOU, 1959, 45).

However, the accelerating enrolment in the early 1960s made many policy-makers begin to doubt the feasibility of keeping the free faculties open to the vagaries of private demand. Still, the work of the U63 Commission confirmed that the traditional policy could rally a majority. The problems of exploding costs and numbers should, according to the Commission, be approached through other measures, such as intensified student counselling, improvement of the efficacy of instruction, and reforms of the study organisation in the free faculties (SOU, 1965, 11).

However, the terms of reference of U68 indicated that a policy departure was in the air. The Commission soon embarked upon the formulation of a proposal for a "total dimensioning" or a *numerus clausus* covering the entire post-secondary system in Sweden. In its final report (SOU, 1973, 2) it outlined a planning model to that effect. In brief it implied that the total number of places in higher education should be determined on a yearly basis through decisions in the Swedish parliament. These decisions should also include the allocation of places to a complex structure of vocational areas, study programmes and courses, although there would be some leeway for regional bodies and institutions in determining the exact distribution. In general, the planning model included three factors or types of considerations: private demand, social demand as determined by manpower analyses, and, equally important, cost considerations. Decisions concerning student numbers were basically political, and would result from the interplay between these three types of considerations. Following a certain delay due to political developments in Sweden (for details, see Premfors, 1979a), the new system for quantitative planning was implemented in 1979.

What has been the role of research in the policy developments briefly sketched above? First, research on the overall contribution of higher education and research to economic and technological development has been cited in support of expansion. At the international level research in economics on the importance of investments in human capital gained momentum in the 1950s. An important result was the identification of the so-called residual factor, mainly consisting of technological R & D and training (for an overview, see, for example, Sobel, 1978). This research was quoted extensively in international debate, and quickly spread through the network of international organisations concerned with economic, scientific and educational policy. It provided an important argument for investment in research and education. In the Swedish context, we may note the role in this process of an economics professor, Ingvar Svennilson, who was also a member of the 1955 University Commission. His views, and the Commission's adoption of them, are reflected in the Commission's major report on quantitative developments (SOU, 1959, 45, p. 166). But the message was also spread in other contexts, particularly perhaps through Sweden's participation in international discussions.

In the late 1960s this element of pervasive expansionist ideology began to be questioned (see Premfors, 1980, Ch 4). This was probably due both to contrary research findings and actual events in higher education, especially growing graduate unemployment and receding economic growth. In later Swedish policy documents the assumption that investment in higher education contributes to economic growth is often present, but in less straightforward and optimistic terms. Most recently, however, the theme is again frequently used, but now with particular reference to research. (The special case of regionalisation is discussed below.)

As we have seen in Sweden, much effort has been aimed at developing the methodology of manpower forecasting. Starting in the 1930s with the work of the Wicksell-Jerneman Commission studies of the labour market for graduates have been carried out regularly. The 1955 University Commission made such studies in a number of professional fields, complaining that it could not cover the entire labour market for university graduates. But, in addition, a plethora of other commissions undertook manpower analyses in specific areas. To make a general statement about the utilisation of this research in policy-making is extremely difficult. An interesting attempt to do so was, however, made by the recent commission on higher education statistics (SOU, 1979, 80). Its analysis of utilisation included the areas of technical personnel with advanced training, social workers, teachers, and librarians. It might be a bit rash to draw general conclusions from the analysis of a limited number of areas, but I doubt if anyone reading the report could dispute the fact that when manpower forecasts have entered policy deliberations they have essentially been utilised as "partisan analysis". These forecasts have generally been so fraught with implicit or explicit values and assumptions, so imbued with methodological difficulties, and have entered policy processes so pervaded by interest group conflicts, that in no single instance do they seem to have been accepted as "authoritative".

From the late 1950s onwards attempts were being made to develop manpower forecasts which would cover the entire labour market. Much energy was spent on methodological work, and here statisticians and economists were heavily involved. In 1967, this development work intensified within the Forecasting Institute of the National Bureau of Statistics, and when U68 was appointed it asked specifically for a comprehensive "flow analysis" linking the entire post-secondary system of education and the labour market. Throughout, however, there existed within the Commission considerable doubts about the effort. Its final report clearly expresses such doubts, and one finds upon closer inspection that the U68 planning model reserves relatively little room for manpower analysis. It is viewed as a complementary source of information to be used in combination with other considerations in the essentially political process of quantitative planning. This relatively modest role for manpower planning based on forecasts is rarely recognised by commentators. No doubt this is partly due to the fact that the Commission so strongly emphasized the need to "vocationalise" the higher education system as a whole (see Bladh, 1982).

U68 also investigated the feasibility of using the rate-of-return approach in determining social demand. A number of Swedish economists were at the time quite enthusiastic about using this tool in higher education planning. The Commission asked for a special report on the topic (SOU, 1972, 23). However, the enthusiasm was never shared by the Commission members. Undoubtedly this was essentially due to the ideological inclinations of the core members. They could not accept the assumption of the rate-of-return approach that the current distribution of income is a valid measure of the contribution of particular occupations to social welfare.

But forecasts have not only been made with respect to manpower needs. Commissions and government agencies have also tried to predict future levels of private demand. To cut a rather long story short, Swedish efforts in this area have not been particularly successful. This is true of all major forecasts of the overall level of student demand. They failed to predict the magnitude of growth in the late 1950s and during the 1960s; they did not in any way foresee the downturn of student demand from around 1970. They were, in addition, grossly inaccurate in predicting the distribution of demand between different fields of study. These observations concerning the lack of success in forecasts of private demand do not of course answer the question of utilisation. No doubt the forecasts were taken into account in planning processes, but quite early on they were viewed with considerable scepticism, as can be witnessed in the U63 report from 1965. The Commission even refused to call them forecasts; instead it termed them "examples" of possible developments (SOU, 1965, 11). Evidently the "forecasts" actually used were more in the nature of general "guesstimates" than precise predictions.

The case of U68 may perhaps illustrate that once such perceptions of future developments have spread, they are difficult to change. The Commission very reluctantly, or so it seemed, realised that student demand was slackening from 1970 onwards. Some would even argue that they never adjusted to the new situation. In a sense this is quite understandable, considering that the Commission's proposals for a system-wide *numerus clausus* was more or less explicitly motivated by the experiences of uncontrolled growth in the 1960s.

*   *   *

In sum, I would like to characterise the role of research in quantitative planning in the following manner. First, research pointing to the important contribution of higher education to economic development was clearly used by the majority of policy-makers supporting the unprecedented expansion of the 1950s and 1960s. Here we encountered a nice illustration of partisan use of research. Second, further examples of partisan use are found in the area of manpower forecasting for specific professions. Third, research in the form of methodological development in forecasting has been important in two ways. On the one hand, from the work of Wicksell-Jerneman in the 1930s manpower planning has at least to some extent been viewed as feasible. On the other hand, discussions of methodological difficulties, especially within the U68 Commission, showed the limits of manpower planning as well as the value assumptions of the rate-of-return approach.

With respect to the major policy departure in quantitative planning during our period of investigation, the decision in 1975 to adopt a system-wide *numerus clausus* and thus reduce radically the role of private demand, research played a minor role. This change of policy must be explained as the outcome of a complex political process (Premfors, 1980).

Social Recruitment

The policy problem is quite simple: How can the enrolment of students be affected so that it reflects the social composition of the population at large? Once the general problem is identified, however, this policy dimension turns out to be not only controversial but also exceedingly complex. A plethora of policy measures are possible – none of which promises to be very effective and all of which to some extent threaten other basic values in higher education policy.

Swedish policy developments may briefly be characterised as follows. The traditional policy was narrow in the sense that it was largely only concerned with two instruments: admission and student aid. The traditional admission policy was characterised by the dualism of free vs. restricted faculties. In the former, students were admitted provided they had a certificate from the academic part of upper-secondary education. In the restricted faculties, admission depended on academic merits. As for student aid, a plethora of existing forms were in 1965 replaced by a single comprehensive system. The new system implied, *inter alia*, the aim of making students independent of parental contributions. It was essentially a loans system, with a minor grant component.

Policy developments from the mid-1960s have implied growing complexity in a number of directions. First, many more aspects of higher education apart from admission regulations and student aid have been considered important to social recruitment. These have included the localisation of institutions, the status of programmes and institutions, governance, curricula, and methods of teaching and learning. In short, the value of social equality became so pervasive in higher education policy that virtually all aspects of the system were to some extent viewed as potential means toward the pursuit of that goal. Second, while policy debates were until the late 1960s only concerned with recruitment in social class terms, since then adult and female participation in higher education have been equally important. Finally, admission policy has become exceedingly complex.

In the late 1960s, the Competence Committee mentioned above recommended that a limited number of courses in the universities should be opened to applicants from upper-secondary education without formal credentials. In practice, such exceptions had already been made on an individual basis in an increasing number of instances. But now it would apply to many more potential applicants. This was the first phase of the well-known 25:5 scheme in Swedish admission policy (for the full story, see Kim, 1982). Later policy developments meant the creation of a complex quota system covering the entire post-secondary system. Compared with traditional policy, it means that much greater weight is given to non-academic merits, primarily age and work-experience.

During recent years public debate and, at least to some extent, policy-making have been characterised by something of a "backlash". The catchword is quality, not social equality. In admission policy small, but significant, changes have aimed at restoring the importance of formal academic merits.

When and in what ways has research entered policy deliberations? As pointed out earlier, much research in Sweden had already been devoted to the problem of social class recruitment in the 1940s and 1950s. Both the 1946 Student Aid Commission and the 1955 University Commission initiated major studies of the "reserve of talent" problem. In both instances it was convincingly shown that such reserves existed. A substantial proportion of working class youth did not pursue higher education, despite their possessing the ability to do so. In both instances research was cited by the respective commissions in support of expansion. More of the same was needed, be it student aid or number of places. However, there was growing insight concerning the successive nature of the selection process in education. Social selection occurred throughout the entire educational system, and, to put it bluntly, there was not very much one could do in higher education. In terms of social equality, lower levels of education were perhaps more important. This general insight entered the deliberations of the 1959 Student Aid Commission. From Olof Ruin's detailed study (1979; Ruin, a political scientist, worked for the Commission, first as secretary and later as expert) we also learn of another research impact. A young economist, Ingemar Ståhl, argued forcefully within the Commission in favour of a loans system. On the basis of income statistics, he pointed out that in a long-term perspective such a system might well be more socially equitable than a grants system. After all, today's students are tomorrow's high-income earners. Ruin shows in his analysis that whereas a majority of commission members were initially intent on proposing a grants system, they came down in the end in favour of what was essentially a loans system. No doubt, research insights about the selection process and about income distribution in the long run both played an important role in this case of policy departure.

The research brought into the deliberations of the *kompetenskommittén* in the late 1960s undoubtedly served to undermine firm beliefs in the predictive value of academic merits for student performance in higher education. In somewhat vague terms, many policy-makers began to adhere to a view which distinguished between "real" competence and academic merit. This distinction was one of the basic underlying ideas of the subsequent reform of admission policy.

More or less routine statistics fuelled policy debates with respect to social recruitment during the entire period. Analyses on the basis of such data showed some progress, but far removed from the dramatic changes that egalitarians had hoped for. Some observers chose to look at overall figures which pointed to a quite considerable improvement in working-class participation during the 1960s. Others, like the researchers working for U68, emphasised the internal stratification of the higher education system, and argued from this observation point that virtually all that had happened was that working-class students had entered the least prestigious parts of higher education. The elite programmes were more than ever the preserve of the offspring of the upper and middle classes (SOU, 1971, 61). Meanwhile the routine monitoring of student recruitment became increasingly difficult, due to deteriorating statistics, and in the mid-1970s Swedish policy-makers knew little about what was in fact happening. In the late 1970s, however, it became increasingly clear that virtually nothing had been accomplished during that decade in terms of social equalisation. Had it not been for the 25:5 scheme, the proportion of working-class students would in all probability have decreased significantly.

No large-scale evaluation effort was undertaken with respect to the 25:5 scheme until carried out within the context of the major follow-up programme mentioned above. With regard to social recruitment, another follow-up project was also initiated. It concerned long-term trends in social class participation and was based on a quite unique Swedish data base containing the educational careers of a large number of individuals. I cannot do justice to the findings of this research here; let me just note that one report from the project very nicely illustrates a general problem of the application of social research to policy problems. The report, entitled "Equality in Progress?", concludes that the answer to the question of whether social equality has increased or not in recent decades depends on precise definitions and general perspectives (Svensson, 1980).

The follow-up project aimed at evaluating the new admission system also illustrates the problem of conclusive findings, but also points to the difficulties of in-house evaluations. The first major report adopted a critical stance toward many important features of the new admission system. This caused considerable controversy within the National Board of Universities and Colleges, and even a delay in publication. In particular the report questioned the basic idea of uniformity and centralisation in admission to higher education. It was argued that equal treatment in admission procedures could in fact create inequities of a worse kind than those that the current procedures were supposed to prevent. In terms of the impact of the new system, the report could show that women were in fact at a disadvantage in competing for places in the more attractive programmes (Kim, 1979). Some of the report's findings were clearly *gefundenes Fressen* for the opponents of the new admission policy. The supporters of that policy retorted that the research was methodologically weak, that most findings were inconclusive for other reasons, and, in particular, that too short a period had elapsed since the new policy was put into effect. Still, the findings were used by the political leadership in Swedish higher education in support of a number of small modifications of admission policy – which, however, clearly point toward a change of direction.

*   *   *

Research relevant to the problem of social equality in higher education has clearly added to our knowledge and understanding of the issues involved. In the 1940s and 1950s, the studies of the "reserve of talent" phenomenon clearly strengthened the expansionist coalition. Thus social equality could be added to economic growth as a major benefit resulting from an overall expansion of higher education. More places to those qualified, in combination with more generous student aid, would do the job.

Increasingly, however, this recipe proved, inadequate to many. Swedish higher education would instead have to change in many and more fundamental ways, in order to adjust to the needs of "new groups". Admission policy was changed radically. Research played a role, albeit a minor one, in pointing to the inadequacy of formal merits as predictors of attainment. Researchers also developed a scholastic aptitude test to be used by some applicants within the new admission scheme.

The next wave of research – spanning from analyses of routine statistics by the National Bureau of Statistics to sociological interpretations of existing data to detailed studies of reform implementation and impacts – fitted well into a growing pessimism concerning the possibilities of changing the social composition of higher education. The interest in social equality waned quickly from the mid-1970s, in Sweden as well as in most other countries (see Premfors, 1982b). Again, the major role of research has been to serve as political ammunition. Sometimes in some areas, when consensus reigns with respect to policy, research knowledge may approach a status where it is considered "authoritative". The expansion of higher education in the 1950s and 1960s was supported by what appeared to be a body of research knowledge of unusual "authoritativeness". Policy-makers primarily interested in economic growth and national competitiveness could unite with egalitarians in pursuing a policy of unprecendented expansion. A series of events – spanning from a critical examination of the research itself to feedback information on policy failures (which radicalised many egalitarians) to economic crisis – dissolved the expansionist coalition as well as eroded the "authoritativeness" of existing research knowledge.

Regionalisation

Elsewhere I have made a detailed study of the role of policy analysis and research in the policy of regionalisation in Swedish higher education (Premfors, 1982a). What follows is a brief summary of that study.

Two basic policy problems seem to appear in any policy of regionalisation. First, policy-makers will ask for the reasons behind regionalisation. What will it accomplish? Second, once the decision is taken to regionalise, there remains the problem of the specific localisation of institutions.

Sweden has since the 1950s made a fairly consistent effort to spread higher education resources across the country. In sharp contrast with the situation prevailing before this time, Swedes can now take at least some types of courses at the higher education level in virtually every town in the country. Three key decisions may be identified in this process of regionalisation: the creation in 1962 of the University of Umeå; the decision to set up four university branches taken in 1965; and the policy of regionalisation adopted in 1975 and based on the proposals of the U68 Commission. What, if any, has been the role of research in these decisions?

The creation of the University of Umeå involved little research. When exploding enrolments in higher education made a fifth university feasible in Sweden, the province of Norrland was the primary candidate for reasons of regional justice, and among the potential specific sites Umeå had in fact no serious rivals (Carlbom, 1970).

By contrast, both the U63 Commission, which proposed four new university branches in medium-sized towns, and the U68 Commission marshalled research evidence to support their proposals for further regionalisation. The latter commission was particularly ambitious. For example, it commissioned a major study from geographers at the University of Umeå concerning the social recruitment of students in a regional perspective. Both commissions tried hard to establish "objective" criteria for the choice of specific sites; neither of them was particularly successful.

The policy area of regionalisation provides us with a particularly clearcut illustration of what may be considered the "normal" pattern of research utilisation in complex policy-making processes. Research enters policy processes at the stage when most participants have already adopted relatively firm positions on major issues. Research is then used to elaborate such positions and to provide legitimacy. Contrary research evidence and cautionary remarks tend to be largely ignored.

Governance

The major problems in governance may be said to concern participation and autonomy. Who should be allowed to participate in decision-making in higher education? And what is the proper degree of autonomy for different decision-making levels and bodies? As that of most other countries of Western Europe, Swedish policy with respect to governance in higher education has changed dramatically in recent years (Premfors, 1980 and 1981).

Very briefly we may identify three major decision-making processes during our period of investigation. First, a number of important changes were implemented in 1964 and 1965, essentially on the basis of proposals from the 1955 University Commission. Second, the Swedish experience with student unrest in 1968 resulted in a series of "experimental activities" with respect to university governance from 1969 onwards (known as "FNYS"). Finally, governance was a key area of inquiry for U68, and subsequently a major part of the 1975/1977 higher education reform.

In terms of policy content, we may, again very briefly, identify the following patterns of change. The 1964 reform implied above all a considerable strengthening of the administrative resources in higher education, both at the central and local level. The major task of the Chancellor's Office – now transformed to a regular central agency with a head appointed by the Cabinet – would be "rolling planning" of all university-level education in Sweden. Equally important, however, was the build-up of administration at the level of institutions. Like all university systems of the Continental tradition, that of Sweden had hitherto been characterised by weak management at the university level. The system had been run largely by Ministry officials at the centre in negotiation with individual professors – although the rector, a professor elected by his peers, had become increasingly important in the postwar years. The 1965 reform somewhat weakened the position of full professors within the institution. Tenured, non-professorial staff were given representation on

Faculties. Students and junior staff also benefited from the reform by being represented on advisory bodies at the departmental level. In sum, the traditional professor's university was modified but not radically changed through reforms in the mid-1960s.

The "FNYS" activities were a direct response to the student unrest of 1968. The general outcome, however, was a dismantling of the professor's university in favour of increased participation in governance by *all* major interest groups in higher education. A governance model based on "professional" authority was replaced by an interest group model. However, the new system was far from based on the one person – one vote principle. Students were nowhere allowed to form a majority in decision-making bodies. Still, the changes were radical enough, especially from the perspective of full professors. From now on they constituted only one interest group among many in formal decision-making bodies (expectedly, however, their influence was much greater than their formal position indicated).

The U68 proposals in many respects merely codified the changes brought about by the "FNYS" activities. But the reform finally adopted in 1977 implied many changes as well. First, one cherished principle of U68 was uniformity. Now the same basic model of governance would apply to all post-secondary education in Sweden. Second, governing bodies throughout the system would now include representatives of the "public interest", meaning political parties and interest group officials. The U68 Commission had even proposed that these representatives should constitute a two-thirds majority at the level of institutions. However, the uproar which this proposal caused at the universities forced the Social Democratic government to withdraw it. A compromise was hammered out with the Centre Party which briefly implied that the share of representatives of the public interest was reduced to one-third at the institutional level while a new regional level was created having a two-thirds majority of the public interest. Finally, the U68 proposals aimed at a considerable decentralisation of decision-making power in Swedish higher education. Although principally affecting "operational" decision-making and although the decentralisation mainly implied a shift of power from the central level to the top-level of institutions, this was nevertheless an important break with a long-term trend in Swedish higher education toward centralisation.

What has been the role of research in these policy developments in the area of governance? Among the major *ad hoc* commissions only the 1955 University Commission went beyond simple fact-gathering in its analysis of governance. As was mentioned earlier, the Commission asked the Swedish Agency for Administrative Development (*Statskontoret*) for assistance. This joint effort would turn out to engender an interesting conflict between contrasting governance or management ideologies. While the Commission's report on university governance (SOU, 1963, 9) was clearly influenced by the rationalistic doctrine espoused by the consultants, the latter would have liked to see more radical changes. The *Statskontoret* analysts argued that the universities ought to be viewed as any public bureaucracy experiencing the same management problems. The inherited "collegial" system of governance was outmoded. What was primarily needed was professional management and a strict division of labour between administration on one hand and teaching and research on the other. The conclusion was evident: Swedish universities needed a considerable build-up of administrative capabilities at all levels.

The 1955 University Commission could not agree with this severe criticism of the inherited forms of governance. The members of the Commission pointed to the special character of academic work and the practical difficulties involved in a strict division of administrative work and academic tasks. One manifestation of the rift between the Commission and *Statskontoret* was their disagreement over the issue of publication. The Commission did not want to see the *Statskontoret* report printed and published in the regular government series, but it lost on this issue. The *Statskontoret* report was published separately in the so-called SOU-series (SOU, 1963, 10). A study of this conflict has revealed some of the underlying motives of *Statskontoret's* behaviour (Nybom, 1980). Its organisational doctrine was a modern management ideology applied to the public sector. Professional leadership, functional division of labour, and a strong belief in economies of scale were important elements.

The "FNYS" reform was the first major response to the growing demands for participation in Swedish higher education. Although it was labelled an "experimental activity", it was clearly no "social experiment" in any qualified sense of that term. The scheme did include different models, but these were seen as adjustments to the varying conditions in different institutions and departments, rather than as parts of an "experiment". The activities were evaluated by a working group appointed by the Chancellor's Office. Although there was an attempt at systematic data collection and analysis, the mode of evaluation was essentially one of "interest group statements". Quite expectedly, no significant policy changes came out of the evaluation exercise. Almost everybody was somewhat disappointed, but virtually nobody wanted to return to the old power structure.

Beginning in the early 1970s, the central R & D programme has, as noted already, supported research related to problems of governance. University-based researchers – representing in particular political science and business economics – have conducted several projects on higher education organisation and decision-making. It was also mentioned above that a study of the organisational aspects of the 1977 reform was an important part of the follow-up programme of the National Board of Universities and Colleges. Have these research efforts affected policy-making in the area of governance? The question is difficult, not least because of the diversity of the research. And only the follow-up project has been directly linked with a clearly identifiable policy process. But even in this case we are confronted with a major problem: the process has not ended yet. It seems obvious, however, that the study – performed by a team of business economists and political scientists – will not result in any major changes. It was focused on the functions of the various decision-making bodies in the post-1977 system, and a number of recommendations for change were included in the final report (Lundin *et al.*, 1981). Most were very general and/or non-controversial, but some were not. Among the latter was the proposal that the regional boards be abolished. This, however, is a highly-politicised issue dividing the political parties and higher education opinion in general. No amount of research in the world could decide this issue. At present it looks as if the regional boards will be strengthened instead of abolished in the future. Many other recommendations were viewed with mixed feelings within the National Board; the final report first aroused some hostility and has then been quietly shelved.

Another piece of research related to problems of governance may prove to have a greater impact on policy. Its story illustrates a case where research affects the general public debate in a way which forces government to respond in some way or other. A team of researchers at the University of Umeå have, with the support of the research programme of the National Board, analysed the quantitative growth of various types of personnel in Swedish higher education. To cut a long and detailed story short, they showed that while the number of students and research positions have grown only slowly during the 1970s, this is not true of the number of teachers and administrators (Lane & Stenlund, 1981a and 1981b). Their analysis has been criticised from a number of angles, including their use of somewhat peculiar definitions. However, many in Swedish higher education, including several national policy-makers, believe that the analysis has highlighted a major problem: beginning well before the 1977 reform Swedish higher education has become heavily bureaucratised. The administration of the system is now too expensive and takes too much time away from the primary tasks of teaching and research. Whatever policy measures will be taken to solve these problems in the future, we may note that a particular piece of research at least helped the issue on to the national agenda.

What about the research which has been less directly linked with current policy and public debate? Although the empirical evidence is quite shaky, I would be prepared to argue that it might be justified to speak of enlightenment (or "endarkenment" if you are opposed to the developments). Expressed in very general terms, it seems as if many national policy-makers, including the most influential officials within the National Board, have come to hold the view that higher education is, after all, peculiar in terms of organisation and tasks. And this peculiarity imposes special requirements on a policy of governance. Some possible sources of such views can be listed. In the early 1970s, the notion of higher education as "organised anarchy" was introduced to Swedish policy-makers (Ramström, 1973). Another study pointed to the special requirements on governance which emanate from the nature of the research function in higher education (Husén, 1975). Political scientists have repeatedly stressed problems of implementation in higher education policy due to the nature of academic work and organisation (see, for example, Premfors, 1980, ch. 7).

However, the major channel of influence has probably been the plethora of conferences, advisory groups and the like which have been an integral part of the R & D activities of the National Board. Here researchers have been allowed to preach their post-rationalist message directly to policy-makers and their staff. And there is scattered evidence that it has percolated, much according to the enlightenment model, into policy deliberations. (See, for example, citations in the National Board Estimates of 1981, and the Board's rejoinder to a National Audit Bureau report on the evaluation activities of the Board.) Admittedly, other evidence can be cited which points in the opposite direction. This would be true, for example, of many recent policy documents concerned with research in higher education. They are often permeated with a rationalistic belief in the possibilities of detailed planning and streamlined management.

*   *   *

Research on governance must be attributed a minor role in the policy-making processes which brought about such radical changes in Swedish higher education in the 1960s and 1970s. The answer given to the basic policy questions concerning the proper degrees of participation and autonomy has depended on the strength of different interest groups and political parties. But we have also noted the underlying issue of the peculiarity of higher education. Here prevailing ideas in organisational research may influence policy. *Statskontoret* said a firm "no" in the early 1960s; the 1955 University Commission's view was a "maybe not so different after all"; U68 leaned towards a "no"; and today many national policy-makers tend toward a "yes". The last-named will, however, experience what is still the major weakness of post-rationalist theories of organisation and decision-making: they are good at criticism and description but poor at prescription.

Teaching and Learning

This is in many respects a different policy area. In particular it is at the centre of what Martin Trow (1975) termed the private life of higher education. While national policy may certainly affect teaching and learning processes, there are obvious limits to its effectiveness. The final control in this area rests with individual teachers and students.

A national policy for teaching and learning in higher education is a relatively late phenomenon in Sweden. Obviously the absence of a national policy reflected the low level of interest in issues of teaching and learning within institutions. Torsten Husén's personal experience may illustrate the point: in 1956 he published a pedagogical handbook for university teachers – he sold very few copies . . . (Husén, 1982). The 1955 University Commission represented in fact the first ambitious attempt to deal with teaching and learning in Swedish higher education. The Commission argued that the emphasis on teaching must become much greater in Sweden than has so far been the case. A major proposal concerned the creation of positions as university lecturers whose sole task would be undergraduate teaching. As for teaching methods, the Commission strongly recommended a development away from infrequent lectures in front of mass audiences toward small group lectures and seminars, a development which has characterised Swedish higher education ever since.

The pressure of numbers and soaring costs in the early 1960s greatly stimulated the interest in teaching and learning in Swedish higher education. From the point of view of national policy-making, it was chiefly a question of efficiency. Routine statistics and other data seemed to indicate that much could be done to improve matters, especially in the free faculties of the universities. There, in particular, attrition rates were high and the periods of study often extremely long. In order to alleviate such problems, a large number of policy measures were adopted from about 1964. Three types of measures were deemed particularly important although many more were motivated by their contribution to the efficiency of teaching and learning. First, the study organisation of the free faculties was reformed. Briefly put, the aim was to force students to adhere to a limited set of options, options which would be more "useful" to themselves and society at large. The proposal – known at the time as "UKAS" – became highly controversial and was the chief substantial element of the student protests in 1968. When finally implemented in a modified and watered-down version (known as "PUKAS") from 1969 onwards, it soon proved to be largely ineffective. Second, resources for study administration and counselling were greatly increased from the mid-1960s. (This is actually a large part of the "bureaucratisation" which has marked Swedish higher education since the 1960s.) Third, and finally, the increasing national concern for teaching and learning was manifested in the programmes for pre- and in-service training of teachers and for R & D activities which have been described in some detail already.

In this last area, the Commission on University Pedagogics (UPU) was particularly important. When rereading its final report from 1970, one is struck by the radical nature of its views and vision. The report expresses a firm belief in the possibilities of educational technology and systematic evaluation of educational processes. Briefly, the teaching process was viewed as consisting of a number of identifiable components. The specific contribution of each component to the efficiency of the process as a whole could be measured and evaluated – provided that objectives were clearly stated. Such objectives were possible to formulate at all levels, the Commission stated, and it outlined how this could be accomplished (UPU, 1970; see also Franke-Wikberg & Lundgren, 1980).

The work of UPU between 1965 and 1970 represented the high point of interest in the efficiency of teaching and learning in Swedish higher education. In the early 1970s policy-makers largely shifted their attention to other problems. No doubt this was partly due to the slackening of student demand; the interest in the efficiency of instruction was felt to be less motivated. In recent years we may again note an increasing concern with efficiency, particularly with respect to postgraduate education. But the visions of UPU will in all probability not reappear. There is a postrationalism in pedagogics as well.

What has been the role of research in national policy developments with respect to teaching and learning? The analysis and policy formulation of the 1955 University Commission involved little pedagogical research. The appointment of UPU, however, signified the arrival of pedagogical researchers to positions of influence in Swedish higher education policy. They loomed large both in the membership and the staff of the Commission. And, as mentioned earlier, UPU soon involved a large number of educational researchers in their work through commissioned studies. As much as UPU itself, these research projects were permeated by the current ideas of educational technologies and rationalistic evaluation.

In the mid-1960s many educational researchers and policy-makers took for granted that the output of graduates was a relatively reliable measure of efficiency. Students who did not manage to obtain a full degree within a reasonable period of time were regarded as failures and as obvious evidence of inefficiency. This was certainly the initial position of UPU and of the Chancellor's Office. Urban Dahllöf (then at the Department of Education at the University of Gothenburg; he had during a brief period been the head secretary of UPU) could, in a secondary analysis of UPU data, show that this measure was questionable if the stated objectives of students were taken into account. A large proportion of them had in fact never intended to pursue a full degree (Dahllöf, 1968). No doubt this finding had important implications for policy, including the current attempts to reform the study organisation of the universities (see Elgqvist-Salzman, 1973).

In many ways UPU was already obsolete when its final report was published in 1970. Research and public debate on teaching and learning processes in higher education soon focused on more "qualitative" problems. Increasingly, research efforts started explicitly from a severe critique of the educational technology paradigm. In particular, a research team headed by Ference Marton of the University of Gothenburg would prove to be influential. In projects supported by the research programme of the National Board, Marton and others have emphasised strongly the need for tailoring teaching and learning strategies to the variable character of individual disciplines. They have also criticised traditional evaluation methods for being overly concerned with superficial, quantitative aspects of learning (see esp. Marton *et al,* 1977). While the research by the Marton team has been widely acclaimed, it is impossible to state anything certain about its impact on policy and practice in higher education. We would expect it to have been an important contribution to the critique of simple notions of teaching and learning in higher education. But its positive influence is more difficult to discern. This clearly has to do with the nature of its conclusions. When policy-makers and practitioners in higher education ask for advice on teaching methods, the short answer from the Marton team is the somewhat discouraging "It depends!" The long answer may, on the other hand, be too demanding for policy and practice.

*   *   *

There is little doubt that national policy has been affected in many ways by research on teaching and learning processes. A particularly clear-cut case was that associated with Dahllöf's reanalysis of output data. And the significant paradigm shift which is illustrated by the work of UPU on one hand and that of the Marton team on the other has been reflected in policy documents. Research has clearly affected the level of awareness of pedagogical problems in higher education. The pertinent question then becomes: do policy documents and research reports effectively change practice? It is probably true that much has changed – but much has also stayed the same in the private life of Swedish higher education, unaffected by any paradigm or other kinds of shift occurring in the public life.

Policy Sector and Research Utilisation

The relationship between research and policy-making can be expected to vary considerably between policy sectors. For example, the problem of utilisation looks very different in sectors where decisions largely involve "hard technology" based on natural sciences, in comparison with social policy sectors. In the former, research knowledge stands a much better chance of being "authoritative" in policy-making.

In this section I will discuss some features of policy-making in higher education which seem to be relevant to the problem of research utilisation. The aspects or variables discussed are taken from a recent article by Janet Weiss (1979). She identifies five broad aspects of sectoral policy-making which seem particularly pertinent to the use of social science knowledge: the degree of centralisation in policy-making; the characteristics of policy-makers, especially their educational and professional background; the nature of decisions in the policy sector; the institutional history and procedures in linking research and policy; and, finally, the availability of alternative sources of information. In the sequel I will comment on each aspect in turn.

Centralisation

This aspect of policy-making seems relevant to research utilisation in many ways. In particular, however, it is reasonable to hypothesise that a relatively high degree of centralisation, implying *inter alia* a concentration of resources for planning and administration at the centre, would further efforts to mobilise research for decision-making. Centralisation also seems to determine to some extent the nature of the research undertaken; the research will largely be tailored to the needs of central decision-makers.

In an international perspective, the policy sector of higher education in Sweden is very centralised. The amount of central regulation and control has traditionally been considerable. Recent developments have, as indicated, implied an important effort to decentralise in many areas. While this decentralisation has been real, we should note some limitations. First, it has mainly concerned operational decisions. Central policy has in parallel become more comprehensive and ambitious, especially with respect to the time perspectives involved in planning. Second, the decentralisation of decision-making has largely stopped at the level of institutions. Finally, and as we have seen already, decision-making in Swedish higher education has now developed into an extremely elaborate process, involving every major interest. The point to be made here is that the decentralisation effort has not been of such a character as to change the capability of using research on the part of central authorities. Quite the contrary, I would argue, since the central level is now concentrating on tasks which seem more amenable to social research than those which have been decentralised (see below).

This said, however, it should also be noted that higher education as a policy sector seems to be relatively decentralised. As organisations, higher education institutions are often classified as professional or "organic". Their key tasks, teaching and research, are in the final instance controlled and assessed by a very limited network of specialists. These networks typically defy the formal authority relations of the organisation.

At least three points seem to follow from these observations. First, the relative centralisation of decision-making in Swedish higher education has probably been an important prerequisite for the considerable efforts made to initiate and support R & D activities. Second, the bulk of research on higher education has reflected the needs of central policy-makers. The type of R & D known as "institutional research" in the United States is largely absent in Sweden, or at least very weak. With the recent strengthening of the institutional level in decision-making, I predict that the demand for such research will increase in the Swedish setting. Finally, the decentralised nature of decisions concerning the primary activities of higher education, teaching and research, may have discouraged utilisation in these areas. Despite the heroic attempt by UPU to develop a technology for university teaching, the policy sector of higher education is far from having any such technology applicable to its core activities.

Policy-makers

It seems reasonable to hypothesise that the attitudes and training of policy-makers is relevant to the extent of research utilisation which occurs in a policy sector. A positive valuation of and an ability to grasp the subtleties of research would seem to further utilisation. At first glance this would make for a high propensity for research use in higher education policy-making. On closer inspection, however, the situation may be less clear-cut. For even if policy-makers in higher education very often appreciate research to an extent which is less common in other sectors, and even if they are trained researchers themselves (which has often been the case in Sweden), this is no guarantee that they find research on higher education relevant to their role as policy-makers. For example, policy-makers with their training in one of the hard sciences are often highly suspicious of much research carried out in the behavioural and social sciences. And many policy-makers and practitioners in higher education are, irrespective of their disciplinary background, highly sceptical about the recipes derived from pedagogical research.

Still, and despite this disclaimer, policy-makers in higher education will probably often be disposed toward involving research in policy-making. Many have taken a personal interest in research. The extreme case is perhaps Sven Moberg, who started as a research assistant in a project commissioned by an *ad hoc* commission in the mid-1940s, wrote a doctoral dissertation on student recruitment, and was himself recruited to government, ending his higher education career as the only Minister of Higher Education that Sweden has so far had. But many other policy-makers have been both interested in research and competent consumers of it.

However, it seems equally important to consider briefly another type of "professional" influence here. In many policy sectors in Sweden, recent years have seen the growth of a specialised planning or policy "profession". Such professionals are found in the relevant ministry, in *ad hoc* commissions and in the relevant central agencies. Characteristically they are quite mobile within their sector, moving back and forth between these various institutional settings. But they stay within the policy sector. While such a professional network exists in Swedish higher education, its coherence and self-awareness is still quite limited. However, and that is the point I want to make here, the growth of what is perhaps best labelled a semi-profession of higher education planners has implied the articulation of a demand for some types of research knowledge. Although this semi-profession is not homogeneous in terms of educational background, it has an increasing proportion of social scientists. Many of them find it natural to turn to the social sciences for both instrumental and conceptual knowledge.

History and Procedures

At any point in time different policy sectors display different "procedures" governing the relations between research and policy-making. These procedures are often the result of historical developments. With respect to the policy sector of higher education, much has been said on both counts in the foregoing sections; let us just recall some of the main features and, in addition, add some comparative reflections. First, we noted the impressive growth of research on higher education since the modest initial efforts in the 1930s. Second, the research was clearly linked with policy-making in terms of timing and contents. Before the 1970s, the procedural setting provided by *ad hoc* commissions was of greatest importance although, from the late 1950s, permanent resources were created for statistical analysis and forecasting. From about 1970 a permanent institutional structure for general R & D work was created.

Neither the historical development of R & D for higher education nor the procedures characterising current relations between research and policy-making in the sector, are unique in any way in the Swedish setting. Many other policy sectors can be described in the same general terms although they differ in many details. The growth of sector-oriented research has in fact characterised most major policy sectors. The earliest efforts occurred in defence, housing and a few other sectors, but during the 1960s the phenomenon spread to most social policy sectors as well, including education (Stevrin, 1978). In the early 1980s there are more than 50 such R & D programmes in Swedish central government.

The schools sector led developments in education, and in the 1960s proponents of R & D for higher education made frequent references to the systematic R & D effort begun in the former sector, arguing that higher education ought to follow suit. Educational researchers had been closely involved in the Swedish school reforms – to a point where it was difficult to see where research ended and policy began (Husén & Boalt, 1968; Paulston, 1968). In the 1960s this relationship was seen as an ideal for many in higher education as well. The influence of educational research in the schools sector was great in the work of UPU and, to begin with, in its brainchild, the new units for R & D in higher education. Interestingly, however, developments in the 1970s would be very different in the two policy sectors. In the schools sector the intimate relationship between researchers and policy-makers continued, resulting in predominantly uncritical and instrumental research knowledge. Research projects were closely monitored by R & D administrators. Almost all research was either in-house or performed in departments of pedagogy. The R & D effort of the higher education sector developed, as we have seen in a quite different direction. Many more disciplinary perspectives were brought in, something which also admitted a broader range of problems to be covered. In particular, the research programme proper encouraged critical research on long-term problems in higher education.

One may speculate about why the R & D effort in higher education developed the way it did. No doubt individual leadership played an important part. In addition, however, it seems as if the "object" itself has been of some importance. In particular, the doctrine of autonomy prevalent in higher education can be expected to have easier access to R & D policy makers here as compared to most other policy sectors. Furthermore, we may hypothesise that the specific nature of supply and demand in higher education R & D may have affected the relationship between research and policy-making. As was noted earlier, higher education problems do not loom large on any discipline's research agenda. In order to attract willing and able researchers, higher education policy-makers may have found it wise to offer something in return, namely greater leeway for researchers than is common in other sectors. Whatever the reason or reasons behind it, the R & D policy of the higher education sector early developed from the engineering model inherited from the schools sector and UPU into something which at least in part reflects the insights provided by the enlightenment model.

Decisions

Here Janet Weiss specifically refers to such aspects of policy-making as complexity, the time perspective involved, and the extent to which policy decisions are controversial. It is not precisely clear from her discussion in what ways such features affect research utilisation, but it may be hypothesised that highly complex and controversial decisions with long-term impacts encourage policy-makers to find research support – if possible. But it also seems obvious that these features make both policy-making and research on policy problems difficult.

As for the complexity of policy problems and decisions in higher education, we have already noted that higher education seems to qualify as one of the more complex sectors. Work and organisation are both extremely specialised at the level of "production". The task of the basic level, i.e. disciplinary departments in most instances, is to create and disseminate highly specialised, and often highly abstract, knowledge. The nature of the primary activities also implies that central policy-making must often stop at regulating aspects which from the point of view of the basic units appear to be secondary functions (see, for example, Becher-Kogan, 1980). To this extreme specialisation of tasks should be added the long-term nature of many decisions and activities in higher education. To a significant degree this results from specialisation; investments are highly rigid. But of equal importance is the relationship between higher education and working life. Decisions in this area should ideally be based on predictions spanning at least a decade or more. Experiences everywhere, including in the planned economies of Eastern Europe, have shown this to be an impossible task. Everywhere policy-makers have retreated to more incremental approaches in quantitative planning.

Without going into detail, we may finally note that higher education decisions have become increasingly controversial in recent years in Sweden. Many aspects of the policy sector have been politicised, both in the sense of arousing party controversies and in the sense that central policy-making is actively resisted within institutions (e.g. Lindensjö, 1981). As the conflicts have spread, demands for knowledge supporting the various policy positions have increased. In such politicised settings, research knowledge stands a slim chance of being regarded as "authoritative" by all major interest groups. It will, instead, serve as political ammunition for those whose interests happen to coincide with selected parts of available research.

Alternative Knowledge

The question here is whether a policy sector is to any significant extent dependent upon research knowledge, or if alternative forms of knowledge could equally well serve as a basis for decision-making. This is, of course, a difficult question – and a central one in the context of this paper. My long answer is provided in the concluding section below; my short answer is that very few areas of higher education policy-making are in any qualified sense dependent on research knowledge. Like most other social policy sectors, higher education has no elaborate technology, more or less linked to established fields of scientific research. Policy sectors with such technologies are, with few exceptions, linked with natural science disciplines. Even among social policy sectors, higher education seems to be among those least dependent upon or linked with established fields of research. Again, this seems to be predicated on the basic nature of work and organisation in the sector. The goals and means of higher education are unusually diffuse and complex (see, for example, Baldridge *et al,* 1978 for a discussion of unclear technology as a basic characteristic of academic organisation; also Clark, forthcoming 1983). While many social policy areas are at any point in time dominated by relatively homogeneous "policy paradigms" – examples are criminal policy, immigration policy, and personal social services in Sweden – this seems less true of higher education. The efforts to formulate such "policy paradigms" – containing relatively clear objectives and a suitable technology – have been only partial and not particularly success-ful in higher education. This does not mean that in the future policies will not be formulated which involve such technologies for higher education – only that they will be unsuccessful since, in my view at least, the policy sector is not amenable to such coherent and simplified approaches to policy-making.

Concluding Discussion

Swedish higher education has experienced tremendous changes in recent decades. As measured by enrolment, the system has grown by a factor of ten since 1945. From catering for the educational needs of a small social elite of Swedish youth, the system now involves a much more diverse clientele, including a uniquely high proportion of women and adults. From four sites having major institutions in the early 1950s, higher education is now offered in some form or other in almost every town of the country. The "system" itself has been redefined to include all post-secondary education within a single unified structure. The mode of governance has been radically transformed: the professor's university has become almost everybody's university. Within institutions teaching and research have also changed dramatically, both as to content and method.

Many of these and other major changes have been the outcome of deliberate policy; others have been unintended consequences of policy; and still others have resulted from factors other than public policy. It seems, however, that change in Swedish higher education has, in the tradition of "social engineering", been more "polity-directed" (Archer, 1979) than elsewhere. And this vast policy-making effort has involved, as I have taken pains to illustrate above, a considerable amount of systematic analysis and research. Throughout this effort, policy-makers have initiated and supported all kinds of research. They have asked for it both in planning future policy and in monitoring and evaluating impacts. They have also engaged in "meta-policy-making" by institutionalising the production of research, both statistical analysis and other forms of R & D activities. The research they have supported has been clearly geared towards the needs of central policy-making; the centralised nature of decision-making in Swedish higher education has made this both natural and feasible.

If such observations – concerning the scale of the research effort, the interest expressed by policy-makers in research, and its fitness with respect to the needs of central policy-making – constitute proof of utilisation, then research has been heavily used in higher education policy-making in Sweden. But in my view such evidence is not by itself sufficient to prove the importance of research in policy-making. Although the empirical evidence marshalled in this report leaves much to be desired, I am prepared to argue that the role of research in policy-making in Swedish higher education has been relatively marginal. Put differently, I have observed no *major* instances of policy change where research made the difference, or instances where similar, if not identical, policy measures could not or would not have been taken in the absence of research.

This said, I have also shown the many *ways* in which research has been used in higher education policy. First, and above all, I think the case of Swedish higher education provides overwhelming support for the thesis that social research in policy-making is mainly used as partisan analysis or political ammunition. Illustrations abound in the Swedish setting. As examples we may cite the use of the research on the "reserve of talent" and on the "residual factor", but there are many others. Now, the observation that research is used as political ammunition is of course evidence of research utilisation, even if many would consider this form of use "inferior" to many other forms. What it indicates is that research knowledge is not accepted as "authoritative" by all parties in policy-making. It is my contention, however, that Swedish higher education policy-making provides no major example where such partisan use of research was decisive for policy change. Research on social recruitment and the economic impact of higher education, for example, reinforced the prevailing positive attitudes toward higher education expansion in the 1950s. But such research did not make many converts, and when the general views on expansion changed, no research knowledge could prevent that change.

Second, while there are examples of situations where research knowledge has been viewed as "authoritative", these have almost invariably concerned minor aspects of policy and/or have been simple fact-gathering exercises. In this report I have consciously used a very broad concept of research in order not to exclude by definition any instance of research utilisation. It seems evident that the type of research which has most frequently been used has been various forms of statistical analysis. While statistics on quantitative trends have probably not been decisive for the basic features of quantitative planning, there is plenty of evidence that they enter specific decisions on numbers. And forecasts of manpower needs have been used as one of the inputs – together with the views and actions of professional groups, cost considerations, etc – in real-life manpower planning. That simple statistical exercises can be important for policy-making is also illustrated by the decision models applied by U63 and U68 in determining the specific sites for the localisation of higher education institutions.

Third, we noted above that research in the form of methodological development was important in the area of quantitative planning. Interestingly, such work both pointed to the possibilities of and the limits to manpower planning in assessing social demand. Here, incidentally, I think we have the only area where policy-makers were truly dependent upon research contributions. Without them, Swedish higher education planning would at least be very different in character.

Fourth, Swedish higher education provides at least one example where research caused a reinterpretation of what was widely held to be a "fact". I refer to the contribution by Urban Dahllöf which changed the interpretation of "attrition" as a measure of efficiency or, rather, inefficiency. No doubt the reinterpretation was aided by the fact that higher education looked more effective as a result! If you, by contrast, assume that students *should* complete their degrees – irrespective of their own intentions – little was changed by Dahllöf's analysis.

Finally, there is some evidence that research has had an impact on policy-making in line with the so-called enlightenment model. Two instances have been cited in the earlier analysis. First, research on policy-making and organisation in higher education seems to have been instrumental in spreading the message of post-rationalism in general, and the notion that higher education is peculiar in particular, among at least a number of policy-makers at the national level. Second, the criticism of educational technology by Ference Marton and others and their preference for discipline-focused approaches to teaching and learning have increasingly become the prevailing doctrine among national policy-makers. Through pre- and in-service training and through other forms of R & D dissemination this doctrine has probably affected practice in higher education. Interestingly, however, we may also note that both these instances of enlightenment were better at description and criticism than at prescription. Their main function has been to discourage simplistic solutions to policy problems in higher education. Need I say that this is in itself a worthwhile contribution of research?

References

Archer, M. (1979) *Social Origins of Educational Systems*. Sage, London.

Baldridge, V. *et al* (1978) *Policy-Making and Effective Leadership*. Jossey-Bass, San Francisco.

Becher, A. & Kogan, M. (1980) *Process and Structure in Higher Education*. Heinemann, London.

Bladh, A. (1982) *The Trend Towards Vocationalism in Swedish Higher Education*. University of Stockholm: Group for the Study of Higher Education and Research Policy, Report no 21.

Bulmer, M. (1982) *The Uses of Social Research*. Allen & Unwin, London.

Carlbom, T. (1970) *Högskolelokaliseringen i Sverige 1950–1965*. Almqvist & Wiksell, Stockholm.

Clark, B. (forthcoming 1983) *The Higher Education System: Academic Organization in Perspective*. University of California Press, Berkeley.

Elgqvist-Salzman, I. (1973) *Är avbrott och genomströmning meningsfulla effektivitetsmått för universitetsutbildning?* University of Umeå: Pedagogisk Debatt 10.

Franke-Wikberg, S. & Lundgren, U. (1980) *Att värdera utbildning. Del 1*. Wahlström & Widstrand, Stockholm.

Husén, T. (1975) *Universiteten och forskningen*. Natur och Kultur, Stockholm.

Husén, T. (1976) Sweden, in Noel Entwistle (ed.), *Strategies for Research and Development in Higher Education*, pp. 202–219. Swets & Zeitlinger, Amsterdam.

Husén, T. (1983) *An Incurable Academic*. Pergamon Press, Oxford.

Husén, T. & Boalt, G. (1968) *Educational Research and Educational Change: The Case of Sweden*.

Härnqvist, K. (1958) *Reserver för högre utbildning. Beräkningar och metoddiskussion* (SOU, 1958, 11).

Johansson, E. (1981) *UHÄ:s FoU-verksamhet. Del 1*. University of Gothenburg: Department of Sociology, Report no 67.

Kim, L. (1979) *Två års erfarenheter av de nya tillträdesreglerna till högskoleutbildning*. National Board of Universities and Colleges: UHÄ-rapport 1979, 13.

Kim, L. (1982) *Widened Admission to Higher Education: The 25/5 Scheme*. National Board of Universities and Colleges.

Lane, J-E. & Stenlund, H. (1981a) Om byråkrati och högskolans byråkratisering, *Tvärsnitt*, 1 (1981), pp. 3–9.

Lane, J-E & Stenlund, H. (1981b) Tjänster och förvaltning i högskolan, *Tvärsnitt,* 2 (1981), pp. 8–15.
Lindblom, C. (1977) *Politics and Markets.* Basic Books, New York.
Lindblom, C. (1980) *The Policy-Making Process.* Englewood-Cliffs: Prentice-Hall.
Lindblom, C. & Cohen, D. (1979) *Usable Knowledge.* Yale University Press, New Haven.
Lindensjö, B. (1981) *Högskolereformen: En studie i offentlig reformstrategi.* University of Stockholm: Stockholm Studies in Politics 20.
Lundin, R. *et al* (1981) *Högskolans organisation—Hur fungerar den?* National Board of Universities and Colleges: UHÄ-rapport 1981, 13.
Marton, F. *et al* (1977) *Inlärning och omvärldsuppfattning.* Almqvist & Wiksell, Stockholm.
Moberg, S. (1951) *Vem blev student och vad blev studenten?* Gleerups, Lund.
Nybom, T. (1980) Det nya statskontorets framväxt 1960–1965, *Statskontoret 1680–1980,* Liber, Skara.
Orlans, H. (1973) *Contracting for Knowledge.* Jossey-Bass, San Francisco.
Paulston, R. (1968) *Educational Change in Sweden.* Teachers College Press, New York.
Premfors, R. (1979) Social Research and Public Policy-Making: An Overview. *Statsvetenskaplig tidskrift,* 4 (1979), pp. 281–290.
Premfors, R. (1979a) The Politics of Higher Education in Sweden. Recent Developments, 1976–1978, *European Journal of Education,* 14 (1), pp. 81–106.
Premfors, R. (1980) *The Politics of Higher Education in a Comparative Perspective. France, Sweden, United Kingdom.* Stockholm Studies in Politics 15, University of Stockholm.
Premfors, R. (1981) *New Patterns of Authority in Higher Education.* OECD, Paris.
Premfors, R. (1982a) *Analysis in Politics: The Regionalization of Swedish Higher Education.* Group for the Study of Higher Education and Research Policy, Report no. 19, University of Stockholm.
Premfors, R. (1982b) *Numbers and Beyond: Access Policy in an International Perspective.* Group for the Study of Higher Education and Research Policy, Report no. 20, University of Stockholm.
Ramström, D. (1973) The University as an Adaptive Organization. *Utvärdering av en högskolereform,* Chancellor's Office: UKÄ-rapport no. 2.
Ruin, O. (1979) *Studentmakt och statsmakt.* Liber, Stockholm.
Sobel, I. (1978) The Human Capital Revolution in Economic Development: Its Current History and Status. *Comparative Education Review,* 22 (2), pp. 278–308.
SOU series (individual titles in this series of government publications are not given here).
Stevrin, P. (1978) *Den samhällsstyrda forskningen.* Liber, Stockholm.
Svensson, A. (1980) *Jämlikhet på gång?* Department of Education, University of Gothenburg.
Trow, M. (1975) The Public and Private Lives of Higher Education. *Daedalus,* Winter, 1975, pp. 115–127.
Weiss, C. (1976) Research for Policy's Sake: The Enlightenment Function of Social Research. *Policy Analysis,* 3, (4), pp. 531–546.
Weiss, C. (1980) *Social Science Research and Decision-Making.* Columbia University Press, New York.
Weiss, J. (1979) Access to Influence: Some Effects of Policy Sector on the Use of Social Science. *American Behavioral Scientist,* 22 (3), pp. 437–458.
Wildavsky, A. (1979) *Speaking Truth to Power.* Little, Brown, Boston.
Wittrock, B. (1982) Social Knowledge, Public Policy and Social Betterment: A Review of Current Research on Knowledge Utilization in Policy-Making. *European Journal of Political Research,* 10, pp. 83–89.

Development and Research – Foundations for Policy-making in Education: Some Personal Experiences

BY BIRGIT RODHE

INTRODUCTION

My first encounter with the relationship between policy-making and research dates back to June, 1961. Gunnar Helén, a member of the 1957 School Commission, introduced some of the recommendations which the Committee was to submit to the Government a few weeks later. With regard to the issues which had caused a heated debate within the Commission and aroused most interest among educators and politicians, the issue of differentiation and of how to organise the upper level of the 9-year compulsory school, he was not able to reveal any details. He could only say that social and political considerations had had to be given priority over pedagogical ones. He underlined that the Commission had hoped to be guided in its decisions by the extensive research which it had commissioned. The evidence was now available in preliminary form, but Helén did not feel that it was conclusive. There was disappointment in his voice as he added: "The final decision is still up to us, the politicians."

Gunnar Helén's statement warned his listeners against believing in a simple and "linear" relationship between research and policy-making. At the same time, he made it clear that the policy-maker always retains his responsibility for the ultimate decision. In so doing he is guided by his political conviction; but that he has to be willing to compromise, as after all politics is "the art of the possible".

In 1962, the Swedish Parliament passed the bill on 9-year comprehensive school, common to all children in the age range 7–16 years of age, the *grundskola* (the Swedish term will be used in the following, as will the term *gymnasium*, or, after 1971, *gymnasieskola* for the senior secondary school). The parliamentary decision was the terminal point of more than 20 years of commission work, experimental activities and research. Yet Parliament manifested its intention to proceed to reform the school system. This reform would apply to the *grundskola* and also to the educational system as a whole. School reform in Sweden was to

241

be continuous, a "rolling reform", which, among other things, meant that experience gained along the road would guide future reform endeavours.

This was the context for what happened at the local level. For about 20 years I was active in the school system of Malmö, the third largest city in Sweden. It was also one of the few local authorities which introduced the *grundskola* at its earliest possible point, that is, in the academic year of 1962/63. If the following account has an "autobiographical" flavour, it may also serve as a case study of how a local education authority introduced and developed the "grundskola"; how, for its own policy-making, it related to research and to organised development activities; and how, on the national level, use was made of the Malmö experience. A case in point here was the later reform, the *Lgr 80*, based upon a bill passed by Parliament in June, 1979, when I was the responsible minister of education.[1]

The Creation of a *Grundskola*.

In spite of 10 years of nationwide experiments with the comprehensive school, after the parliamentary decision of 1962, the *grundskola* was still a school which had to be created. Pedagogical ideas were to be put into practice, principles and guidelines were to be embodied. But how? Only those – or primarily those – who worked in the classroom or close to it would know. The city of Malmö introduced the new *grundskola* as from the academic year of 1962/63, which was an important reason for the National Board to follow closely the development in our city. One of the main reasons for its early introduction was the fact that teacher training was to be organised on a grand scale at the Malmö College of Education, where from 1962/63 subject teachers with a university degree were to be trained to teach at the upper level of the *grundskola* (and the *gymnasium*) in addition to the class teachers for the elementary level. So, in the autumn of 1962, the new school was started with the grades 1, 4 and 7 – with no printed curriculum, very little experience obtained from development work, and with teachers who were to be trained for a school of which teacher educators knew little more than their students. Teachers of the secondary school, mostly from the *gymnasium*, offered to help the Local Education Authority, advising about textbooks, teaching material, laboratory work etc.

---

[1]My curriculum vitae may be summarised as follows:
1940–50 Teacher in junior and senior high school in Uppsala (girls' school)
1950–55   ,,   ,,   ,,   ,,   ,,   ,,   ,,   ,, Karlstad (co-educ. school)
1955–62 Headmistress of secondary girls' school in Malmö.
1962–70, 74–75 Deputy director of education, Malmö LEA
1971–73 City Commissioner for education and culture, Malmö City Council (political office)
1975–77 Headmistress of senior high school (gymnasieskola, co-educ.), Helsingborg
1977–78 Chairman of National Council of Culture
1978–79 Government minister of School Education
1980– Various government services

Groups of teachers were organised for advisory purposes: teachers with experience from different kinds of schools formed "subject area groups", which for several years injected expertise and pedagogical creativity in the construction of the *grundskola* in Malmö. An organisation of local consultants grew out of the subject area groups and also became an important factor in development activities.

Special Pilot Schools. The "Trump Committee".

In Malmö about 10 per cent of the students had belonged to the 9-year pilot schools. The margin for pedagogical development, however, had been narrow, as most of the energy had had to be given to organisational matters. However, teachers from the pilot comprehensive schools were valuable members of the subject area groups. Other kinds of pilot experiments had been carried out in secondary schools, following invitations during the 1950s from the National Board of Education (NBE). Due to a parliamentary decision, the NBE had organised "free experimental (pilot) activities" in such schools all over the country, the idea being that during the time span that the 9-year comprehensive school was created under experimentation in pilot 9-year schools, the secondary schools, too, would have a chance for development through experimentation. After 1958, this experimentation was concentrated on the upper secondary level and on seven schools, of which Malmö school where I was the head was one. The pilot programme was soon geared towards projects which could give useful experience for the realisation of the new comprehensive school and of the *gymnasium*, which was to be built upon this school and which was under construction in a special national commission.

In Malmö, experiments in team teaching and flexible group size grew out of the "special experimentation activity" and proved valuable for later development. However, no provision had been made for evaluation of the experimental activities in the seven "special experimental schools" and there were practically no links with research. Sixten Marklund, in his recent book *Skolsverige 1950– 1975* (Marklund, 1982), attributes to the secondary school experiments a certain ultimate value. Yet, primarily due to lack of evaluation through research, these experiments could not serve as a basis for a comprehensive, all-round objective and free comparison with the experiments in the 9-year comprehensive school, as seems to have been intended by Parliament.

Later, a more serious attempt was made to evaluate experiments of the kind that had been tried in Malmö. In January, 1963, the National Board of Education appointed a group with the task of "preparing experiments with varying class size and team teaching starting from school year 1964–65". The group was also to analyse the organisational and pedagogical problems which might arise. As the experiments were to test patterns worked out in the USA within J. L. Trump's *Experimental Study of the Utilization of the Staff in the*

Secondary School, the Swedish committee was called the "Trump Committee". In a report, published in 1964 (Skolöverstyrelsen, 1964), suggestions for the evaluation of experiments of this kind were given. It was made clear in the Swedish text that strictly scientific evaluations were foreseen with control classes for comparison with the "experimental classes", and with the preparation of detailed plans for the work in these classes, plans from which no deviation should be allowed.

Though attempts were made to measure certain aspects of the "Trump experiments", the whole road to "really systematic experimentation" or evaluation was never achieved. In my view this was due not only to lack of time and other necessary resources, but mainly to the very nature of this kind of experiment.

Education Development Centres (EDCs).

When the *grundskola* was to be introduced in Malmö in the school year 1962/63, I left my "special experimental school" in order to help develop the *grundskola* in the city as Deputy Director of Education. The idea of widening the scope of experimental activities from one school to the whole school system and to integrate other experiments which had been carried out in Malmö was only a step away. The idea was conceived to form what was to be called an "Education Development Centre". By a parliamentary decision of the spring of 1964, NBE was authorised to establish EDCs, and the first two centres began their work in the city of Malmö and the county of Kalmar respectively. The objective was to find *"practicable ways of giving effect to the intentions of the educational reforms proposed or already decided, also on levels higher than that of the compulsory school, and to facilitate the continuous school reform"*. It was presupposed that the centres would *"lead to a fruitful cooperation between pedagogical theory and practical pedagogical activity"*. The centres were advised to address themselves to essential pedagogical problems. A state grant was to be matched by a contribution from the local authority and was combined with the condition that results gained would benefit the school system as a whole through the agency of the National Board of Education. It was not defined what kinds of results were to be expected, nor were methods of evaluation recommended or discussed. Although it was affirmed later that the work of the EDCs has been of considerable value for the continuous Swedish school reform, it is my conviction that their contribution could have been still more substantial, had their objectives been more clearly defined and their relationship to research better worked out. This possibly was not feasible at the start, but the intention by the central authorities, and a continuous effort on their part, to define the platform and role of the EDCs would have been of great importance. What was at stake was not just the role of the educational development centres, but the role played by development work in schools, in local or regional school systems, in relation to research, and in their turn to policy-making on the whole.

The creation of the EDCs in Sweden followed closely in time upon the organisation of a unit for Research and Development at the NBE, the unit L4, led by Nils-Eric Svensson. Applied research and development work was to be the focus of the projects, which the new unit was to support. The main objective was "the realisation of intentions behind the parliamentary decision concerning the goals and the methods of work within the new school". Thus there was no clearly defined difference between the objective of the R & D work, related to and financed by the unit L4, and that which was to take place, also under the auspices of NBE, through the EDCs. To me it seemed logical that both instruments for the "realisation of the intentions . . . of the goals and the methods of work within the new school" should be placed within the same unit of NBE.

I remember a private conversation with Nils-Eric Svensson shortly before the start of the work of the EDCs, where I pleaded with him to take on the responsibility of the EDCs. As I recall his answer, he said: "No, I want to be responsible for the one unit within the NBE, where one knows what one is doing". Thus, from the very beginning the term *development*, as in Research and Development, bore a different meaning from *development* in the context of Education Development Centre. The difference implied was that in R & D work one would know what results had been achieved and, probably, what use could be made of them in policy-making. This would not be the case with development activities within the EDCs.

The EDCs were placed under the Department of Instruction and not under the one responsible for R & D. There were, of course, good reasons for this, as development work can be said to be an integral part of all school activities. But the placement underlined the difference between the two kinds of development work without defining the difference. For a couple of years, NBE defined the development work in the EDCs as "teacher-led experiments", a definition which was both incorrect and incomplete. The main outcome expected was instructional material to be distributed to local authorities with no EDCs, an expectation which the EDCs proved less suitable to live up to than some of the research projects supported by the unit on R & D.

The Malmö EDC and the Malmö School of Education.

In Malmö the EDC was fortunate to be able to start its work from the very beginning in close cooperation with the School of Education (SofE), specifically its Department of Educational and Psychological Research (DEPR). The Rector of the SofE became a member of the planning group of the EDC, which was headed by the Director of Education of the local authority. Another member was the head of the DEPR, Professor Åke Bjerstedt, who took a keen interest in the EDC both as an idea and reality. One of the researchers of the

DEPR, Ebbe Lindell, became the scientific adviser and a member of the EDC executive committee. Later, a research assistant was employed by the EDC working under the supervision of Lindell. She came to devote her main work to the relationship between preschool and school, a project started within the EDC. Presently she is a member of a National Commission on this issue; and in 1982 she presented her doctoral dissertation on the transition from preschool to school (Gran, 1982), an interesting but not very common linkage between development work, research and participation in policy-making.

At an early date, the discussion began in Malmö about the position of the development activities within the EDC in relation to the R & D work in the DEPR. As an early reflection of this discussion in the first annual report of the EDC (Rodhe, Lindell & Bjerstedt, 1965; also Bjerstedt, 1968) Bjerstedt described "a continuum of different types of planning R & D in the educational field from basic research towards experiments in natural classroom situations". He saw *development work* as "a systematic use of scientifically based knowledge with the intention of producing new or essentially improved products (processes, systems etc.)", whereas he reserved the term *experimental activity* for "an activity which is not made permanent or given definite form until the result is seen". If one desired systematic evaluation of the results and wanted the activity to be successfully directed by the outcome, one might speak of *research-linked experimental activity (action cum research)*.

Bjerstedt's attempt at describing the continuum of research and development activities, and of defining the various aspects of work, was helpful to us who worked within the EDC, although we did not really recognise our work in terms of either his "development work" or his "experimental activity". Naturally enough, his vantage point was research. The classroom was to be the testing ground for products originating from applied research, not the starting point for new pedagogical ideas or new practices as we saw it within the EDC. At this time – the late 1960s and the early 1970s – educational technology supplied the pattern for most R & D work in Sweden as in many other countries. In Sweden, the so-called IMU project aimed at producing individualised instructional material for the teaching of mathematics at the upper level of the *grundskola*. The project was based at the Malmö DEPR and was seen by NBE, and not least by its Director General, as a model project for school development. We tested the IMU material in connection with team teaching within the EDC programme and felt that the concentration upon the individualisation of instruction which it represented could be a danger to the other basic objective of our schools, social education. Furthermore, our teachers felt that in using the IMU material and to some extent the material–method system for the teaching of German, also produced at the Malmö DEPR, their own role became passive and their pupils did not receive enough of a personal teacher–pupil relationship. Evidence existed, both through practical experience of teachers and through systematic research, that this was particularly harmful to less gifted pupils.

However, the technologically inspired development of method/material systems had a very short heyday in Sweden, as well as in most other countries, whatever the reasons may have been. In a report on school research and school development, submitted in 1980 by a government commission (*Skolforskning och skolutveckling*, 1980), it is maintained that the discontinuation of the development of educational technology in Sweden depended less on non-satisfactory learning than on the fact that its methods were founded on theories and principles in conflict with new dominating views within the education society. "Dialogue pedagogy" had succeeded "transmission pedagogy". I agree with the general view held in the report that the Swedish debating climate both in the educational field and in other areas tends to have a certain similarity with a flock of chattering magpies settling down in a tree for a time; after a while the birds are chased away, never to be seen again, but another flock can be heard chattering in the same tree. However, I find this explanation too simple, as I think that the technological methods only partially fulfilled the aims of the Swedish school reform, as has been said above. On the other hand, the rejection of the results of some of the technologically based projects was probably too radical; some of the gains of the very comprehensive and costly work within this field might have been saved, and valuable use made of them.

The Programme of the Malmö EDC; Cooperation, Flexibility, Integration.

The focus of the development activities encouraged by the leaders of the Malmö EDC – and to a certain extent inspired by them – was *the school as a whole*. Teachers in their practical classroom situation reported their great difficulties in fulfilling the objectives of the new *grundskola*, as they tried to use the traditional teaching methods. They then tried to develop alternative methods, often in informal cooperation with their colleagues. On the part of the local authority, we tried to assist them in their efforts and found elements of innovation, often of great interest, but, lacking resources and encouragement, not fully developed. Such innovative efforts became the origin of projects within the EDC programme. Other projects were inspired from earlier experimentation, for example, in the "special experimental schools" or from ideas and intentions by leaders of schools or the local authority. Gradually, something of a vision appeared of how a school might work in order to give body and shape to the new school in Swedish society. In many respects these developments represented attacks on the traditional organisation of schools: one teacher for approximately 30 pupils at a time in a closed classroom, the school forming a secluded entity in a society as a whole. With something of a cliché I called this new conception of a school, which grew out of our development activities (and not only of ours), a "two-way open school" (Rodhe, 1972). In other words, it signified a new concept of the "ecology" of the school. In 1975, a ten-year report on the education development work in Malmö was published (Engquist, Gran & Lind, 1975). A concluding chapter summarised the characteristics of the Malmö activities under three main headings: cooperation, flexibility and integration.

Quite a few of these characteristics of the Malmö development activities have become more or less integrated into Swedish school development as a whole – thus team teaching was included in the curriculum of 1969 (Lgr 69), as was coordinated and special teaching, all early concerns of the Malmö EDC. Again, it should be underlined that this happened not only through the development work in Malmö. Parallel activities were tried out in other EDCs and elsewhere in Sweden, some inspired from Malmö, some independently. We in Malmö, for our part, were inspired by and used experience from elsewhere, not least from other countries.

How much of all this activity was "scientifically evaluated"? If some of the Malmö activities influenced national educational policy-making, what research was available to "prove" that the results of the development work were worth disseminating?

These questions are not easily answered. From the activities during the 1960s there is, with a few exceptions, little research-based evaluation. There are at least three reasons for this:

(a) The staff resources for research were limited; no funds had been specifically earmarked for this purpose.

(b) There was a great uncertainty as to what role research should and could play in relation to such educational development activities as those in the EDCs – possibly also because far-reaching and valid results were not expected.

(c) Many of the development projects of the Malmö EDC were extremely difficult to evaluate because of their complex character. Examples: flexible grouping and teamwork of teachers, open plan schools.

Already earlier in this paper I have mentioned the uncertainty about what kind of result might reasonably be expected from the EDCs. On the other hand, the dominant expectation from development work at this time was products in the form of material and methods. The method in its turn was to be based on "a systematic use of scientifically based knowledge". This was the "linear" model used primarily in science and technology. Our development work in Malmö started from problems in the classroom, primarily in relation to the implementation of goals and objectives of the new curriculum. Through the organisation of the EDC, teachers or groups of educators who were developing new ways of implementing pedagogical objectives could draw upon resources of researchers, but the initiative rested with themselves and with those resources of assistance which were otherwise available in the experimental community from the executive committee of the EDC. What model was available for describing a development process of this kind?

Resources which are available in the shape of involvement from central, regional and local school administration, from heads of schools, teachers and other school personnel, from students and parents and from research workers with different specialities need to be linked together into a model which takes care of, both organisationally and in practice, the integrity and freedom of all parties at the same time as their cooperation becomes as efficient and as constructive as possible. (Rodhe-Andersson, 1970).

Is this just a dream? Maybe. But any model which does not include any of the parties mentioned or which violates any of the principles contained in this description would fall short of the real potential of a school development based on an interplay between research and development activities as a foundation for policy-making. At the same time, of course, there are aspects which are not included even in this rather comprehensive model. The influence of an outstanding and inspiring leader of a school or a school system, or even of a prophetic visionary, has not been mentioned.

Some of the fields of the Malmö development activities were less difficult to evaluate than others. This can probably be said about the important area of the integration into normal classes of students who had earlier been taken care of in special classes. Good reports were produced by Ebbe Lindell and Birgitta Gran. Practice preceded and followed up the research work. Special classes were abolished at a rate which was well ahead of that of the country as a whole. Special education was transformed into coordinated education, a classroom situation, where students requiring special attention are helped by specially trained teachers who assist the class teacher for certain periods of time. Similar development work was carried out in other school systems, and the coordinated special education has become the rule in Sweden. Even the integration of many severely handicapped children has followed, with the assistance in the normal classroom of teaching assistants and special teachers.

It proved more difficult to evaluate team teaching and flexible grouping. Still harder was the task when new school buildings, often called open plan schools, emerged, partly as a consequence of new teaching practice (new building techniques and the need for lowering building costs formed other presuppositions for the new types of school buildings). As a group of local education authorities formed an organisation to develop and build these flexible open plan schools, parents, teachers (particularly through their unions) and policy-makers increasingly – and not without a cutting edge – asked whether these schools were really better than traditional schools. One hoped that research would provide an answer. Obviously, educational research in a narrow sense could not provide a definite answer. Architects, sociologists and others were also engaged. This trans-disciplinary cooperation in itself presented not only new possibilities but new difficulties, when the researchers – as well as participating practitioners – found that they had to learn new languages if their cooperation were to be effective. Even greater problems were faced by the complex character of the research tasks.

Also, those of us who had to take decisions on what kind of school buildings were to be built in the future wanted answers from research, although some of us had limited expectations. The timetable was tight. Thus, researchers were up against impossible demands, and disappointment was unavoidable. The research projects which were based upon the activities within the Malmö EDC and the MPU, mainly on team teaching and flexible grouping and on work in the open plan schools, produced a long series of valuable reports well into the 1970s but on the whole too late to influence essential decisions. Not until 1981 was a book published in which Bertil Gran and Göte Rudvall, who were responsible for these research projects, tried to summarise their results (Gran & Rudvall, 1981). The book places the school which emerged from the development activities in Malmö, in the framework of present-day society. One problem, however, is that the activities, the buildings they have researched, were produced in order to solve problems which school and society of the late 1960s and early 1970s raised. The setting of the problems of the early 1980s is in many respects different. The time-lag between research and reality, between research and policy-making, constitutes a basic problem in the relationship between the two.

This is not to say that research did not play an important role for policy-making in the Malmö area before its results were published in its final form. Cooperation with the research workers, which became increasingly close during the late Sixties and the Seventies, led to better planning and increased precision as to objectives and methods. Research influenced the *process* of development work and thus indirectly affected the policy-making more than the final decisions. Yet, even these were influenced, as preliminary research results were made available and discussed during the course of the development process, which in itself changed direction due to these preliminary reports. As far as the Malmö experiences were able to influence national policy-making, this was certainly due to the unique interaction between local development work and pedagogical research, which emerged through the Education Development Centre and the Department of Educational and Psychological Research at the Malmö School of Education.

The Education Council (Pedagogiska nämnden).

In 1971, according to parliamentary decision, the government appointed *Pedagogiska nämnden*, a council which was to assist NBE as "a counselling body to prepare questions concerning research and development, including evaluation of educational development". Parliamentarians of the different political parties, research workers and politicians from local bodies were the members; I belonged to the council between 1971 and 1975. This body could have become a platform for study and debate of the relationship between research, development and policy-making, and to some extent it functioned this way. It was authorised to take decisions on the placement and programme of educational development centres and showed an active and positive interest in the activities at these centres. However, the council did not exert a very active influence on the direction of R & D work in the university institutions – though it might have done so – nor did it actively define the consequences for policy-making of emerging results from development and research work. It did not become what I had hoped, "a centrally placed body, planning for the future of Swedish education". Its work was discontinued in 1981 (see the final report of the Council, Skolöverstyrelsen, 1981).

A Minister of Education Faces Research.

Having become, in mid-October 1978, a cabinet minister of school education, I saw two main tasks ahead of me:

1. The completion of a bill on the curriculum of the *grundskola* to replace the Lgr 69 (see above). This task included the problem of marking in Swedish schools.

2. The elaboration of short-term measures of education for the 16–19-year-olds in view of the growing unemployment in this age group, and the ensuing necessity to widen both in size and in character the kind of education offered to this age group.

Other issues emerged, such as:

3. The future of small schools, primarily in sparsely populated areas and with decreasing birthrate, but also in other areas where large schools had growing problems.

4. The future of private schools, of which there are very few in Sweden, but those which exist had financial difficulties and there was an increasing interest in them on the part of parents, as the *grundskola* faced growing problems.

5. The follow-up of parliamentary decisions with the school area, in the first hand the so-called SIA decision of 1976, regarding the inner work of the school.

6. With my background in development work, it was natural that I would look for new development tasks.

For a minister with a short-term mandate (general elections were to follow in September, 1979) the possibilities of commissioning research on current issues were excluded. What was feasible was to enquire about what research results might already be available and to consult scholars who could give advice and orientation. Had I been able to anticipate a longer term of office, more systematic plans for cooperation could and should have been worked out. Also, I would have wanted to draw more extensively on research results from other countries, often collected through international organisations or agencies. One essential case in point, which was brought to a conclusion a short time after I left office, was the 1979 OECD Review of the Swedish educational system – a most valuable document which, I feel, was discussed and made use of far too little in Sweden (OECD, 1980).

Let me give some indications as to what was the outcome of my drawing upon research and development work resources in the areas related above.

1. As one of the consequences of the parliamentary SIA decision, the NBE had been commissioned to work out a proposal for a new curriculum for the *grundskola*. The proposal had been published in April, 1978 and, as is common procedure in Sweden, distributed to interested parties for comments. The proposal had proved controversial and a rather heated debate followed regarding both the main principles and many details. Officially, comments were to be returned on December 15, 1978. It seemed impossible to me to produce a bill between the early weeks of 1979, when the gist of the comments might have been extracted, and April 1, when, at the very latest, the bill had to be dealt with during the parliamentary spring session, the last one before the elections. Thus I announced that it would probably be impossible to submit a bill before May – parliamentary action would then follow after the elections – as I regarded it to be of prime importance to study carefully what was being said in the official comments. For many years I had been on the other end, among those who had to submit comments, and had often felt that due consideration was not given to them as bills seemed to be written before comments were rendered. This announcement met with appreciation from those who had been or were in the same situation, although others placed greater weight on the political side of the issue: that the curriculum bill should have a chance of being passed by the present parliament.

The main criticism against the NBE proposal was that it was felt to imply decisive steps in the direction of a totally homogeneous upper level of the *grundskola*, that is the age group 13–15 years. The system of electives offered through the Lgr 69 was felt to discriminate against socially and/or intellectually less privileged pupils and also to discriminate according to sex. Thus, the NBE proposed a system where electives would be offered only on the basis of language – the choice being between a second foreign language or a general linguistic subject, called Communication. Very few were satisfied with this new ''subject'', the main reason being that it was artificial and would be chosen for negative reasons by those who thought they could not master a second foreign language and/or did not aim at further education after the *grundskola*. Social discrimination would again be the consequence.

Alternatives seemed to be on the one hand a totally homogeneous integrated curriculum, where all pupils would follow a common course, *or*, at the other extreme, an early selection according to ability – against the very idea of the *grundskola*.

However, in its annual report of 1977/78, the *Pedagogiska nämnden* (Skolöverstyrelsen, 1978) referred to research, for which Kjell Härnqvist was responsible. The main outcome was, to put it briefly, that it would not be possible to create an elective system where discrimination would be totally eliminated. In fact, discrimination was not limited to, or even operated mainly through, the selective system, but in the subjects common to all pupils. This was a new aspect. We started to search for ways in which methods of work of a non-discriminatory, or at least less discriminatory kind, could be found in subjects such as Swedish, social studies and science. It proved possible to combine curriculum time given to these subjects with time allotted to free activities. Thus, a possibility would be given to dedicate about 1/3 of the time to project studies, where individual interests and differences could be drawn upon. It would be up to the teachers and students together to shape these projects. Also proposals for electives – beside the second foreign language – were to be offered locally.

Through such arrangements the upper level of the *grundskola* would offer considerably more freedom of choice than had been the case so far. On the other hand, there had been strong pressure on the school to give greater attention to "basic skills". Research had shown that a not negligible part of the students left the *grundskola* without satisfactory skills in reading, writing and mathematics (the mass media had vastly exaggerated the research results, but they were alarming enough). More than had been done in the NBE proposal, my bill stressed the need for developing in every student who passed the *grundskola* a minimum level of basic skills. Tests such as those developed within a reading project at the Linköping School of Education would be used to assess the level of competence.

Though research was useful for other aspects of the curriculum work as well, experience during this period also suggested major areas where, so far, sufficient knowledge is not available. It is possible to define operationally "basic skills" in mathematics and possibly in reading and writing (though the task is considerably more complex than is generally taken for granted). But what is "basic knowledge" in history, religion, chemistry or physics? Efforts at producing such definitions had given discouraging results as, during the early 1970s, the NBE conducted a project called MUT, later discontinued without having been brought to an end. Possibly, the very character of such subjects defies efforts to define a basic core of knowledge.

On the whole, there is in Sweden a need for planned curriculum development of which there has been so far too little. For my curriculum bill there was not time even to sketch a curriculum theory, although efforts were made (Lundgren, 1979). Lack of time was the negative side of another more positive development. First drafts of the complete bill were ready in late February/early March, 1979, still with the intention to submit the bill in May. Professor Urban Dahllöf, who read a draft, suggested that here was the foundation for the curriculum bill and that it should be possible to place the proposal on the table of Parliament by April 1st. Since also the reactions of the teacher unions and contacts with other political parties were positive to the basic ideas of the proposal, a serious effort was made to complete the bill at an earlier date than had been announced. The bill 1978/79:180 *Läroplan för grundskolan* was submitted to Parliament on

April 2nd, and was passed on June 5th with very few changes and, on the whole, unanimously.

2. In the years of 1977 and 1978 unemployment of youth 16 to 20 had increased. Measures against this process were to be taken both by the Ministry of Education and the Ministry of Labour. As there was little hope that a radical improvement in the situation would occur, long-term plans as well as short-range measures were needed. It proved possible to offer school places to practically every young person who asked for one, but not all unemployed youth wanted to continue school after having completed the *grundskola*, even if school meant training in the vocational branches of the integrated *gymnasieskola*. Sweden, having practically abolished the apprenticeship system in favour of vocational schooling several years earlier, started again to look for ways of reintroducing the kind of close relationship between trainer and trainee which the apprenticeship system can offer.

Comparative research as to the virtues of the different systems was not available in Sweden, for natural reasons. In the Nordic Council, a project on the 16–19-year-olds was in process and results were presented to the Nordic Ministers of Education in August, 1979 – too late to guide my action in this field. As I would not have time for study visits in different countries to see how similar situations were dealt with, I turned to the major international organisations in order to draw upon their collective experience. Visits to the ILO, the OECD, Unesco and the Council of Europe in December, 1978 showed a concern in all these organisations for the problems of the training of 16–19-year-olds. The International Labour Office, not surprisingly, had assembled the most substantial research and experience material. It was my hope, during my period in office, to organise a seminar in Sweden of experts both from abroad and from the Ministries of Education and of Labour to review available knowledge on the two systems of vocational training, schooling and apprenticeship, and possible combinations between them. The seminar never materialised, due to the burden of day-to-day work in the ministries. I still think that some of our uncertainty and fumbling with these matters in the last few years could have been avoided had we in time, and in a more systematic way, made use of experience and knowledge available in the international field. I have no doubt that there are still rich sources to draw upon and information available, in no small way based on research and development. A short visit in November 1978 at the Aspen Institute in Berlin on the future of institutional education added valuable aspects to the discussion of the problems of schooling and adolescents. It confirmed my general view that we have to make better and more systematic use of international research efforts and collections of data. Some of the knowledge available from such sources can be applied even on relatively short term basis (see Husén, 1979).

3. A rather heartrending experience for a Minister of Education is to listen to complaints of representatives of small schools which the authorities want to

close down. The *grundskola*, with its elaborate elective system, had been seen from the very beginning to require large schools. Consequently, many village schools had been closed and children were being transported, mostly by bus, to central school units. With dramatically falling birth rates and a rapid urbanisation, more schools were threatened. This was felt to accelerate the movement away from areas with dispersed population to the detriment of the social, cultural and economic life of neighbourhoods and regions. Several years earlier, a research project had been started under the leadership of Urban Dahllöf with the aim of finding out, among other things, the respective virtues of small and large schools. The possibilities of constructing an ungraded upper level, in a small school, was also considered. Preliminary results of this project became available during my time of office (Andrae, 1980). The conclusions as summarised by Annika Andrae were, among others, the following:

> The aim of this study has been to answer the question whether nongrading in lower secondary education is an acceptable alternative when pupil supply diminishes and school consolidation would otherwise be a reality.
>
> Summing up from the results we can draw the following conclusions.
>
> – results on standardised tests and school marks are as good in nongrading as in grading;
> – attitudes towards the school, schoolmates and the family are more positive in nongrading than in grading;
> – the teaching process of nongrading differs from the teaching process of grading, for example:
> teachers spend more time on planning,
> planning, organisation and content include the stage grade 7–9 as a whole,
> collaboration between colleagues is more common,
> work is more flexible both for teachers and pupils,
> guidance is more common as a teacher activity,
> pupils are more active during the lessions.

The study also showed that even when grading was maintained in small schools or a combination of grading and nongrading, "schools seemed to be able to survive" and that such results as summarised above held true. These results provided incentives for efforts to maintain small schools and, possibly, even to create small schools or small units in large schools.

4. Sweden has, compared to other Western countries, very few private schools. As during the 1970s the school debate has become increasingly heated and criticism against the public schools has increased, more parents than previously have asked for alternatives to the public *grundskola*. Private schools can be instituted by permission of the local education authority if the education given in them "in kind, scope and general direction corresponds to that of the *grundskola*" and if the school has a competent head. However, there is no general provision for state grants to private schools and only a few of them receive public grants. State grants are given only by parliamentary decisions. Of these, one Rudolf Steiner school, the Kristofferskolan in Stockholm, had received grants both from the state and from the local authority for some years. A number of small Steiner (Waldorf) schools have come into being during

recent years but they do not receive any state grants. The same is true about a number of confessional schools. Both Christian groups and groups affiliated to the Waldorf school movement now demand grants, referring among other things to the declaration of human rights by the UN, the Council of Europe and Unesco. In order to review this issue in the light of these declarations, and of the general school situation in Sweden, I appointed a Commission in August, 1979. One valuable source for the work of the Commission was a report on the activity of the Kristofferskolan by the Uppsala School of Education on behalf of NBE – a good example of how a school can be evaluated in both a positive and critical way. Another source of valuable material for the Commission has been the collection of essays *Alternative Schulen?* (Gold-schmidt-Roeder, 1979), dedicated to Hellmut Becker, which contains a wealth of material from many countries.

Some conclusions

As indicated in the beginning of this paper, my role as a policy-maker has been acted out within the framework of the Swedish school reform, specifically in its character of *continuous reform*. On various levels, I have had the task of implementing the reform and, in fulfilling this task, to identify where and how the next steps would have to be taken, and how the reform would have to be modified in order to achieve better its objectives.

What, then, has been my relationship to research?

1. First of all, it seems obvious to me that reform, not least continuous reform, for the process of policy-making needs *research* but *development* as well. This does not necessarily mean *R*esearch *and* *D*evelopment in the fixed combination in which it is often used. What I mean, rather, is research and development as parallel or preferably interacting activities, both necessary as preconditions for policy-making. This in itself is not new. I began this paper by reminding myself and my readers of the role played by research, commissioned by the Swedish school reformers, on the issue of differentiation. Though the results of this research did play an important rôle for the policy-makers, the model for the upper level in the comprehensive school was largely taken from spontaneous development work in one of the pilot schools, Österåker. The Österåker model was never systematically tested by research, although it turned out to be compatible with the main research results. To policy-makers, who wanted proof that their political ideas about differentiation were feasible, the Österåker model did good service. However, I think it can be said that school reform in Sweden has never made systematic use of *both* research and development foundations for continuous change.

2. Seen in this perspective, research and development would have to play different roles with regard to policy-making. They will do this in varying relationships to one another. The role of *research* is less one of producing

actual foundations for policy-making than of offering new knowledge in the shape of analysis, development of concepts, or new models of thought (see SOU, 1980, 2). Sometimes research can form a direct base for development, as in the traditional R & D model, though this model in its "linear" form is more useful in the field of science than in education, which should rather be seen as an art than as a science. When, as in educational technology, research has been expected to include development and to deliver ready-made products, the lasting outcomes have been strikingly limited. On the other hand, in an R & D project of a broader and more complex model than technological ones and where ample scope has been given to autonomous development efforts by participating schools and teachers, the results have been much more useful for policy-making and will probably be more lasting ones.

More often, however, the importance of research in relation to policy-making will be more of an *indirect* one. Basic questions of the Swedish school reform – and of any school reform in a democratic society – are still unsolved, for example, under what conditions can children of different abilities and interests profitably learn and work together, how can individualisation be combined with social training, and how can individualisation truly further the less gifted and not only the more gifted pupils, as is often the case in technologically based individualisation?

New questions have come to the fore with the increase for instance of children of non-Swedish origin in Swedish schools: what is the relationship between learning the "home language" and the "adopted language", under what conditions can true bilinguality best be achieved (even: does it exist?)? Can Swedish as a foreign language be taught to children with different home languages in the same school class?

Research can be commissioned and /or be specifically supported by policy-makers, but they must know where to stop when formulating their questions and interpreting the results. The independence of research has to be respected and the outcome honestly utilised. This, obviously, is not always the case.

3. *Development* can be a link between research and policy-making, but there are other types of development with a different origin. They start rather from the problems of implementation of the curriculum – as did the first education development centres – or from the more general task of teaching small children, as did the Oxfordshire primary schools and similar schools in other English counties. Such development activities are difficult to evaluate and possibly cannot be truly appreciated in a scientific way. One risks missing the dynamism of the development – which may be described but not measured – or entering into the process too late, or even contributing to ending it. This is not to say that research can have no relationship to this kind of development; the ideal seems to me to be what in German has been called *begleitende Forschung*, a kind of "accompanying of research", helping to analyse, define, advise, not to control, govern or measure. It would seem to me that this kind of develop-

ment is mostly of a limited life-time. As an American researcher pointed out (Rowland, 1969), there seems to be a kind of defreeze or thaw effect, which makes the dynamic process possible, a creative phase, the result of which is change. After a time the change is institutionalised, the institution may be "frozen". Ideally by that time the movement should have caught on in other places and in other schools, which should not necessarily be expected to copy the original but to face the same basic problems and to work, with its own dynamism, to find its own models of solving them.

4. Probably it is in this kind of dynamic process that researchers may find more important and worthy objects than in just evaluating outcome. There will be "knots" in the developmental process which have to be analysed and if possible untied. There is the whole process of what causes the thaw and the freeze to be studied; there is the question of what causes innovation, or why reform is always implemented in depth.

Several years ago, Professor Karl-Gustaf Stukát, after careful studies in many Swedish classrooms, stated that "individualisation is a rare bird in the Swedish classroom". Callewaert & Nilsson (1980) maintain that this is still the case and that, in general, the teaching method in Swedish schools is very traditional, defeating the basic objectives of the school reform. It can be said, as they would do, that schools are just products of society, whatever their objectives, as defined by idealistic (or opportunistic) policy-makers.

Even if I want to be realistic, I still try to be optimistic. According to the 1980 curriculum – based on my bill of 1979 – each school has to work out a plan for its pedagogic and social activities for the school year, the idea being that teachers and other school personnel, together with their students, should base the work both on their problems and their resources in their given setting. They will find patterns and advice on national, regional and local levels. But basically, it is my hope that this model of work – to which my successor has added resources for local development activities – will release forces of dynamic development. It is my conviction that researchers will find fruitful tasks both in accompanying such development and in working at untying the "knots" and analysing the basic problems which will no doubt present themselves. It is, I think, in fruitful interaction – certainly not without tension and conflict – that hope for a continuous reform can be placed.

REFERENCES

Ader, Jean (1975) *Building Implications of the Multi-option School.* OECD, Paris.
Andrae, Annika, (1980) *Grundskola i glesbygd.* Försöksverksamhet med årskurslöst högstadium. Uppsala Studies in Education, Uppsala.
Bjerstedt, Åke (1968) *Skolan och det pedagogiska utvecklingsarbetet.* Gleerups, Halmstead/Lund.
Callewaert, Staf & Nilsson, Bengt A. (1980) *Skolklassen som socialt system.* Lektionsanalyser. Lunds Bok- och Tidskrifts AB, Kristianstad/Lund.
Bennis, Warren G., Benne, Kenneth D. & Chin, Robert (1970) *The Planning of Change.* Holt, Rinehart and Winston, London.

Engquist, Olle, Gran, Bertil & Lindh, Sune (1975) *Pedagogiskt utvecklingsarbete i Malmö under tio år.* Skolöverstyrelsen, Stockholm.
Goldschmidt, Dietrich & Roeder, Peter M. (hrsg.) (1979). *Alternative Schulen?* Gestalt und Funktion im Rahmen öffentlicher Bildungssysteme. Klett-Cotta, Stuttgart.
Gran, Bertil & Rudvall, Göte (1981) *Skolan som utvecklingsmiljö.* Lärarhögskolan, Malmö.
Gran, Birgitta (1982) *Från förskola till grundskola.* Villkor för barns utveckling i åldrarna kring skolstarten. Gleerups/Liber, Malmö/Lund.
Husén, Torsten (1979) *The School in Question.* A Comparative Study of the School and its Future in Western Society. Oxford University Press.
Lundgren, Ulf P. (1979) *Att organisera omvärlden.* En introduktion till läroplansteori. Liber, Borås/Stockholm.
Marklund, Sixten (1982) *Skolsverige 1950-1975. Del 2. Försöksverksamheten.* Liber, Helsinborg/ Stockholm.
Pedagogiska nämnden (1978) Redogörelse för verksamhetsåret 1977/78. Skolöverstyrelsen, Stockholm.
Pedagogiska nämnden (1981) Redogörelse för verksamhetsåret 1980/81. Skolöverstyrelsen, Stockholm.
Proposition, Regeringens (1979) *Läroplan för grundskolan.* 1978/79, 180.
Rapp, Nils Jan (1979) *Skolan som satte segel.* Om projektorienterad undervisning på Öckerö. Liber, Falköping/Stockholm.
Rodhe, Birgit (1972) *A Two Way Open School.* In Prospects in Education, 1972, 1. Unesco, Paris.
Rodhe, Birgit (1976a) *Teachers and School Building* in Teachers and Innovators, New Patterns of Teacher Education and Tasks. OECD, Paris.
Rodhe, Birgit (1976b) Teachers and School Building. OECD, Paris.
Rodhe, Birgit; Lindell, Ebbe & Bjerstedt, Åke (1965) *Pedagogiska utvecklingsblocket i Malmö.* Synpunkter på verksamheten läsåret 1964/65. Lärarhögskolan, Malmö.
Rodhe, Birgit & Andersson, Ruth (1970) *Pedagogiska utvecklingblocket i Malmö.* Synpunkter på verksamheten läsåret 1969/70. Lärarhögskolan, Malmö.
Rodhe, Birgit & Gran, Bertil (eds.) (1974) *New Patterns of Teacher Tasks.* School of Education, Malmö.
Rowland, Monroe K (1969) *A String of Beads.* International Learning Corporation, Fort Lauderdale.
Silberman, Charles E. (1979) *Crisis in the Classroom.* The Remaking of American Education. Random House, New York.
Skolöverstyrelsen (1964) *Varierande klasstorlek och lagundervisning.* Karlshamn.
SOU (1980) *Skolforskning och skolutveckling.* Betänkande av skolforskningskommittén, Stockholm.

Researchers, Policy Analysts and Policy Intellectuals

BY MARTIN TROW

Models of the Relation of Research to Policy

In a paper presented to the conference which gave rise to this volume (Husén, 1982), Torsten Husén argues that the relation of research to policy is far more complex, far more indirect than it formerly appeared. Drawing on the informed writings of Carol Weiss and Maurice Kogan, among others, and from his own rich experience, he dismisses as irrelevant, at least to the field of education, two classical models of the application of research to policy that Weiss lists among seven different models or concepts of research utilisation: the "linear" model, which leads neatly from basic knowledge to applied research to development to application, and the "problem-solving" model, in which research is done to fill in certain bodies of knowledge needed to make a decision among policy alternatives. These are dismissed on the grounds that they simply do not even roughly describe what happens in the real world. The remaining five models he merges into two. One is an "enlightenment" or "percolation" model, in which research somehow (and just how is of greatest interest) influences policy indirectly, by entering into the consciousness of the actors and shaping the terms of their discussion about policy alternatives. The second, the "political model," refers to the intentional use of research by political decision-makers to strengthen an argument, to justify positions already taken, or to avoid making or having to make unpopular decisions by burying the controversial problem in research.

Of these two models, the "percolation" model is the more interesting, for both Husén and myself, since it is the way through which research actually has an influence on policy, rather than merely used to justify or avoid making decisions. Moreover the percolation model and its mechanisms and processes are so subtle that they challenge study and reflection.

The bulk of Husén's paper is devoted to an exploration from various perspectives of the complexities in the relation of researcher to policy, with special attention to the variety of forces and conditions that come between the researcher and the policy-maker. These help explain why it is that research, when it does have a bearing on policy, does so in complicated indirect ways rather than through the simpler more direct ways of the classical, but now discredited models.

In Husén's words:

> The "percolation" process is a very subtle, and, in many respects, intangible one. The direct contact, either face to face or through the reading of scholarly reports with all the paraphernalia of technical jargon, seems to play little role. The role of "middle-men" should be carefully studied, because this appears to be a key one. One can identify entire "informal networks" of intermediate linking mechanisms. Newspapers, journals with popularised versions of research findings, friends of the politicians, and their staff members play important roles. Certain research-promoting, private bodies can also play an important role in spreading the information that relates to the idea of fiscal neutrality and equality of finance. The "percolation" is of particular importance to the staffs of legislators and top administrations in a ministry of education or state board of education. (Husén, 1982, p. 5).

In a recent, unpublished paper by Ulrich Teichler describing some of his preliminary thoughts about a study on "research in higher education and its impact", he notes that:

> The underlying hypothesis (of the study) is that the way that research on higher education develops and has impact on decision-making is highly influenced by the general climate of interaction between researchers and decision-makers. In the Federal Republic of Germany, the conditions are not very favorable for research on higher education: Administrators tend to prefer very controlled ways of major data collection, believe in the strengths of administrators to solve almost all problems without relying on research and mistrust the political inclinations of researchers. There are however, exceptions as regard to the administrators, the researchers accepted as well as the topics of the research desired. On the other hand, researchers are heavily inclined to take over political roles themselves. (Teichler, 1982)

Similarly, Premfors, drawing on the writings of Lindblom and Wildavsky, argues that analysis, a category broader than research, including "intellectual cogitation" with or without the data base that we associate with research,

> . . . is generally accorded an exaggerated role in studies of . . . public policy-making. Social scientists tend to underestimate the importance of various forms of social interaction as problem-solving mechanisms, even in contexts where analysis seemingly provides the basic criteria for policy choices. Social interaction – which has two basic forms in problem solving contexts: politics and markets – is more often than not the major determinant of outcomes. When analysis or intellectual cogitation appears in various guises it is normally as "partisan analysis" i.e. analysis tailored to policy positions already adopted. (Premfors, March, 1982, p. 1)

But Premfors, like Husén, does not wholly agree that research and analysis are merely devices for legitimating policies whose sources and determinants lie elsewhere. He continues:

> However, we are dealing with a complex relationship. The literature on knowledge utilisation in social problem-solving has in recent years taken pains to illustrate the many ways in which policy analysis and social research may enter such processes . . . A lack of impact in the short run does not preclude considerable effects in the long run. The fact that analysis does not provide the "objective" criteria often sought by policy-makers and analysts, does not preclude that such activities slowly permeate the definition of problems and the formulation of choices. (Premfors, *ibid.*)

Premfors here is suggesting that analysis and research, on one hand, and social interaction on the other, are not alternative forms of reaching decisions, but are complementary. Both market behaviour and political behaviour are affected by analysis and research, but as all these commentators appear to agree, more commonly through a process of percolation whereby knowledge and ideas "slowly permeate the definition of problems and the formulation of choices".[1]

In exploring this complex topic it is desirable to avoid premature cross-national generalisations. Even if we confine ourselves to the field of education, countries differ enormously in where and how educational decisions are made, how centralised or dispersed those decision points are, and what kinds of decisions are made at what levels. They differ also in the development and organisation of research and analysis about education, where that work is done, at whose initiative, and under what constraints. And countries differ also in what Teichler calls "the general climate of interaction between researchers and decision-makers". Indeed, Teichler warns that "one has to compare the 'interaction climate' in different countries in order to explain the potentials and the short-comings of the impact of higher education research in a given country". (Teichler, 1982, p. 4)

A New Actor—the Policy Analyst

In his paper Husén speaks throughout of "researchers", by which he clearly means social scientists employed in universities. In part his discussion of the gulf between researchers and policy-makers arises out of the quite different training, time constraints and work situations that characterise the university social scientist as compared with the decision-maker, the politician or civil servant.

I want to contribute to this discussion of the influence of research on policy in education by talking about a different kind of actor in the process – an actor who is sometimes very much like a researcher, defining a problem, doing analysis and gathering and interpreting new data; sometimes like a "middle-man", bringing together and interpreting for decision-makers the findings of research by others; and sometimes himself a decision-maker. This actor has come to be called a "policy analyst" in the United States, but he may have his analogues and counterparts with different names in other countries.

The past decade has seen in the United States, and to some extent elsewhere, the emergence of a profession, that of the policy analyst, whose training, habits of mind and conditions of work are expressly designed to narrow the gap

---

[1]How market behaviour is affected by research is an interesting but separate problem. It seems likely that some actors in markets, for example, students choosing a college or career, use the findings of educational research as these are publicised and interpreted by commentators, popularisers and school and vocational counsellors. A useful line of research is one pioneered many years ago by Coleman and others, who studied the role of personal influence in decision-making. (Coleman, *et al.,* 1957; Katz, 1957).

between the researcher and the policy-maker, and to bring systematic knowledge to bear more directly, more quickly and more relevantly on the issues of public policy. Let me try to compare and contrast the researcher and the policy analyst to see how this breed of staff analyst/researcher, inside as well as outside government, may affect the ways in which research comes to bear on policy. My comparison is not intended to be invidious, that is, I am not implying that the invention of policy analysis has in any way solved the problems of the relation of research to policy that Husén, Carol Weiss and others have identified. But it may be of interest to see how this emerging profession affects that process, and how it generates new intellectual, political and moral – as it solves some of the old.

Policy analysis developed as a formal discipline about 10 years ago through the coming together of a number of strands of work and thought in the social sciences. These included operations research developed during World War II on a strongly mathematical basis for improving the efficiency of military operations. Added to this were new forms of micro-economics developed in the 1950s and 1960s; the long standing tradition of work in public administration; the newer and increasingly strong strain of behaviourism in the political sciences; organisational theory; certain lines of applied sociology and social psychology; and the emerging interest in the role of law in public policy. Graduate schools of public policy were established in a number of leading American universities about 1970 – for example, the Kennedy School at Harvard, the Woodrow Wilson School at Princeton, the LBJ School at Texas, schools of public policy at Michigan and Minnesota, and the Graduate School of Public Policy at Berkeley.

Twelve leading universities now have genuine graduate schools of public policy; there are literally hundreds of others which offer programmes which include some measure of policy analysis in their schools of management, public administration, or business administration.

To the mix of social science and law some schools have added scientists, engineers and others interested in public policy problems. These graduate schools for the most part offer a two-year postgraduate professional degree, ordinarily for the Master of Public Policy. Their graduates go directly into public service at national, state or local levels, or get jobs in think-tanks or private agencies concerned with public issues – for example, organisations concerned with the preservation of the environment, with education, overseas trade and so forth. These latter "private" organisations, however, are directly involved for the most part in public policy – indeed, much of what they do is to try to influence public policy, so the conditions of work for public policy analysts in them resembles that of those analysts who enter governmental service itself.

There are several aspects of the training of policy analysts that need to be emphasised. As must already be clear, the training of the policy analyst is intensely interdisciplinary. This is required first because of the diverse nature of its intellectual antecedents; the field itself reflects the coming together, the mutual links among diverse currents of what Harold Lasswell called the "policy sciences". (Lerner and Lasswell, 1951.) But more important, the training has to be interdisciplinary because that is the way the problems present themselves to decision-makers. Real decisions, as we all know, do not respect the boundaries of the academic disciplines: they always have political, economic, and organisational components; they may well have also legal, educational, biological or other technical implications as well.

Perhaps the most important distinguishing characteristic of the policy analyst as contrasted with the academic research social scientist in the university is that he or she is trained, indeed required, to see and to formulate problems from the perspectives not of the academic disciplines, but of the decision-maker. In his work he accepts the constraints and values of the decision-maker – the political pressures on him, the political feasibility of a proposal, its financial costs, the legal context within which it will operate, the difficulties of implementing it, of shaping organisations, and of recruiting, training, and motivating people to work in the service of its purposes. He is, if effectively trained, sensitive to the costs and benefits of programmes, to the trade-offs in any decision, and to the alternative advantages of government and the market in achieving social purposes. In a word, he tries to see problems from the perspective of the decision-maker, but with a set of intellectual, analytical and research tools that the politician or senior civil servant may not possess. He is, and is trained to be, the researcher in government[2] at the elbow of the decision-maker, or if not in government, then serving the "government in opposition" or some think-tank or interest group which hopes to staff the next administration or agency on the next swing of the political pendulum.

By contrast, the faculty members of schools of public policy are not, for the most part, like the students that they train: the former are almost without exception academic social scientists with Ph.D.s trained in and drawn from the social science disciplines, specialists originally who have a particular interest in public policy, and who do research on policy issues, but not on the whole like the research that their students will be doing in their government or quasi-government jobs. The faculty members of these schools are for the most part what James Q. Wilson has called "policy intellectuals", while their students are policy analysts – the staff people and bureaucrats serving their policy-oriented clients in and out of government. That relationship of the policy intellectual in the university to the policy analyst in government bears on the issue of "knowledge creep" and "research percolation" that Husén and Carol Weiss speak of, and to which I want to return.

---

[2] Of course, not all policy analysts are "researchers", as the university conceives of research. But what they do, bringing ideas and information to bear on social "problems" in a search for "solutions", is the kind of "research" that has the most direct influence on public policy.

The Policy Analyst as Compared to the Researcher

Let us look at some of the characteristics of "researchers" as Husén describes them, and at some of the "disjunctions" between research and policy that the nature of the researcher in the university gives rise to. The field of policy analysis and the new profession of policy analyst were, one might say, invented precisely to meet the need of policy-makers for analysis and research carried out within the same constraints that the policy-maker experiences. Policy analysis thus aims to narrow those "disjunctions" between research and policy of which Husén speaks. He describes three conditions under which researchers work that are different for policy analysts.

1. "Researchers are usually performing their tasks at . . . universities. . . . They tend to conduct their research according to the paradigms to which they have become socialised by their graduate studies. Their achievements are subjected to peer reviews which they regard as more important than assessments made by the customers in a public agency." (Husén, 1982, pp. 4–5.) Analysts by contrast work for the most part in government or in shadow governmental agencies like Brookings and Rand, or in large private business organisations. The paradigms of research that they acquire in graduate school emphasise the importance of serving the client, of defining or clarifying the nature of his problem, or identifying the policy options available to him, of evaluating those alternatives in terms of their cost, probable effectiveness, political feasibility, ease of implementation and the like – the same criteria which the decision-maker himself would use in planning and choosing a course of action. The analyst is trained then to make recommendations among the action alternatives that he has identified, supporting his recommendations with appropriate arguments and evidence.

Much, perhaps most, of what such analysts do is not published, is not reviewed by peers, and will almost certainly appear, if at all, in greatly modified form, either anonymously or under someone else's name.

The analyst's reputation will be made *not* in an academic setting, but in his agency, and more importantly among the small but active community of analysts in government agencies, on legislative staffs, in think-tanks and special interest organisations, who do know of his work and its quality. Incidentally, it is in that arena of discussion and assessment – the analyst's analogue to the scholar's "invisible college" – that we need to look for the mechanisms of information "creep", and for the processes of percolation through which research and evidence come to influence policy.

2. "Researchers operate at a high level of training and specialisation, which means that they tend to isolate a 'slice' of a problem area that can be more readily handled than more complicated global problems." (*Ibid.*, p. 5)

By contrast, analysts are trained to be as interdisciplinary as possible, to follow the requirements of a problem in their choice of ideas, theories and research methods, rather than to allow the theories and methods of their discipline to select and shape their problems. That is not wholly successful, in part because their teachers in these schools are not themselves equally familiar with the variety of research methods and perspectives across disciplinary lines, and because their students, the fledgling analysts, inevitably come to be more familiar and comfortable with some kinds of analysis rather than others. Nevertheless, the requirement that they see problems as the policy-maker would were he an analyst requires analysts to transcend the constraints of a single discipline and to tackle problems as wholes rather than by "slices".

3. "Researchers are much less constrained than policy-makers in terms of what problems they can tackle, what kind of critical language they can employ and how much time they have . . . at their disposal to complete a study." (*Ibid.*, p. 5.)

Analysts, by contrast, ordinarily are assigned their studies, or do them within circumscribed policy areas. That does not wholly preclude their exercise of discretion; and indeed, they may exercise very important amounts of initiative in how they formulate their problems, and in the range of responses to the problems they consider.[3] From the researcher's perspective, the captive analyst is merely "a hired gun" doing what he is told by his political or bureaucratic superiors. But from the perspective of the analyst, discretion, even within the constraints of a given policy problem or area, may be very considerable. How to control air pollution in a given area, for example, allows a variety of regulatory solutions, from setting standards for allowable emissions for different kinds of plants and industries, to setting charges on pollutants, requiring polluters to pay for each unit of pollutant emitted. The issues are political, technical, economic, legal and normative – and they are not always decided *a priori* by political or administrative decision-makers.

It is true that analysts are ordinarily held to a closer time frame than are academic researchers; in my own School, students become accustomed to doing analyses of various policy problems, drawing upon the best available data, research and advice, within 48 or 72 hours, exercises designed to prepare them for the fierce time pressures of legislative hearings or the negotiations that accompany the writing and revision of legislation. Other exercises allow them a week, and a major piece of research equivalent to a master's essay will take up to 6 months. Time constraints on the job also vary; analysts become skilful in knowing who has been working on a given problem area, and where published or unpublished research or data on the issue can be found. For the analyst, knowledgeable people are a central research resource, and the telephone is part of the student's equipment alongside calculators, computers and the library.

But as he develops the skill of rapidly bringing ideas to bear on data, and data on ideas, the analyst becomes heavily dependent upon existing statistics

---

[3]See Arnold J. Meltsner, (1976), especially Chapter 3, "Policy Selection," pp. 81–114.

and on research done by others. He is often skilful, and even bold, in drawing analogies between findings in different areas of social life, allowing him thus to use the findings of research in one area for informed decisions in another. The analyst cannot often meet the scholar's standards of depth and thoroughness in his research – for example, in his review of the research literature, or in his critical evaluation of the findings of relevant research. Yet working under time and other pressures in the political milieu, the analyst knows that the alternative to what he is doing is not a major university-based research project, but more commonly the impressions, anecdotes and general wisdom of a staff conference. His own report, which includes a discussion of alternative lines of action based on data regarding their comparative costs and benefits, must, he believes, be better than an unsystematic discussion among friends and advisers.

Policy analysts in government, as we have described them, have some of the characteristics of researchers, but are more narrowly constrained by their bureaucratic roles. They also have some of the characteristics of Maurice Kogan's middle-men, professionals who serve a liaison function (Kogan, Korman and Henkel, 1980, pp. 36–38), though they are more active and ready to take research initiatives than the term "middle-man" implies. But they also are not infrequently the decision-makers themselves.

One almost always talks about research *influencing* decision-makers – and if the researcher is a university social scientist then the decision-maker is almost certainly someone a distance away with his own concerns, political commitments, interests, and prejudices. But the policy analyst has the advantage of acting within the bureaucracy to make or directly affect a myriad of administrative decisions that rarely get into the newspapers, are not debated by politicians or on floors of legislatures, but nevertheless have very large consequences. Sweden can surely supply a myriad of illustrations of administrative decision-making, some of which may even have been informed by research done inside or outside the bureaucracy.

One illustration comes from the University of California, half of whose budget, the half which pays the operating costs of the University, faculty salaries and the like, comes from the State of California. The preparation of the University's budget and its incorporation into the Governor's budget, is a complicated procedure. Very substantial parts of the University's budget are governed by formulas, relating, for example, support levels to enrolment levels which have been negotiated over the years between the budget analysts in the central administration of the University and their counterparts in the State Department of Finance. These formulas, essentially bureaucratic treaties, are mutual understandings which give the University a greater degree of fiscal security and predictability than one would ever guess by reading the newspapers, which almost never report these matters, but only the visible debates in the legislature and the speeches by the Governor.

The formulas, of course, do not cover all contingencies, especially in an institution as fluid and diverse as the University, with so many different sources of energy and initiative, creating new programmes, facilities and claims on public funds all the time. Claims for resources, old and new, are argued out or negotiated annually between the University analysts and the State Department of Finance analysts; they speak each other's language, and often have been trained in the same graduate schools and departments, not infrequently in Berkeley's School of Public Policy.

In these negotiations, "good arguments" by the University are rewarded; that is, requests for additional support funds which are supported by a good bureaucratic argument are often accepted, and new activities are built into the Governor's budget. The arguments made for these programmes are the arguments of analysts, often based on analogies with existing State-funded activities, and backed by data showing the actual nature of the activity and its costs. For example, the University wants the State to revise the formula allocating funds for the replacement of scientific equipment used in teaching; it wants more generous provision for teaching assistants; it wants the State to assume the costs of certain athletic facilities; it wants the State to support remedial courses for underprepared students; and so on. In support of these claims the University analysts do research on the actual useful life of laboratory instruments in different scientific departments, and on how that record compares with the life of instruments in other universities and in commercial labs; it studies the use and distribution of teaching assistants in the University and how their work contributes to the instructional programme; it studies who uses the athletic facilities and for what purposes; and so on. These are not matters of high principle; there exists a broad area of value consensus between the negotiators, but the quality of the research backing those claims is crucial to whether they are accepted, and indeed whether they ought to be accepted. The sums of money that are allocated in these ways are in the aggregate very large.

There are many areas of public life in which civil servants exercise wide decision-making discretion, though they are often wise enough to deny that they are in fact making policy or decisions, but merely "implementing" them. Nevertheless, when we reflect on the influence of research on policy, we should not neglect the realm of bureaucratic and technocratic decision-making in the public sector, where researcher and decision-maker come together in the person of the policy analyst. University-based researchers need to be reminded that not all research has to percolate down through a complex network of relationships to enter another complex process of "decision accretion"; some research has access to decision-makers quickly and directly, and is done for and by them.

The newly emergent field of policy analysis seems to be thriving in the United States, at least in a modest way, even in the face of budget cuts and hiring freezes in the federal and in many state and local governments. Policy analysts are in demand whether public expenditures are rising or falling; the problems posed to government by budgetary constraints are even more severe than those posed by expansion and the proliferation of public programmes and services. And with all the cuts, most governments are not reducing the absolute level of public expenditures on social services, but merely reducing their rates of growth. In any event, public life is becoming increasingly more complex and there is no shortage of work for policy analysts.

Four Problems Facing the Policy Analyst

But it should not be thought that the emergence of the policy analyst, and of the infrastructure of graduate schools, journals, professional associations and meetings which gives definition and self-consciousness to their intellectual community and neo-profession, solves all the problems of the relation of research to policy. For if policy analysts solve some of those problems, they also create new ones. I would like to discuss three such problems in the realm of policy analysis as currently practiced, though I do not mean to imply there are only three. These are all problems which in significant ways affect the quality of the analyst's work and his influence on policy and decision-making.

First, and this is a problem that the analyst shares with much academic research in education, policy analysis makes relatively little use of ethnographic field methods, the method of direct observation of customary behaviour and informal conversation. One consequence of this is that the policy analyst, as I have suggested, is a captive of existing and usually official statistics; where those statistics are wrong, misleading or inadequate, the analyst's work is also flawed, misleading and inadequate. By contrast, university researchers are more likely to question the quality of research data.

Second, the outcome of public policy analysis, its reports and recommendations, are affected not only by the analyst's own preferences and biases, and those of his client, but also by how the analyst bounds his problem, the phenomena and variables that he will take into account. These boundaries are sharply constrained by his position within the bureaucratic work setting, more so than for the university-based researcher.

Third, for every policy analyst outside the university there is tension between the needs and requirements of his client, on one hand, and his own professional commitments to intellectual honesty, to the searching out of negative evidence, to his freedom to speak and publish what he knows or has learned, on the other. Bureaucratic research settings put severe strains on those scholarly and professional values. Indeed, the moral issue of how a given analyst deals with his dual loyalty to his professional identity as a policy analyst and to his political masters and clients is at the heart of policy analysis, and not, as moral issues often are, at the margins.

Finally, I would like to deal with the relation between policy analysts and policy intellectuals, as that relation bears on the nature of communication and persuasion in the political arena, and more broadly on the processes of "decision accretion" through enlightenment and the percolation into the decision-making process of research findings, ideas, and assumptions.

The Absence of Ethnography and its Consequences

The near absence of ethnography from the research armamentarium of the policy analyst places a major limitation on the policy analyst's contribution to public policy. Ethnography, the direct observation of customary behaviour, and the reporting and evaluation of the significance of that behaviour, is extremely expensive of time. It involves the primary collection of data rather than the analysis of data, for example, statistics gathered by agencies of government. Policy analysts often work under severe time constraints, and it is almost impossible to reduce the real time required to come to know and be accepted by people whom one is living among and observing closely. Those who use other methods of research can substitute money and assistants for time, but that is not possible for ethnographers.

One source of resistance to ethnography by policy analysts lies in the canons of verification held in the various disciplines which have contributed to the faculty of public policy schools. Ethnographic methods are, for the most part, non-quantitative, and it is hard to use them to "prove" hypotheses. Part of the resistance to ethnography lies in the difficulty that its users have in demonstrating control over researcher bias. This control is built into the training and the systematic, though qualitative, methods of the professional ethnographer, but that is hard to demonstrate to laymen. Unlike anthropology, which is written for other anthropologists, a good deal of policy analysis is addressed to laymen, including politicians, and it has to persuade laymen. Field methods are not sufficiently esoteric to be persuasive to laymen, and that is an important weakness of that kind of data for policy analysts. A persuasive methodology is central to policy studies. This surely accounts for the high, and often inappropriate, formalisation of policy analysis, its esoteric forms of modelling and statistical manipulation. By contrast, ethnography simply is not enough like the esoteric hard sciences to borrow their persuasive authority.

Another reason that ethnography does not appeal to policy analysts is that it tends to force a degree of disaggregation of phenomena that is incompatible with the generalising tendencies of public policies. Public policy analysis is not really interested in the fine structures of social life, partly because it is generally impossible to develop legislation, rules and policies appropriate to the variability of the specific circumstances in which policies are actually implemented. Policy analysis for the most part rests on certain brutal simplifications, the chief one being that the activities, people or phenomena that are grouped within a category are in fact sufficiently alike so that they can be dealt with under a common set of assumptions and by a common set of rules and regulations. Ethnographic studies continually reveal the inadequacy of the categories which underpin policy and policy analysis, and thus are in a way subversive of broad and uniform laws and rules. At the same time ethnographic studies provide another perspective, that of the objects of policy, one that could strengthen the capacity of policy analysis to be responsive to the rich variability of social and economic life.

Ethnography is also suspect to analysts because it tends to uncover politically inconvenient facts. When ethnographers study organisations or communities they often learn quite a lot about how rules and laws are bent or broken, and by whom. But analysts and their bureaucratic superiors are not interested in or rewarded for muckraking, which ethnography often makes possible and even unavoidable.

Finally, ethnography does not seem to be a really serious and hard-to-acquire skill. Analysts can imagine themselves spending time in the library or even better in front of a computer console or at their desks with calculating machines and recorder. They find it hard to imagine themselves "hanging around" a streetcorner, or in a classroom, or in the other ordinary places where the objects of social policy usually hang out. That simply does not seem like dignified work appropriate to people with the high skills and rare abilities to analyse public policies. And not least, very few policy analysts have been trained to use themselves as the chief instrument for recording, describing and understanding social life. They are, in short, not anthropologists, and they find it much more difficult to acquire the skills of ethnographic field work, than, say, to acquire new skills in the use of computers or the ability to do survey research.

These are only some of the reasons that policy analysts so rarely employ ethnographic methods. Some of these reasons apply to university-based researchers as well. But the failure to employ ethnographic methods is a serious handicap to making research useful and relevant to public policy. And that is because without field methods we are severely handicapped in learning why it is that some of our public policies are successful, while so many others fail.

One example: in all advanced industrial societies, I think without exception, the national statistics on the labour force show a rise in unemployment rates among youth in recent years, even larger than one would expect as the effects of the current economic recession. These figures are much discussed, many explanations are given for them, and large and expensive public projects are developed to do something about this grave and growing social problem. Yet almost no one goes behind the published statistics to ask what they mean, whether there are in fact growing numbers of young people who are anxiously seeking gainful employment and are unable to find any. What we ought to do, and most policy analysts do not do, is to question the quality and meaning of the published statistics on this issue. What statistics on youth unemployment do not reflect, for example, are certain developments in modern industrial society in recent years, reflecting a liberalisation of welfare policies, which make it easier for young people to get public assistance, but only if they are "unemployed". The statistics also do not reflect the rapid growth of the grey or "subterranean" economies, which employ young people in casual but uncontrolled, unreported and untaxed occupations. (Trow, 1979.) Moreover, they do not reflect the development of youth cultures and attitudes toward work and leisure which make young unmarried people far more discriminating about the kinds of jobs they will accept and for how long. (Roberts, Noble and Duggan, 1982.) Field studies using direct and participant observation of youth cultures are, I believe, necessary to get a better understanding of the varied and changing attitudes toward work among different kinds of youth; they would help to give us a better sense of the extent of the unrecorded subterranean economy and the role of youth in it; and would even be of some help in seeing the effects of liberalised welfare provisions in encouraging young people to be "out of work" for periods of time after leaving school and before they marry or "settle down".

I hasten to add that I am not saying that there is no real problem of youth unemployment in western societies, but only that the official statistics tell us very little of its character and extent. The statistics on youth unemployment, on which policy analysts are so dependent, do not provide a good data base for the creation of effective public policies aimed at ameliorating the problem. If in fact youth unemployment as a national phenomenon is not accurately reflected in the official statistics, if, for example, it is really two or three quite different problems, then our public policies and programmes ought to be responsive to its true character and not to the common sense notions so crudely measured by the central statistical offices.

But in this policy area, like others, the constraints on the policy analyst's time, on the nature of the problems he pursues and how he attacks them may make it impossible for him to go behind the published figures. Moreover it is hard to imagine an analyst in one branch of government making a fundamental critique of the work of the central statistical office of the same government. It remains for the relatively free university researcher to question the quality and meaning of published statistics about youth unemployment, and about many other aspects of life on which government agencies gather statistics. Policy analysts are dependent on published figures, and that I fear is a serious limitation on their contribution to good public policies, at least in some policy areas.

What I have been saying may be less true for Sweden than for many other countries, by virtue both of the quality and extent of its public record-keeping, and of the relative homogeneity of its population. When a culture is widely shared, its participants may not have to do research into its character; they live it, and to know how people feel they need only observe life around them and reflect on their own experience. And this applies to researchers as well as to civil servants and policy analysts. Ethnography becomes more important as one's national culture becomes more diverse, and as more of it becomes foreign to one's own experience and understanding. In order to understand our own complex world we have to study the society that we live in. This is of course true to an extreme degree in the United States, with its extraordinarily varied population and ethnic subcultures.[4] But I suspect it is becoming true for Sweden as more of its population comes to have its recent origins in other countries and especially in Mediterranean countries. Moreover, it is those groups that are disproportionately liable to be the objects of public policy.

My second illustration is drawn from the important and influential study published in 1966 known as "Coleman I". (Coleman, 1966.) The major findings of the first Coleman report were that differences in a number of readily measured characteristics of schools – per pupil expenditures, pupil/teacher ratios, teacher education, building quality and the like – have little or no effect on academic achievement once you control for aspects of family background. Moreover, this was true for both whites and blacks. The study also seemed to show that there were some gains in achievement for blacks enrolled in integrated schools without any evident loss for the whites in the same schools. But these findings, showing very slight effects of school characteristics compared with the much larger effects of home environment, were seized upon as evidence of the desirability, indeed the necessity, of integrating the schools forcefully, and by bussing if necessary.

Subsequent analysis and discussion led many to believe that the Coleman report's measures of "school effects" were simply not powerful enough to capture the subtle aspects of schools and schooling that do indeed make a difference to whether and how much children learn in them. These include such aspects of the school as how teachers conduct their classes, how principals manage their schools, the degree of order and discipline in them, and much of what might be called the school "ethos", its institutional values and culture. These characteristics of a school are all difficult to capture through large scale survey instruments, and the processes through which they have their effects are even more elusive. But ethnographic studies of schools as institutions and communities help us to learn more about the subtle but powerful forces that make some schools and teachers much more effective than others with the same kinds of pupils. Policy analysts, and indeed many other educational researchers, tend to focus on the inputs and outputs of schools. Ethnographic studies allow us to get inside the black boxes that schools are to researchers to see what goes on inside them, not only the specifics of pedagogic techniques and teaching but the life of the school as a community. James Coleman wrote about many of those matters years ago in his book on the adolescent society in the school. (Coleman, 1961.) We need to go back to some of those ideas and insights and

---

[4]For example, the few ethnographic studies of the life of American blacks in northern cities reveal patterns of life and values at variance with the assumptions of social welfare programmes designed to help them. See Liebow, (1967) and Stack (1974).

see to what extent the social pressures that he saw at work in high schools 20 years ago can be found at work today.

The study of school effects through close observation may give us a research base for developing better public policies for schools. (Wax, Wax and Dumont, 1964.) But I think this work will have to be done by university-based researchers rather than by policy analysts in public agencies.

The Bounding of Problems

Another major limitation on the policy analyst is the effect of his work setting on the way he bounds his problem in time, space and relevant variables. One illustration of the effects of the bounding of research on its implications for policy can be drawn from how policy-makers used the Coleman report referred to above which addressed the effects of school and home characteristics on student achievement. It was, of course, a central referent in the heated debate over school integration during the next decade and a half. The racial integration of urban schools, and especially their forced integration through bussing, as Coleman and others subsequently pointed out, accelerated the flight of white families from the cities where bussing was imposed, and thus helped both to defeat efforts at school integration, and also profoundly affected the character and viability of many American cities. If these unintended and unanticipated effects of bussing were known, it is likely the debate over bussing would have been conducted quite differently, and perhaps with different outcomes. The bounding of the problem, as Coleman saw and studied it, was constrained both by the legislative charge to his study group, and by his and our ignorance of the effects on residential patterns and mobility of forced integration within the political boundaries of the big cities.

My point is that no one saw then that the quality and character of American public education would be affected not only by the characteristics of the schools themselves, but also by the characteristics of the cities in which they were located, and that in turn might be substantially affected by policies directed rather narrowly at changing the racial ratios of urban public schools. We are all continually being thwarted and defeated by the unintended and unanticipated consequences of our purposeful social action. I drew my example from a policy-oriented university-based research, but I suspect that policy analysts, constrained as they are by their bureaucratic work settings, are even more narrow in bounding their research inappropriately, and are more likely than other social scientists to be unpleasantly surprised by the inextinguishable inventiveness of society's responses to political intervention into its life and institutions.

Another illustration of the effects of the bounding of problems is drawn from a bit of counter-factual history. Some years ago I reflected on the significance of the historical fact that the United States did not establish a national university supported by federal funds as was warmly recommended by George Washington during his presidency and by the five presidents who succeeded him. (Trow, 1979.) While exploring that event, or non-event, I asked myself what I or any of my colleagues concerned with higher education might have advised President Washington if we had lived then and he had called on us to offer him advice about the wisdom of creating a University of the United States. If we can imagine policy analysts before 1800, then I am sure that we would at that time have strongly urged President Washington, and anyone else who would listen, to carry through his proposal to create a national university, one that would immediately become the strongest institution of higher education in the young country, and would undoubtedly exert a powerful, and to our minds, positive influence on the other colleges and universities in the country, public and private, and on its secondary schools as well.

I will not go into the nature of our recommendations except to say that they would meet all the requirements of good policy analysis. But we would have been wrong. I believe the University of the United States, however attractive it seemed to Washington and would have seemed to policy analysts at the time, would in fact have had bad effects on the evolution of American higher education.

But the hypothetical advice of policy analysts to that President would only come to be seen to be bad advice in the perspective of nearly 200 years, from the point of the view of the whole system of higher education and even more broadly, of the welfare of society as a whole. The problem, as we analysts would have surely bounded it, would have addressed itself narrowly to the viability and character of one specific federal university and its relatively short term effects on other existing institutions of higher education. Moreoever, and this would be taken as an absolute assumption beyond question by any analyst, our aim, like Washington's, would have been to assess the possibilities of creating in this country at that time a university of strength and high quality, firmly funded, with a distinguished faculty, a progressive curriculum, and the highest academic standards. A University of the United States, if it had been established as Washington wished and urged and as we policy analysts would have encouraged, would have been that kind of institution. But that capstone university, however excellent it might have been, would almost certainly by its dominance have thwarted and inhibited the rapid and uncontrolled growth of colleges and universities of every shape and description all over the United States over the next 150 years, and perhaps effectively prevented the emergence of that diversity, arising out of almost uncontrolled growth, that has made the American system of higher education appropriate to the society in which it has developed.

No policy analyst can reasonably be expected to make a recommendation about a problem at hand while taking into account all of the ramified consequences of a decision on other institutions of the society across a time span of two centuries. He can only do that in this case retrospectively and speculatively; I cannot really know what other third and fourth order effects might have occurred if the University of the United States had been created as Washington urged. And yet without trying to play God, and to see all the possible futures that might have occurred had that event been different, there is a principle that emerges from our reflections on the case of the University of the United States that may have more general significance. And that is that the kind of advice we offer to decision-makers is almost always focused rather narrowly on the quality of the programme under consideration, and on its very short-term effects on narrow target populations. This, I think, is inherent in the policy analyst's training and in his work situation. It is not to the same degree a constraint on the researcher in the university, who has the time and freedom to take into account a much wider range of factors and forces over a longer period of time. Here we see one of the central limitations on the work of the policy analyst as compared with that of the university-based social scientist. It is simply that they do not have the same freedom to define their problems and to bound them broadly. This is the great strength, at least potentially, of the free intellectual – that he can raise any question, question any assumption, and seek connections among causes and consequences as broadly as he can stretch his imagination and find empirical chains of linkage.

This is not to say that the analyst, even the government analyst, has no discretion in his choice of problems or in the way he formulates them. Analysts do have and do exercise considerable discretion in their research, but the extent and nature of that discretion will vary in the agencies of different societies, and in the same country under different governments, in different ministries, and indeed in different sections of the same ministry. A research problem worthy of our attention would be to explore the scope of discretion that is available to analysts under different working situations, and to see whether and how they take advantage of the discretion available to them and what difference that makes to their work and to their influence on public policy.

Tensions Between Professional and Bureaucratic Roles

A third major problem that faces the policy analyst in government is the continuing tension between his professional role and that of his role as an employee in a government department, and thus indirectly a servant of the government currently in office and of its programme and purposes (Trow, 1980).

One set of moral issues for policy analysts arises out of the fact that they are employees and professionals, often civil servants, and sometimes political appointees. For each of those social groups there are reasonably clear norms and expectations. But the analyst is not exclusively an employee, professional, civil servant, or politician, but something of them all. This is the source of great uncertainty as he confronts the questions of what his guiding principles are and where his primary loyalties lie, questions that arise constantly in his daily work.

Related to this is the issue of who is the analyst's "client". Toward whose interests is he oriented? To his immediate superior, or the divisional chief, or the secretary of the department, or the agency's external clients or constituency, or "the public interest"? And to what extent is he responsible to his profession and its norms of truth-seeking and truth-saying, a set of expectations quite different from those of the various other constituencies who claim his loyalty. The multiplicity of the policy analysts' "clients" contributes to the difficulties analysts face in their professional lives, and introduce moral complexities that university-based researchers do not face, or can choose to ignore.

Policy Intellectuals and Policy Analysts

In his paper identifying several models of connections between research and policy, Torsten Husén is drawn, as I am, to the "enlightenment" or "percolation" model. He quotes Carol Weiss to describe research as permeating the policy-making process, entering the policy arena not through specific findings or recommendations, but by its "generalisations and orientations percolating through informed publics in coming to shape the way in which people think about social issues". (Weiss, 1979.)

There is, I think, broad agreement that much of the impact of research on policy (I would not say all) occurs in this subtle, difficult-to-measure way. But is this not at variance with the image of the policy analyst directly at the policy-maker's elbow, preparing papers and reports at his request, speaking to issues and problems that the policy-maker will be facing even if he does not yet recognise their character or his options? This image of the policy analyst is in fact compatible with the metaphor of the "percolation" of research, and of the notion of research entering into the general debate about an issue going on among interested publics, an ongoing debate that crystallises into policy at a moment when a political actor chooses to place it on the agenda for action and not merely discussion. The analyst in government cannot often do basic research; he cannot do long-range studies; he is to a large extent a consumer and adapter of research, part of the attentive audience for research, and among the most active participants in the critical discussion about the issue and the literature that grows up around it. In the United States the analyst who is educated at a school of public policy is especially trained to take part in that discussion because his former teachers and his teachers' peers in other policy schools and professional and academic departments do the research and comment on the research of others in such journals as *The Public Interest, Policy Analysis, Public Choice, Policy Studies Journal, The Journal of Policy Analysis and Management,* among others. These university-based writers and researchers, some of whom teach in the schools of public policy, are what

James Q. Wilson calls "policy intellectuals". And his view of their influence on policy is not far from that of the "percolation" model. Reviewing the role of policy intellectuals over the past decade, Wilson observes that:

> If the influence of intellectuals was not to be found in the details of policy, it was nonetheless real, albeit indirect. Intellectuals provided the conceptual language, the ruling paradigms, the empirical examples . . . that became the accepted assumptions for those in charge of making policy. Intellectuals framed, and to a large degree conducted, the debates about whether this language and these paradigms were correct. The most influential intellectuals were those who managed to link a concept or a theory to the practical needs and ideological dispositions of political activists and governmental officials. (Wilson, 1981)

Wilson goes further than most of us in downplaying the role of research *per se* as compared to the power of the arguments of skilful intellectuals.

> At any given moment in history, an influential idea – and thus an influential intellectual – is one that provides a persuasive simplification of some policy question that is consistent with a particular mix of core values then held by the political elite . . . Clarifying and making persuasive those ideas is largely a matter of argument and the careful use of analogies; rarely . . . does this process involve matters of proof and evidence of the sort that is, in their scholarly, as opposed to their public lives, supposed to be the particular skill and obligation of the intellectual in the university. (*Ibid.,* p. 36)

But Wilson would agree that there are some – James Coleman is one, and Torsten Husén another – who are *both* researchers and policy intellectuals, and whose contributions to the ongoing policy discussion is an odd mixture of their research work and their policy analysis in a more qualitative and rhetorical sense. One might almost suggest that their research work and findings get into the policy discussion chiefly by way of giving greater weight and authority to their writing as policy intellectuals; indeed in both cases their research findings have been seized upon by others after publication, and put to uses rather different from their own interpretations and preference.

The role of the policy intellectual in policy debates, independent of his research, is of great importance, and deserves to be studied more closely. The influence of such informed discussion and argument will, I think, vary in different policy fields. But of special interest is the combined effects of policy intellectuals based in the universities and the policy analysts whom they have trained, or who were trained to read them, to understand them and to use their arguments in the preparation of their reports for decision-makers in government. These staff papers, reports and memoranda give the policy intellectuals' ideas and work access, in ways that the intellectuals themselves do not always have, to the committee rooms and governmental conversations where decisions are made.

Policy Analysts versus Interest Groups

The structure of government in the United States, both in Washington and in the state capitols, is changing, becoming even more open and responsive than it has been to vocal, well-organised special interest groups, less and less managed by traditional elites. In the field of education, says Jerome Murphy,

State policy stystems, no longer the captive of state education establishments, are now far more accessible to interest groups and open to public view. The adoption of a large number of policy reforms reflects a new responsiveness on the part of state government to these groups.

Within government, the most important change is the heavy involvement of legislators and governors in educational matters. Spurred on by worries about money, school quality, and social issues (e.g. integration), general state government has used its new staff and expertise to challenge education professionals and to remove education from its privileged perch "above politics".

There's a different cast of participants outside government as well . . . Some of the new lobbies promote equality, representing such interests as urban areas, the poor, blacks, Hispanics, the disadvantaged, the handicapped, girls. Reform of state school finance laws has been promoted for the past decade by a network of scholars, foundation executives, lawyers, government officials, community organisers, and citizen groups. Other groups work for efficiency and effectiveness, lobbying for comprehensive planning, improved budgeting, accountability laws, standards for graduation, competency tests for students and teachers. More recently, some of these groups have been promoting tax limitation measures and controls on expenditures. Still other lobbies promote "the public interest". (Murphy, 1981, p. 128)

All this energy and activity (in part a consequence of mass higher education) generates an extraordinary level of noise, demands, charges and counter-charges, court actions and so forth. Pressures of every kind are felt by legislators, elected officials and their staffs. Policy analysts inside government provide some counterweight, some degree of stability, predictability and rationality through their professional patterns of response to these pressures and demands. This is not to say that the political activists and their pressure groups are not often successful. But how a government agency responds to organised political pressure may well be shaped by the anonymous analysts in the executive and legislative staffs and agencies. And it is through them that a larger, or at least a different, set of ideas comes into play in these discussions, and these ideas at their best are less narrow and parochial, more likely to be illuminated by historical and comparative perspectives and by the ongoing discussion that policy intellectuals carry on among themselves in the professional journals.

* * *

The structure of politics, the character of the policy arenas in which discussions and debate about policies are carried on, are quite different in Sweden than in the United States. Careful studies of actual policy formulation and implementation in specific areas must illuminate the patterns of "social interaction", which more often than not are the major determinants of outcomes in the policy arena. (Premfors, June, 1982, p. 2.) In these increasingly complex networks of social interaction, the relations between policy analysts in government and policy intellectuals in the university are of large and growing importance in the United States, with close analogues in Sweden and other western societies.

Conclusion: Research and the Rhetoric of Politics

It is natural that we members of the research community be concerned that the research we do be true and illuminating accounts of the institutions and processes that we study. Some of us also are interested in whether our research has any influence on the shaping of policy and the making of decisions, and if it does, how it enters the decision process, and with what effects on the outcomes of those decisions.

But it may be useful, and not wholly subversive of the research itself, to reflect that policy research has value independent of its truth or quality or its influence on policy. That is because social research is one of the ways in which political discussions are carried on in democratic societies, a way that is supportive of liberal democratic politics. Political argument is increasingly conducted in the language of research and analysis; concepts like "cost-benefit" and "trade-off" have found their way into the daily language of politicians and bureaucrats. Moreover, social research and democratic politics have some close affinities. For one thing, like democratic politics, social research is a process not of assertion or demonstration but of persuasion. Moreover, it is a form of persuasion that appeals to reason and evidence, rather than to supernatural authority, or tradition, or the charisma of an individual, or the authority of a legal order. The appeal to research findings is very far from the coercive domination of others by force or threat, and equally far from political manipulations which depend on the exploitation of a differential of knowledge and awareness between manipulator and the manipulated. The appeal to "research findings" is the appeal to the authority of reason, to a rationality that connects means and ends in ways that are consistent with strongly held social values. Max Weber has said that the contribution of sociology to politics is not to affirm ultimate ends, but to help clarify, if possible to "make transparent", the connections between means and ends so that choices can be made in greater awareness of the consistency of the means chosen with the ends intended. Insofar as social science attempts to do that, it becomes part of the persuasive mechanism of politics, rooting politics, at least in part, in persuasion based on an appeal to reason and knowledge. It need not weaken our professional concern for the quality and truth of our research to suggest that social research makes its largest contribution to liberal society not through its findings, but by its steady affirmation of the relevance of reason and knowledge to the politics of democracy.

References

Coleman, James S., Katz, E., and Menzel, H. (1957) The Diffusion of an Innovation Among Physicians. *Sociometry*, **20**, pp. 253–270.
Coleman, James, *et al.* (1966) *Equality of Educational Opportunity*. U.S. Government Printing Office, Washington, D.C.

Coleman, James (1961) *The Adolescent Society: The Social Life of the Teenager and its Impact on Education.* The Free Press of Glencoe, New York.

Husén, Torsten (June, 1982) Two Partners With Communication Problems: Researchers and Policy-Makers in Education. Paper presented at the Symposium "Researchers and Policy-Makers in Education: How Do They Relate?" held at Wijk, Lidingö-Stockholm.

Katz, E. (1957) The Two-Step Flow of Communication: An Up-to-Date Report on an Hypothesis. *Public Opinion Quarterly,* **21,** pp. 61–78.

Kogan, Maurice, Korman, Nancy and Henkel, Mary (1980) *Government's Commissioning of Research: A Case Study,* Department of Government, Brunel University, pp. 36–38.

Lerner, Daniel and Lasswell, Harold (Ed.) (1951) *The Policy Sciences,* Stanford University Press, Stanford, California.

Liebow, E. (1967) *Tally's Corner,* Little, Brown, Boston.

Meltsner, Arnold J. (1976) *Policy Analysts in the Bureaucracy,* University of California Press, Berkeley.

Murphy, Jerome T. (Summer, 1981) The Paradox of State Government Reform. *The Public Interest,* **64,** pp. 124–139.

Premfors, Rune (March, 1982) Analysis in Politics: The Regionalization of Swedish Higher Education. Paper presented at a conference on "The Functions and Problems of the Urban University: A Comparative Perspective," City University of New York, New York, New York.

Premfors, Rune (June, 1982) Research and Policy-Making in Swedish Higher Education. Paper presented to the Symposium "Researchers and Policy-Making in Education: How Do They Relate?" held at Wijk, Lidingö-Stockholm.

Roberts, Kenneth, Noble, Maria and Duggan, Jill (January, 1982) Out-of-School and Out-of-Work . . . Is It An Unemployment Problem?. *Leisure Studies,* I (No. 1).

Stack, C. B. (1974) *All Our Kin,* Harper and Row, New York.

Teichler, Ulrich (April, 1982) Some Remarks Regarding a Project Proposal 'Research on Higher Education and its Impact. ' (mimeo).

Trow, Martin (1979) Aspects of Diversity in American Higher Education. In Herbert Gans, Ed., *On the Making of Americans: Essays in Honor of David Riesman,* University of Pennsylvania Press, Philadelphia.

Trow, Martin (April, 1980) Moral Dilemmas of Policy Analysis and the Policy Analyst. Graduate School of Public Policy Working Paper, **104,** University of California, Berkeley.

Trow, Martin (1979) Reflections on Youth Problems and Policies in the United States. Margaret Gordon, Editor, *Youth Education and Unemployment Problems,* Carnegie Foundation for the Advancement of Teaching, Washington, D.C. pp. 127–164.

Wax, M. L., Wax, R. H., and Dumont, R. V. Jr. (1964) *Formal education in an American Indian community.* An SSSP Monograph. Supplement to *Social Problems,* **11** (No. 4).

Weiss, Carol H. (September, 1979) The Many Meanings of Research Utilization. *Public Administration Review,* pp. 426–431.

Wilson, James Q. (Summer, 1981) Policy Intellectuals and 'Public Policy.' *The Public Interest,* pp. 31–46.

Planning, Pluralism, and
Policy Intellectuals

BY BJÖRN WITTROCK

Researchers and Policy-Makers: The Problem of
Knowledge Utilisation

The growth of public programmes in all the industrialised, Western countries during the post World War II period entailed a growing role for social and policy research. Funding for such activities was forthcoming on a scale previously unheard of; social scientists and policy analysts were brought into newly created government offices for advice, planning and evaluation; and systematic endeavours were made to link up social knowledge and public policy-making. Numerous tags, such as programme budgeting, social indicators, policy analysis, future studies and sectoral research, bear witness to the same pervasive "scientification" of policy-making and administration.

However, in the 1970s it became increasingly clear that the original promises of these various efforts were not being fulfilled. Policy-oriented research seems to have had little or no direct impact on policy-making. And when it is used, it is often in partisan and distorted ways that grossly deviate from expectations of a systematic input into a well-ordered planning machinery (Aaron, 1978; Coleman, 1979; Wilson, 1978).

The notion of a mismatch between supply and use of policy-relevant social knowledge has been succinctly formulated by Carol Weiss, a leading scholar in the field of knowledge utilisation:

> Our starting point is the general contention that social science research is largely ignored by government officials as a basis for decisions. Observers in government and out find few instances in which research conclusions visibly affect the course of policy . . . Yet at the same time governments, particularly the federal government of the United States, spend substantial sums of money to support social science research . . . There is an avowed and explicit intent to use research results to inform action . . . The discontinuity between government commitment to social science research, as evidenced by the expenditure of money and the surrounding rhetoric, and its neglect of the results that social science research produces, presents a paradox (Weiss, 1980, 3f).

Part of this sense of disillusion might be traced to some of the models trying to relate social research to public policy-making. These attempts were largely based on a highly rationalistic conception of the policy process. Policy-makers, objectives, alternatives, and the costs of different courses of action were assumed to be clearly definable, and policies to be shaped by a sequence of carefully calculated choices. But suppose policy-makers are better understood in terms of interconnecting networks than in those of planning individuals, policy problems as fuzzy and wicked rather than clearly delimited, and that policy-making is conceived as a moving process rather than a set of discrete events? Then, obviously, the conditions of the use of social knowledge will differ accordingly.

In the past decade there has been a growing number of empirical and theoretical studies that elaborate on the problems and potentials of knowledge utilisation. An emerging consensus among these researchers, perhaps, can be summed up in three propositions.

Firstly, the very concept of knowledge utilisation is highly complex. The standards of utilisation might range from the perception and cognition of policy-relevant information over its role in the formulation of policy problems and its adoption in policy decisions to the actual implementation and impact of policies (see, e.g. Knott and Wildavsky, 1980).

Secondly, knowledge utilisation is determined by the structure and characteristics of the relevant policy-making system, where social research will only form one component among many types of information experiences and beliefs (see, e.g. Weiss, 1978).

Thirdly, it is necessary to work out the conditions of knowledge utilisation in all those situations that cannot be adequately grasped by means of a strictly rationalistic conception of policy-making. Social research can and does have an impact other than by serving as a basis for a well-defined planning process.

Several scholars have argued that social research will tend to be used less to solve a specific and clear-cut problem than in a more circuitous process to help formulate and conceptualise problems, and less as a neutral piece of information than as ammunition in political controversies. Conversely, should there be some consensus among policy-makers, social research "corrodes the simple faiths on which political movements are built; this effect is particularly strong when, as in the late 1960s and early 1970s, the actions of political leaders tend to destroy those faiths and events make them implausible" (Aaron, 1978, p. 159).

One prominent theme in the literature is the call for an "enlightenment model" that can account for the indirect uses of social knowledge that affect policies by providing a background of ideas and empirical evidence:

> What we come to is a distinction between the social engineering model of research use and the enlightenment model. Researchers as social engineers are expected to answer specific requests for information and knowledge in a straightforward manner. They are expected to take the government's ends as given and to devise means to achieve them. Since research is planned, done, and transmitted, it is expected to be applied. The enlightenment model, on the other hand, assumes that social science research does not so much solve problems as provide an intellectual setting of concepts, propositions, orientations, and empirical generalisations. No one study has much effect, but, over time, concepts become accepted . . . Over a span of time and much research, ideas . . . filter into the consciousness of policy-

making officials and attentive publics. They come to play a part in how policy-makers define problems and the options they examine for coping with them . . . At this point in their development, enlightenment may be the wisest use of the social sciences" (Weiss, 1978, 77f).

Obviously, the dichotomy of engineering and enlightenment is rather crude. Some research, for example, might well have a direct impact without ever having been commissioned in the way envisaged by the engineering model. Such instances can be found in several cases during the protracted controversy over nuclear power in Sweden in the 1970s. If the circumstances are propitious, unplanned but important uses seem quite possible (see Majone and Wildavsky, 1978; Wittrock, 1981).

However, attractive as it is, the enlightenment model also leaves a number of crucial issues wide open. What is the relationship between social research and other forms of knowledge and beliefs? How, more precisely, does knowledge "creep" into decision making, or, rather, decision accretion? How does better understanding contribute to the amelioration of social conditions and the cure of social evils? And in what sense is it reasonable to call something a social problem in the first place?

Linking Analysis to Action: The Dispositional Approach

Thus, even if the thesis of a mismatch between social research and policy-making is accepted, there is a need for an account which does not necessarily accept the dichotomy of engineering and enlightenment, and which lends an insight into the mechanisms which link the activities of researchers and intellectuals to those of policy-makers and administrators. Important steps in this direction have been taken by James Coleman in his account of the role of policy-oriented research in adversary processes where findings tend to be used in ways envisaged neither by the researcher nor by those policy-makers who originally might have commissioned the research (Coleman, 1979 and in this volume p. 131 ff; Husén, 1981). Swedish examples of cases in which results from policy-oriented studies in the energy field, commissioned by the government were used by the opponents of the government policy rather than by the government itself, testify to the relevance of the adversary model beyond the American setting (see Wittrock, 1981). Torsten Husén's introduction of the notion of "percolation" as well as Maurice Kogan's discussion of the role of middle-men also outline important linking mechanisms (Husén in this volume p. 7 ff; Kogan *et al.,* 1980; Kogan and Henkel, 1983 and Kogan in this volume p. 261 ff). Martin Trow has taken up the challenge of actually showing how linkages between researchers and policy-makers function in terms of different sets of actors, who embody essentially new roles in both academic and policy-making environments.

The emergence of policy analysis as a professional activity is, Trow argues, largely a phenomenon of the early 1970s when a number of policy-oriented branches of inquiry, often rooted in a tradition of systems analysis and micro-economic theory, gradually merged into a new field of scholarship and professional training. New schools, set up in leading American universities, began to train members of a new profession who would know how to use an array of intellectual instruments to tackle problems in the face of the constraints in terms of time, resources and feasibility inherent in a policy process.

True enough, these constraints impose a series of limitations on the policy analyst's work in bounding his or her problems. A focus on the short or, at best, medium-term problems and on a definite group of clients and customers constitute some of these limitations. However, – and this is a major thrust of Trow's argument – besides policy analysts in government, agencies, and organisations there will be policy intellectuals who make up the faculty of schools of policy analysis. This group will have both a professional capacity to analyse policy problems and the privilege of doing so free from the constraints of a policy-making environment. Together these academic intellectuals and the analysts educated by them might have a considerable direct and indirect leverage. Thus, they might leave an imprint on the way a problem is delimited in apparently technical background papers. If conditions are ripe, the impact of policy intellectuals may be considerable also in cases of public controversy. The research findings of the academic intellectuals might provide excellent ammunition for the guns of debate, especially if they are manned by these same policy intellectuals or people trained by them.

This account has three highly attractive features. It helps locate key actors which are conducive to knowledge utilisation. It focuses on important changes in the domains of both research and policy-making in terms of demands for new types of analysis. Finally, it outlines an explanation which avoids the simplistic sequential view of the early formulation of the engineering model as well as its neglect of activities in the borderline zone between traditional academic research and policy-making proper. Instead, it proposes a conception of knowledge utilisation which might be termed dispositional; the process is neither arbitrary and haphazard, nor entirely preprogrammed; important policy research must be there to be utilised and if conditions are propitious and important actors available, these findings might well have an impact. Such an account seems, furthermore, to be well in line with many of the experiences from the field of education reported by Coleman, Husén, Ruin and other contributors to this volume.

However, it poses major dilemmas. These concern firstly the intellectual origins and legitimacy of policy analysis as a scholarly activity. Secondly, the nature and implications of the changes in policy-making, which have precipitated the expansion of policy research and policy analysis as a profession, must be assessed. Thirdly, the account is open-ended in terms of its reliance on – to use James Coleman's terminology – a pluralist or a cybernetic conception of society.

Dilemmas and Constraints

Firstly, then, there is little doubt that the last decade and a half has witnessed the establishment of policy analysis within Academia. It is, however, an open question whether this has involved a major change in the relative prominence of policy-oriented scholarship. In fact, historians of social thought remind us that policy-orientation in a broad sense formed an important component of the very process of the emergence of professional social research towards the end of the nineteenth century and in its growth, not least in the United States, in the 1920s and 1930s (see Soffer, 1978; Bulmer, 1980).

The concept "policy sciences" was also introduced more than 30 years ago by Harold Lasswell to outline a field of policy-oriented and value-conscious scholarship in terms of three main characteristics, namely multi-disciplinarity and diversity of methods, problem-orientation, and contextuality. Lasswell warned against "the suggestion that social scientists ought to spend most of their time advising policy-makers on immediate questions" and against an emphasis "upon the topical issues of the day" (Lasswell, 1951).

Some of Lasswell's warnings are echoed in Carol Weiss' current admonitions:

> Adherence to all the traditional strictures – acceptance of decision-makers' constraints, focus in manipulable variables, timeliness, jargon-free communication, and the like – seems to increase the application of results only minimally . . . quick and dirty *ad hoc* studies, which cut methodological corners in order to meet an arbitrary deadline or satisfy an impatient client, are more likely to muddy than to clarify the issues. To serve the longer-term policy needs of officials, research should be grounded in relevant theory and existing knowledge; it should look at the issues comprehensively in all their multivariate complexity . . .(Weiss, 1982).

This, certainly, suggests a dilemma. To the extent that policy-oriented research takes the form of a management dominated analysis, which basically accepts the constraints and strictures of the decision-maker, then it will correspondingly reduce its potential to serve any real enlightenment function. Thus, Trow's description of the expansion of policy analysis suggests that this might entail a growth of the points of contact between the realms of research and policy-making. But if policy research does not go beyond a managerial approach and thus, heeds the warnings of Lasswell and Weiss, the value of the individual contributions of policy researchers might well dwindle.

Secondly, the dispositional approach to the linkage problem reflects a growing interest in the 1960s and 1970s among policy-makers all over the Western world in engaging in analytically more ambitious exercises in planning, budgeting, implementation and evaluation. From the mid-1960s and onwards a plethora of new bodies for these kinds of activities in agencies and ministries has grown up in most of these countries. Higher education is no exception to this development. Despite a decade of scholarly criticism of rationalistic planning and many practitioners' disappointment with some of the early experiences, the current stringent financial conditions seem to have brought about renewed enthusiasm for long-range planning as well as evaluation in both higher education and science policy.

The crucial question is whether these developments in policy-making environments signal any real improvement in the conditions under which research is linked to policy. If efforts to set up policy analytical units and to draw on their resources in exercises in planning, budgeting, and evaluation are seen to constitute a decisive change towards a more rationally managed policy process, then such conditions must indeed be deemed more favourable in the vein of the dispositional approach. If, however, these phenomena of administration and policy-making are seen as little but window-dressing for traditonal political bargaining and conflict and administrative muddling through, then we simply witness a new element of ritual in a process no more amenable to analyses and research than before.

Some observers of higher education planning have been arguing that the ritual component is increasingly prominent even in a system such as the Swedish one which traditionally has been ascribed highly rationalistic characteristics (Lindensjö, 1981; see Floden and Weiner, 1978; Gustafsson, 1983). Still, even if some of the points of this argument are granted, it seems safe to assume that the changes in the higher education policy process associated with the increasing role of analytical exercises will in many cases exhibit an uneasy mixture of elements of rationality and ritual (see Wittrock, 1982). After all, even symbolic uses of research cannot be disregarded. Thus, the pervasiveness of the changes of policy-making, which partly determine the strength of the dispositional approach to the linkage problem, seem to be open-ended. But it is hard to deny that a series of changes have occurred, whether in the guise of changes in policy style or as new practices leaving an imprint on policy outcomes.

Thirdly, the dispositional model, espoused by Trow and others, poses the problem of the societal ramifications of such a model. James Coleman argues (p. 131) that most policy research has been performed according to a "cybernetic" model of social problem-solving with a view of society as a single rational actor and the policy analyst assigned to the role of the princely adviser. He juxtaposes this conception with a pluralist one, in which there will be a multiplicity of actors often engaged in adversary processes and in which policy relevant information is a public good available to all rather than a private good of a single actor. However, attractive though it may be, this model implies that the policy intellectual will be in a precarious position. His or her findings will be used in ways which might well erode their intellectual legitimacy and credibility.

Coleman's proposals to manage this dilemma include such institutional mechanisms as science courts and the practice of having more than one research project investigating the same policy-relevant issue. However, the strains on the intellectual legitimacy of policy research seem to be quite a deep-seated structural characteristic of a full-fledged version of the pluralist model which can only be partially handled through the institutional procedures outlined.

This, however, is not to say that any other model of social problem-solving will assign an unambiguous role to policy intellectuals and analysts and establish the societal legitimacy of their activities.

Policy analysis originated as a part of endeavours to handle the link-up between research and knowledge on the one hand and policy-making on the other. These endeavours were often accompanied by exaggerated hopes of achieving a more rational management of administrative and policy problems. But they also provoked opposition. An expanding "hybrid" sector inhabited by "technocratic" administrators and planners has been envisaged as a threat both to academic freedom and to the traditional virtues of bureaucracies. The politicisation of science and the scientification of politics and administration have been regarded as a mixed blessing in both radical and conservative circles. Nor should such objections be lightly dismissed. But they show that the problem of the societal legitimacy of policy-oriented analysis is a problem which is related to more encompassing developments in society.

One such development concerns science policy in the advanced industrial Western nations. Policy-makers are trying increasingly to relate research to social and political objectives, possibly – so the critics argue – at the expense of a longer-term and freer-ranging search for knowledge unbound by considerations of direct utility and immediate returns. (For overviews of recent Swedish science policy, see Elzinga, 1980, and Wittrock, 1980).

Another feature of relevance to the problem of the societal legitimacy of policy analysis and policy-oriented research concerns the explicitly political characteristics of various types of such activities. Questions such as these are closely linked to problems related to the role of the state in contemporary society, and on what some observers see as the emergence of a new stratum of intellectuals and functionaries assuming a leading position and acquiring new elitist privileges (see Bruce-Briggs, 1979, Gouldner, 1979).

Obviously policy analysts cannot be expected to solve broad social and analytical problems of this kind. But a minimum requirement, formulated by Jonathan Gershuny can be suggested: policy analysts and forecasters should not let themselves be mistaken for neutral instruments in the politicians' hands (Gershuny, 1981).

References

Aaron, H. J. (1978) *Politics and the Professors.* Brookings, Washington, D.C.
Bruce-Briggs, B. (ed.) (1981) *The New Class?* McGraw-Hill, New York.
Bulmer, M. (1980) The Early Institutional Establishment of Social Science Research. *Minerva,* **28**, 51–110.
Coleman, J. (1979) Conflicts Between Policy Research and Decision-Making. In H. Skoie, (ed.), *Scientific Expertise and the Public.* Oslo: Institute for Studies in Research and Higher Education, 14–21.
Elzinga, A (1980) Science Policy in Sweden: Sectorization and Adjustment to Crisis. *Research Policy,* **9**, 116–146.

290 *Björn Wittrock*

Floden, R. E. & Weiner, S. S. (1978) Rationality to Ritual: The Multiple Roles of Evaluation in Governmental Processes. *Policy Sciences,* 9, 9–18.

Gershuny, J. L. (1981) What should Forecasters Do? A Pessimistic View. In P. R. Baehr and B. Wittrock (eds.), *Policy Analysis and Policy Innovation,* Sage, Beverly Hills, 193–207.

Gouldner, A. (1979) *The Future of Intellectuals and the Rise of the New Class.* The Seabury Press, New York.

Gustafsson, G. (1983) Symbolic and Pseudo Policies as Responses to Diffusion of Power. *Policy Sciences,* 15.

Husén, T. (September, 1981) Coleman II – Another Case of Politics and the Professors. *Change,* 13 (No. 6).

Husén, T. and Boalt, G. (1968) *Educational Research and Educational Change.* Almqvist & Wiksell, Stockholm. John Wiley, New York.

Knott, J. and Wildavsky, A. (1980) If Dissemination Is the Solution, What is the Problem? *Knowledge,* 1, 537–78.

Kogan, M. and Henkel, M. (1983) *Government and Research: The Rothschild Experiment.* Heinemann, London.

Kogan, M., Korman, N. and Henkel, M. (1980) *Government's Commissioning of Research: A Case Study.* Brunel University, Uxbridge.

Lasswell, H. D. (1951) The Policy Orientation. In D. Lasswell and Lerner (eds.), *The Policy Sciences: Recent Developments in Scope and Method.* Stanford University Press, Stanford, Ca. 3–15.

Lindensjö, B. (1981) *Högskolereformen: En studie i offentlig reformstrategi.* Stockholm Studies in Politics, Stockholm.

Majone, G. and Wildavsky, A. (1978) Implementation as Evolution. In H. E. Freeman, (ed.), *Policy Studies Review Annual,* 2, Sage Publications, Beverly Hills.

Soffer, R. (1978) *Ethics and Society in England: The Revolution in the Social Sciences 1870–1914.* University of California Press, Berkeley and Los Angeles.

Weiss, C. H. (ed.) (1977) *Using Social Research in Public Policy Making.* Lexington Books, Lexington, Mass.

Weiss, C. H. (1978) Improving the Linkage Between Social Research and Public Policy. In L. E. Lynn, Jr. (ed.), *Knowledge and Policy: The Uncertain Connection.* National Academy of Sciences, Washington, D.C., 23–81.

Weiss, C. H. (1980) *Social Science Research and Decision-Making.* Columbia University Press, New York.

Weiss, C. H. (1982) Policy Research in the Context of Diffuse Decision-Making. In D. B. P. Kallen *et al* (eds.), *Social Science Research and Public Policy-Making: a Reappraisal.* NFER-Nelson, Windsor, 288–305.

Wittrock, B. (1980) Science Policy and the Challenge to the Welfare State. *West European Politics,* 3, 358–372.

Wittrock, B. (1981) Future Studies Without a Planning Subject. In P. R. Baehr and B. Wittrock (eds.), *op. cit.,* 119–150.

Wittrock, B. (1982) Managing Uncertainty or Foreclosing the Options. *European Journal of Education,* 17, 307–318.

Appendix I

List of Participants at Symposium

Hellmut Becker, Professor and Director Emeritus of the Max Planck Institute for Educational Research, Berlin; former Vice-President of the German *Bildungsrat*.

Gunnar Bergendal, Rector, School of Education, Malmö, former Secretary-General of U68.

Alain Bienaymé, Professor of Economics at the University of Paris; former Advisor to Edgar Faure.

Eskil Björklund, Head of Programme on Research on Higher Education of the National Board of Universities and Colleges, Stockholm.

James S. Coleman, Professor of Sociology, University of Chicago.

Urban Dahllöf, Professor of Education, University of Uppsala; former Chairman of the Government Committee on Research and Development in the Swedish school system.

Lars Ekholm, Head of the Department of Higher Education, Ministry of Education, Stockholm.

Ingemar Fägerlind, Associate Professor of International Education, University of Stockholm.

Mats Hultin, Senior Educational Advisor in the World Bank, Washington, D.C.

Torsten Husén, Professor Emeritus at the Institute of International Education; former Chairman of IEA.

Kjell Härnqvist, Professor of Education, Rector of the University of Gothernburg.

Maurice Kogan, Professor of Government and Social Administration, Department of Government, Brunel University, England.

Lennart Levin, Director, Research and Development Bureau, National Board of Universities and Colleges, Stockholm.

Esse Lövgren, Director, Bureau of Research and Development, National Board of Education, Stockholm.

Inger Marklund, Head of School Research Programme in the Department of Research and Development, National Board of Education, Stockholm.

Sixten Marklund, Professor, Institute of International Education; former Director, Department of Research and Development, National Board of Education, Stockholm.

Ingrid Munck, Liaison Officer on Research, University of Stockholm.

Richard Noonan, Associate Professor, Institute of International Education, University of Stockholm.

Lennart Orehag, Director General, National Board of Education.

James A. Perkins, President, International Council for Educational Development, New York; former Vice-President, Carnegie Corporation.

T. Neville Postlethwaite, Professor, Department of Comparative Education, University of Hamburg; Chairman of IEA.

Gunnar Richardson, Associate Professor, Department of Education, University of Uppsala; former member of the Advisory Panel of the National Board of Education.

Birgit Rodhe, former Minister of School Education.

Olof Ruin, Professor of Political Science and Dean, Faculty of Social Sciences, University of Stockholm.

Nils-Eric Svensson, Executive Director, The Bank of Sweden Tercentenary Foundation.

Martin Trow, Professor at the University of California, Berkeley, and Director, Graduate School of Public Policy, Berkeley.

Sigbrit Franke-Wikberg, Professor of Education, University of Umeå.

Björn Wittrock, Associate Professor of Political Science, University of Stockholm.

Name Index

Subject Index